CHINA'S MINORITIES:
Yesterday and Today

THE WADSWORTH CIVILIZATION IN ASIA SERIES
Laurence G. Thompson, University of Southern California
Series Editor

China's Minorities: Yesterday and Today
    Wolfram Eberhard (University of California, Berkeley)
An Invitation to Japanese Civilization
    Robert S. Ellwood, Jr. (University of Southern California)
Essentials of Chinese Literary Art
    James J. Y. Liu (Stanford University)
The Chinese Economy: Past and Present
    Ramon H. Myers (Hoover Institution, Stanford University)

CHINA'S MINORITIES: Yesterday and Today

Wolfram Eberhard
University of California, Berkeley

Wadsworth Publishing Company
Belmont, California
A Division of Wadsworth, Inc.

Acknowledgments

Excerpts on pp. 43,114,134,145 from *Among The Mongols* by James Gilmour, Religious Tract Society, 1888. Used with permission of Lutterworth Press, England. Excerpts on pages 44, 114 from *Chinese Agent In Mongolia by Ma Ho-t'ien*, translated by John DeFrancis, 1949. Used with permission of Johns Hopkins University Press, Baltimore, Maryland. Excerpts on pp. 103, 141, 142, 143 from *Among the Tribes in South-West China* by Samuel R. Clarke, 1911. Used with permission of China Inland Mission, England. Excerpts on pages 107, 110–111 from *The Uigur Empire* by Colin Mackerras, 1972. Used with permission of University of South Carolina Press, Columbia, South Carolina. Excerpt on page 112 from "Sino-Mongol Relations, Part 3" by Henry Serruys in *Mélanges chinois et bouddhiques*, vol. 17. Brussels 1975. Used with permission. Excerpts on pages 119, 135 from Liu Mao-tsai, *Die chinesischen Nachrichten zur Geschichte der Ost-Türken*, 1958. Used with permission of Verlag Otto Harrassowitz, Germany. Excerpts on pages 125, 126, 127, 128 from *Smithsonian Miscellaneous Collections*, volume 123, "Songs and Stories of the Ch'uan Miao," by David Crockett Graham: pages 27–31. Washington, D. C.: Smithsonian Institution, 1954. Reprinted by permission of the Smithsonian Institution Press. Excerpt on page 130 from *Strong Tower* by A. J. Bromhall, 1947. Used with permission of China Inland Mission, England. Excerpt on page 131 from *Mongolische Volksdichtung* by N. Poppe, 1955. Used with permission of Franz Steiner Verlag, Germany. Excerpts on pages 144, 145, 146 from *Shen Ts'ung-wen's Vision of Republican China* by Jeffrey C. Kinkley, 1978. Used with permission of Jeffrey C. Kinkley.

Series Editor: *Laurence G. Thompson*
Asian Civilization Editor: *Sheryl Fullerton*
Production Editor: *Toni Haskell*
Designer: *Jane Rockwell*
Manuscript Editor: *Susan Weisberg*
Technical Illustrator: *Jane Rockwell*

Library of Congress Cataloging in Publication Data
Eberhard, Wolfram, 1909–
   China's minorities.
   (Civilization in Asia)
   Bibliography: p.
   Includes index.
   1. Ethnology—China. 2. China—Race relations.
I. Title. II. Series.
DS730.E17   305.8′00951   82–2629
ISBN 0–534–01080–6   AACR2

Printed in the United States of America
1 2 3 4 5 6 7 8 9 10---86 85 84 83 82

CONTENTS

Foreword

Civilization in Asia is a series intended to make available to college students and teachers the current state of scholarly thinking in various Asian subjects. The proliferation of specialized monographs of high quality during recent years makes it possible to write well-informed general summaries in many fields, and makes it essential to bridge the ever-widening gap between specialist knowledge and undergraduate education.

To write texts of the sort described is a task that requires the best scholarly awareness of the current state of the art, the ability to compress and summarize without distorting the subject, and a style of writing that is lucid and literate. Fortunately, the sound rationale for this series has attracted some of the best-qualified scholars in the field as its authors. These are all persons who have distinguished themselves by published research that gives them high reputations in the profession. That they have willingly devoted their learning and talents to provide sound, basic texts is a sign of their recognition of an urgent need.

Perhaps the most overriding concern shared by all who are involved in *Civilization in Asia* is that American education should continue, and increase, its efforts to bring all of humankind within the purview of our students, who must function intelligently and humanely in what is now undeniably one world.

Laurence G. Thompson
Series Editor

Transliteration of Foreign Words

The system used in this book is based on *Matthews' Chinese-English Dictionary*, which was developed by English and American scholars for use by English-speaking people. We do not use the system developed by the present Chinese regime, because it is not regarded as final and because it does not differentiate between the sound *u* and *ü*, so that, for instance, *lu* (the road) is written exactly like "green," which we would write as *lü*. French and German writers use their own system, and books written about China before 1900 again used different systems of transliteration. Therefore, in Western books the names of some of the tribes mentioned in this book are transliterated in several different ways. In such cases we added variant spellings in parentheses.

Extracts from original Chinese sources have been translated by the author, unless otherwise indicated. Works in Chinese are divided into chapters, and the chapters into pages. Each "page" is, in our terminology, a double page and in quoting we add to the page number the letters *a* and *b*, sometimes *r* (recto) and *v* (verso). Most Chinese books have been reprinted many times. Sometimes the pagination changes, often it does not. Because chapters are usually not very long (10 to 20 pages), quotation of the chapter number suffices.

Preface

This study addresses itself mainly to students in fields like ethnic studies or Chinese studies. Students who use it to compare the treatment of minorities in the United States with that in the Far East will see that there are many similarities. Students in Chinese studies will find here a different picture of Chinese society from that usually given by Chinese and by many non-Chinese scholars. This book attempts to see both sides—that of the Chinese as well as that of their minorities.

China is a good field for studies in minority relations because written documents spanning more than three millennia exist. We can therefore see the processes as long-time developments, from the beginnings, when different ethnic groups coalesced into a nation (in the second millennium B.C.), to the present, when small ethnic groups are overwhelmed by almost a billion Chinese who decide over their fate. Over its history China has several times, and often for long times, been ruled by foreigners—always a small minority ruling masses hundreds of times larger than their own people and endowed with a higher, more complex culture. Similar situations have existed in other countries, especially in the nineteenth and early twentieth centuries, in what we call colonial systems. But this book is not really a political book, though political scientists may be interested in some chapters; the stress lies upon social and cultural factors.

History does not easily fit into sociological theories—often documentation is too fragmentary, or the documents are obviously one-sided, or we know only one or two factors but nothing about the many, many other factors that may have determined a particular development. Thus, we can do no more than put forth some general thoughts and hope that the description of each minority fits to some degree into our theoretical scheme. It is important to remember that each case represents a unique situation.

Wolfram Eberhard

Background: On the Subject of China's Minorities

Part One

Introduction

1

Calling groups that are part of a larger society *minorities* is a new concept. People have always been aware that in their country were people—gypsies and Jews, for instance—who differed from the majority in their dress, certain physical traits, language, religion, or all of these factors. However, calling such people *minorities* implies not simply difference but dominance and subordination. The term may mean several things: (1) The minority are fewer in numbers than the dominant group. Sometimes—in colonial countries, for instance—the largest group of people is not the ruling group, and we now often speak of a ruling minority. (2) They differ in a number of aspects, such as those mentioned above, from the majority. (3) They feel themselves to be "different" from the majority. (4) They are in a subordinate position, socially or politically, in the society. In other words, minorities exist in societies that are socially or ethnically stratified.

RACE AND "DIFFERENCE"

In China, in contrast to the West, the question of minorities is not a question of race. To understand what we mean by this, it is important first to understand what we mean by *race*, a term that is often used imprecisely and is frequently misunderstood. As the term is usually used today, *race* refers to physical traits observed by others. In China, however, what are commonly called races do not necessarily have any visible biological uniqueness; their identity is defined by social perceptions.

The people we know as the Chinese—those who referred to the country in which they lived as Chung-kuo, *the Country of the Middle*, did not describe themselves. Only occasionally in an old text do we find an expression like *the black-haired masses* (if this translation is correct), but this expression seems to have meant only the common people as opposed to an upper class. Chinese did not describe their neighbors in terms of "race," which was formerly used to differentiate large groups of people. Throughout Chinese history the specific physical traits of China's neighbors or minorities were of no great interest to their historians; for them the Chinese were beautiful and other people were simply more or less ugly, looked like monkeys, or were tall or short. If their hair (which we often use as a racial characteristic) is mentioned, the hair style is of interest rather than the color of the hair or whether the hair was straight, curly, or wavy. Only when, later in history, the Chinese got acquainted with blond and blue-eyed people in Central Asia or even later with red-blond Europeans, is hair color mentioned because such people looked to the Chinese like the demons described in popular novels. In fact, the expression *red demons* (*hung kui-tse*) was often used in the nineteenth century.

In general, physical characteristics such as hair style, tattooing, or clothing were less important for the Chinese than innate physical traits. Once a non-Chinese lived in China, behaved "civilized"—that is, like other Chinese—and had a Chinese education and a Chinese name, that person was accepted, though the stigma of "barbarian" descent remained with his or her descendants for several generations. Today the word *tsu* is used in the vague sense of *race* as it is found in vulgar language. So if we use the old term *tsu*, all Chinese belong to the Mongol, or "yellow" race, with a skin color that is a yellowish white and straight black hair. The only true exceptions today are some communities in Sinkiang (Chinese Central Asia) who are said to belong to an Eastern branch of the "white" race. But within that "Mongol race" we find people who are not citizens of China, such as Koreans, Japanese, and many Southeast Asians; and people who are subjects of China, such as Tibetans, Mongols, Manchus, or the tribes of Taiwan, but are linguistically and culturally different from the Chinese. The Chinese are right when they say that, "normally," northern Chinese, Koreans, and Mongols are taller and more heavy-set than southern Chinese; that the Taiwanese aborigines have hair that is not totally straight; that the inhabitants of Sinkiang have more body hair than Chinese usually have. But often even the Chinese find it difficult to say to which group a person may belong.

When Chinese authors speak of a specific subgroup, they like to use the term *min-tsu*, which is sometimes translated as *race*, but which really means an ethnic group other than the majority of Chinese, such as a tribe.

THE DEVELOPMENT OF AN IN-GROUP FEELING AND A WORLD CONCEPT

To further understand the concepts of racial difference and minorities, we have to go back in history to the time before the emergence of "states," to the time when there were only tribal societies on earth. In some parts of the world, such as Mesopotamia, this period had already ended around 3500 B.C., while in others, such as parts of Africa, it ended less than a century ago.

Patterns of Historical Development

In an attempt to define some general patterns of historical development, we may differentiate two types: One brings together two or more social groups into a new unit. It seems to have begun in prehistoric times and can still be observed in our century. The second one is a breakdown of once-unified societies into smaller units that assure or reassure their right to independence by fighting or by migrating to new homes. This process may have started only with the beginning of history. It seems that beginning in the twentieth century, developments of the second type will become quite common, but they were evident as early as the fourth century.

The first type, the coalescing of groups that had regarded themselves as different from another or several other groups, can be the result of a change in an earlier symbiotic relation between these two or more groups. For instance, to take an example from Southeast Asia, in a mountainous area some groups who live high up in the mountains may begin by living in symbiosis with valley dwellers. One group supplies the other with wood and lumber or with venison and skins, and in return is supplied with vegetable food such as rice or other grains. This symbiosis can be broken, for instance, if the greater fertility of the valley dwellers leads them to move up the hills and cut down the forests to establish new fields, forcing the mountain dwellers to become a depressed and subordinated group. Or one group may inhabit a steppe (a semidesert area), raising cattle or sheep. Their neighbors in adjacent fertile areas, who produce more than sufficient agricultural products, can exploit the steppe dwellers by not buying their meat, fat, butter, milk, and skins except for very low prices. Two possibilities may result: (1) The animal breeders may become a military society and attack the plains dwellers, taking what agricultural products they need by force. In the end they may conquer the plains dwellers and set themselves up as a ruling class, while the farmers become a lower class. (2) The plains dwellers may be much more numerous or have a superior technology so that they can successfully defeat the animal breeders and enslave them.

Another process of this type may be started by a new form of social organization (the reasons for which may not be apparent)—for instance, the change from small, nomadic groups, which we usually call *tribes*, to a federation of such tribes by means of political marriages (which will be discussed further later in this chapter). Such federations, in which not all members are equal, may gain so much power that they can subjugate other tribal units and force them to supply materials or weapons. In all such cases of federation formation the result is a stratified society in which some units are social leaders and other units are, to a greater or lesser extent, enslaved.

The second type of historical development starts with a stratified society in which one or several of the sectors begin to demand their freedom and independence. This may happen through a rebellion in which the rebels try to assure their own, separate identity—or invent such an identity. It may also happen if the leading group or class is unwilling or does not try to prevent such a development. Members of the ruling group or class may actively support the rebellion even though it will, in the end, lead to the loss of their status or even their lives. We may think here, to take an example from the present time, of Rhodesia (now Zimbabwe) and South Africa.

The earliest tribal societies we know had no production; they consumed what the area in which they lived produced. Men hunted; women collected roots, fruits, and small animals. Population density was naturally very low, and each small group had a large territory it regarded as its own. There were contacts with other groups, friendly as well as hostile, but they were not very close, and one group did not know much about another. Other groups were just regarded as "different." What was seen as different was not always the same from group to group. It could have been skin color or hair texture, but it could just as well have been certain rituals or customs. A feeling of "we" versus "them" arose, and this led to a kind of self-definition and a definition of the "others" as "inferior" and as "barbarians," to use a term coined by the Greeks and adopted by later peoples.

Myth and Identity

The anthropologist Paul Radin once pointed out that we find in all societies, small or large, two types of leaders, whom he called the priests and the thinkers. The priests are men who have acquired a certain knowledge, usually about ways and means to communicate with the supernatural powers. They can perform the necessary rituals or other actions, and stress that success depends upon the exact performance of these actions; any deviation would mean failure. The priests, then, represent the conservative leaders of societies. The thinkers are the leaders who try to bring order into the mass of ceremonies and rituals by creating logical ties between them—by unifying them, by developing a "system" or, we may say, an ideology. They are the progressive leaders of societies, *progressive* meaning not that what they do is better or more desirable, but simply that it is more coherent and logical than what the priests did. In all societies both priests and thinkers, though sometimes in conflict with one another, in the end cooperate and mutually strengthen their position in society.

It is the thinkers who dream up the myths, especially the myths that explain the uniqueness and superiority of their societies. Often such myths are a direct continuation of the myths about the creation of the universe and the world. The classical example is the first chapter of the Old Testament, where first the world is created and then the human race, but clearly only the Jewish "race" as the text makes it clear that there were other "races" living nearby at the time of Adam and Eve. With this was joined the idea that the God they venerated was their special God, a God who had special interest in them. Other people had their own Gods, who did not care about the Jews.

The thinkers tried to explain not only why their society was unique and in a special relation to the supernatural power(s) but also how their society had become what it was in their time. In this case perhaps the best example is from Chinese society. Over the course of time Chinese thinkers developed a theory of cultural development where almost every single element of the material or spiritual culture was created by a great man, a culture hero, as we like to call these figures. Chinese culture heroes were always emperors because, as far as we know, these myths were developed relatively late, at a time when China had already long outgrown tribal society and formed one or several states. There was the emperor who "invented" clothing, the one who "invented" marriage, and the one who "invented" medicine and pharmacology. It is interesting that these ancient Chinese "theories" about the origin and development of their culture were quite similar to nineteenth-century Western anthropological theories, which postulated an age of wood, when all implements were made of wood, followed in turn by an age of stone, an age of copper and bronze, and an age of iron. Indian and Greek thinkers, too, had similar ideas. Such a classification of historical periods also allowed the thinkers to regard other societies as inferior or backward. We should not believe, however, that all the thinkers in any one society developed the same ideas. Probably in no culture did all the cultural and social elements make a logically coherent and balanced system. Thinkers proceeding along different lines set up "equations" or "parallels," usually following a dualistic or sometimes a tripartite system, such as sun/moon, heaven/earth, or, in China, *yin/yang*. Such a system can be constantly enlarged over many centuries. For instance, sun/moon come to be equated with day/night, with light/dark, and, even further, with human races. I think it was always an important factor in European society that white was identified with good, God, heaven, life; and black with bad, Satan, hell, and death. Out of such myths and theories emotional attitudes toward dark-skinned people developed.

A modern Chinese creation myth expresses a similar thought: When the creatress created humanity, she modeled the people in clay and then put them into a kiln. The first group remained too long in the kiln and came out black; the second group was taken out of the kiln too early and were still white. Only the last group was as it should be, yellow. In traditional Chinese belief black is the color of the north (the place of death) and white the color of the west (the place of old age). Yellow is the color of the center, formerly the color only the emperor could use for his clothing and the roofs of his palace.

Other physical traits, such as the shape or color of the eyes or the color or texture of the hair, may also be identified with philosophies, leading to the society's definition of a standard of beauty. This in turn may have biological consequences, as persons defined as beautiful may have a better chance of marrying and reproducing, so that over centuries a specific physical type may become predominant. Such selective processes, of course, were never fully operative—many brides in early times were not selected for beauty but were taken captive from another tribe and became mothers whether they were beautiful or not.

During the many centuries when large parts of northern China were ruled by "non-Chinese," many mixed marriages with Chinese women occurred. We even know of cases in which several generations of foreigners again and again married Chinese, choosing their brides according to physical traits, so that a certain selectivity was operative. Furthermore, Chinese in the border or newly conquered territories very often married local women for the simple reason that the bridal price was much lower than the price of a woman from home. This process is still going on in Taiwan. In the long run, such processes can change the appearance of Chinese as well as of non-Chinese. It may well be, for instance, that the small differences between northern and southern Chinese are the result of such intermarriages.

As we shall see, all the processes we have been considering were operative in Chinese society to some degree and affected the development of minority groups.

NATION FORMATION AND NATION DISSOLUTION

In the year 1910 there was no Pakistan. There were no Pakistanis. Even the word *Pakistan* did not exist. At that time those who later became Pakistanis were settled among the Indians, and both were subjects of Britain. They were of the same ethnic stock, had a common culture, and differed from each other only in their religion and their literature: One group was Muslim and used an Arabic script for their literature; the other was Hindu and used the Hindu script. Today there is a Pakistan and there are Pakistanis, and when we visit their country, we feel that they differ in many ways from their neighbors, the Indians. Two men, Gandhi and Jinnah, had visions of the shape their nation should take, and their visions created two different nations. Much blood was shed before this was achieved.

In 300 B.C. there was no France, no England, no Germany; there were no French, no British, no Germans. In the area occupied by their countries today lived numerous tribes that spoke different languages, practiced different religions, and had different cultures. As in the case of Pakistan and India, there were no physical differences. Unlike Pakistan and India, there were no great men who created separate countries. All three countries were originally partially under the colonial rule of the Roman Empire. Out of the dissolution of the empire the nuclei of France and Germany developed and soon extended their power over tribes that had not been part of the empire. A similar thing happened in England, but after the end of Roman rule Saxons and later Normans became dominant and, in a long process of mutual assimilation, what we now know as England developed.

In 1500 B.C. there was no China, and there were no Chinese. The area that is now China was then inhabited by a great number of tribes with different cultures. Though the majority of them belonged to one or another branch of the Mongoloid race, other races were represented. Again, there was no great man who created the first Chinese empire; it grew out of a long, slow process of assimilation and integration over centuries. It is this process and its consequences and results we will discuss in the following chapters. It is not a process completed in the past; it is still going on today. As in Pakistan and the European countries, some cracks are still recognizable in China, and no cautious anthropologist or historian would like to predict whether or not the fissures might develop into breaks at some time in the future.

In the last thirty years we have seen not only new states emerging out of the union of different tribes and groups but also cracks developing in the old, united states. Thus, for example, there are the independence movements among the Welsh and Scots, the Basques, the Bavarians and Prussians, and, perhaps the best example, the northern Irish. We do not know whether the states now on the map will still exist after a hundred years. We are no longer as convinced of the stability of old nations as we were some hundred years ago. At that time there was no question of minorities, no discussion of their rights. The inhabitants of the countries of Europe and Asia were just subjects, with few rights. So it was in China until the beginning of the twentieth century. Only from that time was the word *minority* used to describe the situation of the Chinese Empire. But the roots of the problem lie at the beginning of Chinese history; therefore, we must now go back to the beginnings of Chinese history.

THE EARLIEST "STATES" IN CHINA

Naturally, we do not know when the processes of historical development just outlined took place; they probably occurred at different times in different societies. When, however, the first states developed—that is, when large masses of people belonging to different tribes and cultures were forced to obey the leader of the predominant one of these tribes, and when, thus, these different groups came into close contact with one another—two opposite effects seem to have resulted. First, within the new political unit the different tribes influenced one another. Secondly, the ruler and/or his ruling group tried to solidify their rule. This could be done by what are called political marriages, taking wives from different elements within the realm and attempting through them to establish personal links of loyalty. This custom presupposes that the ruler is representative of his people so that, by his marriage, two different peoples are "married" to one another. Remnants of such a belief still existed in the late nineteenth century in Europe, where political marriages continued until the end of the monarchical age.

Another way to establish unity, often used at the same time as the political marriage, was the creation of certain common symbols, which were imposed on all subjects. In other words, symbols of the state as a unit—the concept of a "Pakistani" or a "Frenchman"—setting members of the state aside from those who formerly were very close to them—the "Indian" or the "Celt." Such concepts may not always have been based upon a political reality. There was a feeling of a Hindu culture, a concept fairly easy to define, although there was no political reality of a Hindu state. There was also, in ancient Greece, a common feeling of "Greekness" among the peoples of the numerous small states, although there was no all-encompassing state of Greece. To understand the development of China in these terms, we should try to find out at what point in history the concept of "China" replaced tribal identifications and loyalties.

We now think that a concept of "China" may have developed around 1050 B.C., as Hua-Hsia (the flowering Hsia), but was some 500 years later replaced by Chung-kuo or the similar Chung-yüan (Country of the Center; Plains of the Center). This is a geographically defined ethnocentric term, for which parallels exist in other societies: Their own country was always in the center of the world; the "others," the "barbarians," were on the outside, the borders of the world, which was thought of as being a flat, square plate surrounded by the four seas. Consequently, the capital of China must be in the center of the world. Indeed, when the Chou conquered the Shang dynasty (around 1050 B.C.) and became rulers of "China," they retained their old capital close to Hsi-an (Sian) as political capital but established a second, *ritual* capital near the present-day city of Lo-yang because for the ancient Chinese Lo-yang was the true center of the world. (In fact, Chinese astronomers defined the "actual" center of the world as a smaller place close to Lo-yang and used this place in their calculations.) When the kings of Chou were defeated by their non-Chinese neighbors and had to give up Hsi-an (Sian), they moved to Lo-yang, which became both the political and the ritual capital of China until the end of the dynasty.

This, then, is a picture of the world as ancient Chinese thinkers had developed it. They started from the belief that the sky is round and the earth is a square. There were some regions that were not covered by the sky—these were dark and not fit for humans.

The idea developed that the whole inhabitable world consists of squares. There is the central point of the world: the seat of the emperor, his palace, which is square. Around it is the capital city, again a square, as ideally all Chinese cities were until very recently. Adjustments to natural conditions have always been made, but such adjustments did not alter the ideal. Thus, the emperor's palace was not in the exact center of the world, as defined by astronomers but in a place that was geographically and militarily suitable for a capital. Not all Chinese cities were square; they often had to take into consideration the course of rivers or ranges of mountains. Around the second square was a larger one, often subdivided into nine small squares: These were the original "nine provinces" of China under the direct rule of the Chinese emperor. We don't think that the area under Chou rule was ever actually divided into nine provinces; as far as we know, there were no provinces at all but rather individual feudal states which numbered far more than nine. The concept of the nine provinces occurs in the *Yü-kung*, which may have been composed in the fourth century B.C., and in the *Chou-li*, which is somewhat later—both at a time when the central ruler was powerless and the country divided into more or less independent feudal states. But the magic number 9 (3 times 3; 3 is a strong number, regarded as male) also appears in the smallest unit, the so-called well-field system of nine plots with a well in the center. So this concept remained, though reality had changed, and in the Han time (206 B.C. to 220 A.D.) heaven and earth were still divided into nine squares, corresponding to the so-called nine provinces, with the polar star corresponding to the emperor, and the environs of the polar star, the polar region of the sky, corresponding to the capital city.

Outside of these "nine provinces" came still further squares, each one several times larger than the foregoing one. Tribes that had been forced into a tributary relation to the Chou Empire were in the first *outer* square, and tribes that were still what we would call independent were still farther outside, in the last of the squares. This arrangement corresponded to the concept of "decreasing dependency." In theory, all of the world was in these squares and, therefore, was subject to the orders of the emperor in the center. The closest parallel in the West may be the city of Rome as center of the world, with the papal seat comparable to the imperial palace and the pope comparable to the emperor. The rest of the world was subject to the orders from the center, but with a decreasing degree of loyalty. Clearly, the tribes living in one of the outer squares had no idea of being a part of the Chinese Empire or of having to be loyal to the Chinese emperor. It is equally clear that the emperor realized that the tribes in the outer squares felt themselves to be independent and could not be relied upon; often even those in the first square outside the capital were of questionable loyalty. But this did not lead the early Chinese to change their basic concept of the world.

The logical consequence of this concept is that all human beings are subjects of the emperor. They can have full "civil rights," in theory, by accepting his rule and behaving as Chinese should behave. In other words, whoever accepted Chinese values and morality was, in theory, a Chinese. Thus the concept of "Chinese" is not a racial but a cultural one. Of course, the practice was not always like the ideal. In theory, a person who had accepted Chinese education, even though he looked different from the way Chinese looked, ought to be regarded as a Chinese. However, in most periods of Chinese history such a person remained a foreigner, as did his children. There were some exceptions, but they were few; we will discuss some of these cases later.

Let us return to the term *Hua-Hsia*: Hsia is the name of the first dynasty of China, which we still cannot identify clearly by archeological remnants. Though the Hsia were regarded by the Chou as the founders of Chinese civilization, the stress of the term lies upon the cultural, not the political, aspect. As we saw, *hua* means flowering, in the sense of beautiful, civilized, or refined. This means that Hua-Hsia was an area in which people were civilized: For instance, they were decently dressed, not nude or half-nude like the tribes around them, and they had both ceremonial and ordinary dress, not the same clothing for daily work and sacred services. They had a script, unlike the tribes that had no script or used incised sticks or knotted strings to record messages or events. They had an elaborated ceremony for the service of the deities, in contrast to the surrounding tribes, which supposedly had barbaric, primitive rituals. They had rules of moral behavior, while the surrounding tribes supposedly "knew their mothers but did not know their fathers." Indeed, the "Chinese" soon began to take steps against tribal concepts they regarded as immoral.

We still cannot prove that there was a *state* ruled by a Hsia dynasty; future excavations may establish at least some solid data of Hsia culture. At the moment it seems to be safest to assume that there was a small political unit in the southern part of the present province of Shansi before 1500 B.C. that most likely did not yet have a developed system of writing but may have used copper or bronze. This unit was annihilated by another, more eastern conglomeration, the second dynasty of China, called Shang. The Shang had a system of writing, and we have numerous texts that, to some degree, confirm what later historians have reported about them. Shang texts mention the names of numerous tribes, and probably several tribal confederations or statelets, against which they conducted wars of aggression, leading to an expansion of their originally small territory.

The Shang were annihilated around 1050 B.C. by a federation of tribes with an organization and a culture comparable to their own. One new group, called Chou, seems originally to have had a language different from the Shang, but after the conquest (or even shortly before) they adopted the writing system the Shang had developed and accepted the language of the Shang court. The preserved texts seem to indicate fairly clearly that the people in eastern China, who were formerly subjects of the Shang, regarded the Chou as different from the Shang. The term *Hua-Hsia* seems to have referred in the first period only to peoples of eastern China and only later to have included the Chou and their people. This was after they had established their capital west of that of the Shang, near the present-day Hsi-an (Sian) in Shensi.

We should point out here that the term *Han* for what we call *Chinese* is of relatively recent origin. It refers to the Han dynasty, which ruled from 206 B.C. to A.D. 220. Our name *China* probably comes from the Ch'in dynasty, which came to an end in 206 B.C. after only forty years of rule. The ancient Indian name for China, *Çina*, was also derived from this dynasty. The Russian name, *Kitay*, or *Cathay*, for a time also used in Western Europe, is derived from the Khitans, an ethnic group, mentioned in Chapter 4, that ruled North China from the tenth to the twelfth century. In the countries south of China Chinese are sometimes called *T'ang*, after the T'ang dynasty. Chinese usually refer to themselves as *Chung-kuo jen*, People of the Middle Country, but this includes the political unit of China, minorities as well as Chinese. As Chang T'ing-hsiu (quoted in *Pien-chiang lun-wen chi* 2, pp. 1065–1066) says correctly, "We must say that the 'Han' of the Han 'race' is only the name of a dynasty, not a racial name. That the Chinese race now calls itself 'Han' race comes from purely political usage."

In conclusion, we can say that the early formation of states in China does not seem to be very different from events in western Asia or Europe—events that still go on in our own time. Groups with different physical traits, different languages, and different cultures are brought together by political forces into a new unit, while other sectors of the same groups may remain outside the new unit and be regarded as "foreigners" until (often) they are brought by the forces of the new unit into their "state." There, they change from "border tribes" into "minorities" and finally into ordinary citizens of the new state.

The Setting

In this chapter we will look at three areas that help to define minorities as distinct from the main population of China, those people who are today called the Han Chinese. The first question concerns the existence of groups who looked different and were therefore regarded, correctly or incorrectly, as different races. Secondly, the many different linguistic groups represented in China may give some indications of the origins of specific peoples. Finally, differences in climate and ecology influenced the economy and culture of groups in different parts of the country.

THE QUESTION OF RACE

Our first question now is: What was the racial situation in the Far East at the beginning of history? We use the word *race* here in its most general sense, differentiating between people who are predominantly white-skinned, black-skinned, or brown-skinned. Chinese use the word *tsu* for this.

In 1980 Chinese archeologists found in a tomb in the eastern part of Sinkiang Province a female with red-blond hair. The tomb was dated from approximately 3,200 years before our time. We will have to wait for detailed investigations before we are able to say whether this woman belonged to the Indo-Europeans who penetrated Central Asia, (formerly Eastern Turkestan, now Sinkiang—a province of China) and, according to the investigations of several sinologists, even reached the heart of north China at some time around 2000 B.C. or somewhat later. In any case, we do not know the hair color of these Indo-Europeans (called Tocharians). Chinese sources of the seventh century and later mention a tribe that has been identified with the Kirgis (Chieh-ku) as having had blond hair. But they lived about 5,000 years later than the person in the tomb, and today's Kirgis in Soviet Central Asia do not have blond hair.

Archeological findings from the time of the Shang dynasty (? to 1050 B.C.) give us a different picture. Excavations of royal tombs at An-yang, a site that perhaps was the last capital of the Shang or at least the burial place of their leaders, have brought out many skeletons, some of which seem to belong to non-Mongol races. Although the excavations were done around 1935, the anthropological results are still not fully published, perhaps because the findings were somewhat embarrassing, just as Europeans would feel embarrassed if remnants of a black race were found in the midst of Europe (and there is a possibility that people with dark skin once inhabited parts of Europe). There are also rumors concerning excavations in Korea during the time of Japanese rule, namely that remains of non-Mongol people were discovered there, people who perhaps were related to races found in Siberia. The late Professor Li Chi, the most famous archeologist of China between 1930 and 1960, has made some preliminary comments about the An-yang findings, stating that there were, together with clearly "Mongol" skeletons—which would be ancestors of the Chinese—others that may have been skeletons of a Negroid (that is, dark-skinned) race and of people related to inhabitants of the South Seas (Micronesians). These findings would not contradict the dominant theories about the development of populations in the Far East and the South Seas. We still today find "Negroid" people in Southeast Asia, the so-called Semang and Senoi, and the Melanesians in New Guinea and adjacent islands. Remnants of dark-skinned people are also reported from the Philippines.

Historical sources often speak of black people in Southeast Asia and Ceylon and in Hunan Province in south China. Though none of these people exist in China today, we have no reports that they were exterminated. Professor Li Chi assumed that these dark-skinned people, who are clearly not related to the black populations of Africa, may have spread from south China or, more likely, Southeast Asia to the Pacific. The light-skinned original inhabitants of the Philippines, Taiwan, Indonesia, and parts of the South Seas may also have left a home in south China several millennia before our time. This opinion is in agreement with more recent investigations of Professor Chang Kuang-chih. We know from texts that the Shang made many war expeditions to the South and the West, and they could well have captured people of other races.

We may conclude that the non-Chinese skeletons found in An-yang were once prisoners of war, sacrificed and killed and buried next to the rulers of the Shang, as their servants in another life. Chinese sources admit the persistence of human sacrifices down to much later times, but already at the time of Confucius, around 500 B.C., clay figures of people often replaced the humans. When the first section of the tomb of Shih-huang-ti, the first Chinese emperor (died 210 B.C.), was recently excavated, it revealed a great number of full-size clay figures, who served as supernatural guardians of the emperor's tomb. Among them are figures that definitely do not appear to be Chinese and must have represented non-Chinese. No detailed anthropological analysis of these figures is published yet, and we do not know whether these non-Chinese lived in the heart of old China or came from distant areas. No doubt further surprises will come forth when more excavations have been made.

In general, the Chinese were reluctant to admit the existence of different races even in early times, when the area they inhabited was not yet colonized by Chinese, just as the Japanese are reluctant to admit that there may have been people living on the Japanese islands who were not all physically like the present-day Japanese, or as the Russians try to believe that there was once a common, uniform, prehistoric culture in Russia proper and in adjacent Russian Central Asia and Siberia.

Archeologists have preferred to speak of "cultures" and have mapped out large areas as belonging to specific cultures. These cultures are characterized mainly by material objects preserved in the soil. However, even in Europe, where this kind of prehistoric study is more than a hundred years old, it has been extremely difficult to identify a prehistoric culture with a specific race or even with a tribe or groups of tribes reported later in historical texts. Such study has recently been carried on in China, too, and prehistorians there describe several cultures, some coexisting, some following one another. When these cultures are found within the political borders of modern China, they are described by Chinese prehistorians as "Chinese," even when their area of distribution goes beyond the present-day borders, in the same way the Russians have treated their prehistorical data. Such conclusions are often more politically inspired than scientifically sound. Let us imagine for a moment that in the year A.D. 3000 archeologists excavate sites of a "prehistoric" culture that seemed to have existed around A.D. 2000 between Helsinki and Moskow. If the excavation did not produce any remnants of writing, the archeologists would probably not find out that Finns were living in the area around Helsinki but would assume that a uniform culture covered the whole area. For example, they would find cars of exactly the same or very similar types, although some of these cars would have been made in Russia and others in Sweden, Germany, or the United States. At the present time and with present methods prehistory cannot help us much in defining the racial situation in early China.

THE QUESTION OF LANGUAGE

When we spoke of Mongols or Indo-Europeans, we meant races and not languages. Just as race and culture are not linked, so race and language are not linked.

In general, linguists assume that the Far East is dominated by two large families of languages: the Chinese/Tibetan/Burmese languages and the Thai languages. The Chinese language belongs to the first group. The Thai languages of Thailand and the adjacent areas contain numerous words that seem related to the Chinese language, but it is not clear whether this indicates a relation of both languages or whether the related words are simply loan-words, in this case, Chinese words that were accepted.

In Southeast Asia and Indonesia we find two dominant language groups, one called *Austroasiatic* and the other *Austronesian*. The relation between the two groups is unknown; even the two terms are still under discussion. However, we find minorities in south and southwest China who speak languages that seem to belong to these language groups. The nineteen tribes on Taiwan, for instance, speak languages related to those of the aboriginal population of the Philippines and probably closely related to Indonesian languages. In the north and northwest we find Manchu tribes, today almost completely extinct, who spoke Tungusic languages, Mongols who spoke Mongolic languages, and Turks who spoke Turkic languages. In the opinion of some scholars the Tungusic, Mongolic, and Turkic languages may belong to a still larger cluster of languages, the so-called Uralo-Altaic languages. Korean seems to belong to this great group of languages, and even the original Japanese may have been an Uralo-Altaic language. So we could say that the Han Chinese—in other words, the main population of the "inner" provinces of China—speak a Sino-Tibetan language, while the minorities belong to several different language groups. But the question is somewhat more complex.

Chinese and foreign linguists have, by use of ancient Chinese rhyme dictionaries, attempted to reconstruct the Chinese language, first, of the time around A.D. 600, then working backward, of around the turn of the Christian era or even of a still earlier period. However, these rhyme dictionaries presented only the language of the court; only one (the *Fang-yen*) includes dialectical expressions from other parts of China. This material has not yet been fully studied, nor has the material to be found in the local gazetteers—handbooks for each district prepared for the information of the prefects who came to the district from outside—been used for linguistic analysis of dialects or languages other than Chinese.

The problem in these reconstructions lies in the fact that the Chinese script is not alphabetical like ours but basically pictorial, with one symbol normally representing a word. Many, though not all, symbols have some indicator that gives a clue to the pronunciation, but usually only the ending sound of a word can be reconstructed on the basis of end-rhymes; the initials are uncertain. In addition, even today most words can serve equally as nouns, verbs, adverbs, or adjectives according to their position in a sentence. This makes a reconstruction of word families very difficult. In fact, such an attempt has not yet been started on a large scale. And without the knowledge of word families comparisons of Chinese with other languages and the detection of foreign words in Chinese are as good as impossible. It may be easy to prove that *Hua-sheng-tun* is *Washington* and *Pa-li* is *Paris*. We may even be able to trace some older words—for example, we are fairly sure that the word for grape, *p'u-t'ao*, comes from Greek *bothrys*, and *mi* (honey) may be from Indo-European *miel*. But to what degree were words from one of the languages spoken by the pre-Chinese population of a part of China assimilated into Chinese? There is still a controversy as to whether some words that are found in early Chou texts, say of the sixth century B.C. and earlier, were of foreign origin and should be taken as a proof that the Chou dynasty was originally of non-Chinese, perhaps Turkic or Altaic, stock. The written documents of the Shang period (before 1000 B.C.) contain a large number (estimates are 30–50 percent) of symbols we cannot read and cannot understand. Did the Shang perhaps speak a language that was not Chinese—that is, not related to the language of the period around 600 B.C.? Recently, texts from pre-Christian times have been found in tombs in South China that contain masses of words unknown so far. Are these words only dialectical variants of High Chinese (the language of the court, usually called *Mandarin*), or did they belong to languages different from the High Chinese?

At the present time all these questions remain unanswered. On the basis of language alone we cannot say authoritatively that the Shang were Chinese, although a great number of the writing signs they used are still used by Chinese. We cannot say with authority that the ancestors of the kings of the Chou dynasty spoke Chinese, because some of their names of persons and objects seem to be non-Chinese. And we cannot prove that the languages of those people who later became minorities exercised no influence upon the Chinese language or a Chinese dialect. Perhaps further research will be able to answer some of these questions.

THE IMPORTANCE OF ECOLOGY

Only a few scholars, such as O. Lattimore, K.A. Wittfogel, and R. Ekvall, have paid attention to ecological factors and shown the importance of ecology for understanding the development of the society of China and its neighbors, though numerous questions are still to be clarified.

Roughly speaking, the whole of China can be divided into two different areas, the north and the south. If we go from the extreme north to the south, we begin with an area that is quite cold, has heavy snow, and was originally covered with forest. In most periods of Chinese history this zone was outside the borders of

China. It comprises the central and northern parts of Manchuria and the Altai Mountains and adjacent parts of Mongolia. South of this comes a very dry area, partly true desert, partly steppe. By the term *steppe* we mean an area with some vegetation, mainly plants but no trees, that receives enough rain, usually in the spring, to produce fat grasses and beautifully flowering annual plants. Farming is possible in the steppe area, but a hailstorm may destroy the crops or a dry year may kill the plants. Deserts cover parts of Sinkiang and the Gobi; the steppe covers the rest of Sinkiang and the northernmost provinces of China, such as Kansu, Sui-yüan, Chahar, Jehol (in the People's Republic grouped together as Inner Mongolia) and those parts of Shensi that are often called the Ordos Steppe. Generally speaking, northern China is an arid zone in which rain is irregular and not always sufficient for farming.

Below the formerly forest-covered mountain range, the Ch'in-ling shan, south of the Yellow River (Huang-ho), begins the south and the moist zone of China. Here, the monsoons bring fairly regular rains, often too much rain. Farming is profitable, especially rice farming, for which inundated fields are ideal. But, at the same time, the area is mountainous, with thick, almost impenetrable forests inhabited by many different animals that supply much subsistence food.

Thus, up until modern times, we find in the north people who were animal breeders and nomads because animals could be moved from a place that was too dry to another one with sufficient grass to feed them. In the south, however, we find on the mountains and hills people who specialize in hunting, combined with a form of cultivation called slash-and-burn, or swidden, agriculture. This kind of farming begins with the burning down of forested hillsides so that only the stems of trees remain. With simple implements seeds are planted into the still-warm soil, which is fertilized by the ashes and gives rich harvests for three to four years. Then the fields are given up, and new fields are opened by the same method. In the plains between the mountains we find people who practice an intensive cultivation of rice and tubers on wet fields, often called garden agriculture.

Thus, the non-Han populations of early China can be divided on the basis of ecological factors into the northern tribes, whose economy was based upon animal breeding with some planting of grain, such as millet and wheat; and the southern tribes, who specialized in the planting of rice and tubers and also practiced (at least in the beginning) some hunting. In time the Han Chinese began to occupy both regions, pushing the aboriginal populations out or assimilating them. The Han people specialized in wheat cultivation in the north, soon improving their methods of farming by irrigation; and they specialized in wet rice cultivation in the south, progressing along the valleys and rivers.

But one important question remains unsolved. Were there long-term climatic changes in China, as have been found in the West? Some scholars think so and believe that in prehistoric times, down to about 1500 B.C., north China's climate was warmer than today. Did such climatic changes force people who originally practiced dry farming to become animal breeders and nomads? And were tribes who originally lived in the desert or steppe zone and practiced dry farming forced to invade the wetter areas of north China when the climate became more and more dry? Some scholars seem to believe so. Others point out that changes in climate were caused not by nature but by humans. There are many reports on big forests with high trees in Shansi Province down to the eighteenth century; these disappeared partly because of the need of the court for good lumber and partly because of the needs of increased population for firewood and for topsoil and tree leaves to fertilize their fields. Indeed, down to this century almost all Chinese housewives and cooks in villages and towns used charcoal daily. According to this view, north China changed and became a more and more marginal farming zone because of human action and increase of population, forcing the Han Chinese to adapt to steppe conditions. We shall soon see to what degree these questions influence our understanding of the relations between the Han Chinese and the minorities.

In summary, we can see that, when a group with a strong sense of its identity—an "in-group" feeling—gave itself a name that finally became the name of China, other groups, for various reasons, remained outside, regarded by the Chinese as "barbarians," non-Chinese. Some remnants of these groups lived inside the area the Chinese regarded as their country; others lived outside the borders of China but were later integrated into China by war and conquest. In time, both were largely integrated; today there are some 60 million of them living inside the political borders of China as "minorities."

Minorities in History and Politics: From Independence to Dependence

Part Two

The Barbarians of
Four Directions

THE ORIGINS OF MINORITIES

In this part we will study the minorities of China through history, beginning with the minorities of the Northeast, then those of the West, the South, and the East. In all cases we see that at first these ethnic groups were independent of China, living as free conglomerations or as loosely structured tribes until, at some moment in history, they lost their freedom and were incorporated into the Chinese Empire. From that moment on, they were "minorities," until the moment when they completely disappeared and were "Chinese."

We will leave out of our discussion some small groups that never were neighbors of China but lived as "subimmigrants" in China during some period of its history. Among these we might mention colonies of long-distance merchants who settled, for instance, in Canton in the eighth century for shorter or longer periods until their annihilation in 879 by the rebel Huang Ch'ao. Most of these people seem to have been Muslims from present-day Iraq.

Other foreigners who settled in China were missionaries. There were Mazdaists, Manicheans, and Nestorian Christians, all of them living in Chinese towns since T'ang times (618–906) or later, and disappearing again before 1350. Mazdaism is a religion which originated in Iran; Manicheism, too, developed in Iran, but contains influences of Christianity. Nestorianism was a Christian sect that spread in the Near East until it was persecuted by the mainstream of Christianity and forced to seek refuge in Iran. Only tombstones, a few of their holy texts in Chinese translations, and some traces of their influence upon Chinese folk religions testify to their existence. Perhaps we could include in this group also the Catholic (since the late sixteenth century) and later the Protestant (after 1800) missionaries who lived in small communities or dispersed in various places in China and have left some traces. By now they have left China again, as have the European businessmen who lived during the nineteenth and early twentieth centuries in various "foreign concessions," or special quarters reserved for them, such as Shanghai and Tientsin.

We will rely primarily upon written documents and not on archeology or prehistory. However, for the earliest time, ending about 1500 B.C., we will have to use various data, only some of them written, for a reconstruction of the early history of the Chinese and their neighbors. In historical times we can discern separate periods. New archeological findings and more thorough study of the available written sources may, in the future, allow us to define these periods, particularly the earliest period, in a better way, and perhaps even discern still more periods. The periods are only to some degree characterized by changes in the processes of production or the organization of society. The *first period* may be said to have ended around 250 B.C. In this period there were groups living more or less independently within the core of China proper who became transformed into minorities. In the *second period*, from about 250 B.C. to around A.D. 1000, China expanded to reach about the size of the eighteen provinces of "China proper," that is, excluding the areas still inhabited by strong minorities, such as Inner Mongolia, Sinkiang, and Tibet. During this period some of the foreign tribes began to organize themselves into larger units, such as tribal federations. Some of these foreign neighbors of China ruled for many centuries over parts of the north of China. Finally, in this period most of the old tribal names of the first period disappeared, and new names began to emerge. In most cases we are not able to link the old names with the new ones, and we also have difficulties in linking the tribal names, especially those of the south, with tribal names of the third period. The *third period* covers the time from about A.D. 1000 to the nineteenth century. Tribal names can now easily be linked to still-existing tribes. In addition, there is much more information in Chinese sources about the culture and social structure of the minority groups than before. A fourth period may yet emerge, a period in which Chinese who, in the nineteenth century, had already flowed over the borders of Imperial China into Southeast Asia and Indonesia may include these parts of the world into a new "China." Whether or not this will happen depends not only on China but on the whole world situation. This period would then be characterized as a period in which the neighbors were already organized according to the model of modern democratic or populist states.

THE ROOTS OF CHINESE CIVILIZATION

Our understanding of the earliest time, that is, the centuries before about 1700 B.C., and before the first period, is naturally based to a large extent upon hypothesis. Other reconstructions based on different hypotheses also exist. Let us look at these briefly.

One old hypothesis, developed in the nineteenth century, posits that the Chinese are themselves immigrants from the Near East who brought civilization with them when they settled in the Wei and Yellow river basins. They mixed with the indigenous population, and so the civilization in the east of Asia began. In this form the hypothesis is dead, but it still lingers in a couple of transmutations

1. The Indo-Europeans, tribes that later appear under the name of Tocharians, arrived by migrations in the Far East and stimulated the formation of a state. Perhaps, it is said, they also brought the horse and the war chariot with them, and because of their superior war technology they could establish a state. As we have already said, the date traditionally given for this Indo-European expansion into Central Asia was between 2000 and 1700 B.C., or even somewhat later. The use of the war chariot and horse seems to be, according to what we know now, earlier in western Asia than in the Far East, and the technical similarity of chariots found in Chinese tombs at An-yang and West Asian chariots is astonishing. And the first real state in the Far East probably did come into existence during or shortly after the eastward spread of Indo-Europeans, though the Far East was not without an

already fairly highly developed culture. Recently, attempts have been made to prove linguistic connections between Chinese and Indo-European languages. This theory is highly controversial and strongly opposed by both Chinese and non-Chinese scholars.

2. A related theory is that the painted pottery (and, according to some other scholars, also the so-called black pottery) of China had its origin in the northern parts of Iran, whence it spread also into other parts of the Near East. In Iran as well as in China the recent dating of the painted pottery is nearly the same, namely, sometime before 3000 B.C. Chinese archeologists oppose this theory, saying that the earliest specimens of this type of pottery are found inside China and only the later types are found in West China (Kansu). Some examples of this pottery in China are, indeed, astonishingly similar to samples from North Iran (Anau). One could say that the samples of early painted pottery in Central China are first attempts to imitate the models brought by trade from Iran; or—as has been suggested—that the dating of the West Chinese (Kansu) pottery is too late. Finally, independent invention is another possibility. We cannot make a final decision as to which theory is correct.

A second hypothesis states that the Chinese were a community, physically quite similar to present-day Chinese, who by their genius created all alone a high civilization, which then spread, by imitation or by force, all over the territory of China proper. This theory fits the old Chinese myths of the cultural heroes of China, who, already before 2500 B.C., invented the characteristic implements of Chinese culture. Speaking against this hypothesis, which is clearly ethnocentric, is the fact that the myths of the culture heroes appear in Chinese texts quite late (mostly around 400 B.C.) and may be, on the one hand, euhemerizations that served to explain the origin of culture, or, on the other hand, claims that served political needs of rival clans in the centuries between 400 and 250 B.C.

I would not deny the possibility that some cultural elements may have reached China from western Asia and the Near East. There are many examples of this sort of importation from later times. But even if we accept Russian theories, which assume that essential elements of Chinese culture—for instance, wheat, millet, painted pottery, and later the techniques of bronze manufacture—came one by one from the West over long periods of time, this cannot satisfactorily explain the ethnic composition and the development of the Chinese state. Importations may have done much to stimulate the development, but they cannot have been decisive. On the other hand, when Chinese authors discuss archeological findings, they regard all artifacts that were made within the borders of modern China as "Chinese." Yet the present-day province of Kansu, in which the painted pottery was found, was inhabited not by Chinese but by tribes that were most probably Tibetan, perhaps Indo-European, until certainly the mid-first millennium B.C.; some parts became "Chinese" only at the end of the first century B.C.

STATES AND TRIBES

The hypothesis accepted here, and briefly alluded to above (p. 8), is based upon the fact that none of the other high civilizations of ancient times was created by a "master race"; that all cases of the creation of a "state" involved a fusion of more than one ethnic element. Rather, the process of state formation is usually a fusion of several tribes with different social structures. As far as our knowledge goes, this process, and at the same time the development of the first settlement that deserves to be called a city, seems to have begun in China not much before 1700 B.C. By 1500 B.C. we already find numerous settlements in the form of towns. The societies existing on the soil of present-day China before that period could be called tribal. According to Chinese traditional history, this period would fall into the so-called Hsia dynasty, which the Chinese themselves recognize as their first dynasty but which may not have been what we would call a state (different ethnic groups ruled from a central city).

Certainly the Shang dynasty (around 1500 B.C.? to 1050 B.C.) *was* a state. The Shang produced masses of documents, mainly texts of oracles, though not yet (as far as we know now) historical texts. Nevertheless, we find in these oracular texts numerous names of tribes and also names of towns that were not, or at least not solidly, under Shang rule. We also learn that the Shang waged many wars and captured masses of people and animals, some of which were used as sacrifices, as recently revealed by the excavations of tombs. Most of the tribes and their towns are not yet identified. However, we very often find a name that was still familiar in later times, the Ch'iang. The Ch'iang seem to have been the main enemies of the Shang; they lived close to the center of the Shang state and west of it. Later sources make it clear that the Ch'iang were tribes belonging to Tibetan stock, relatives of other Tibetan tribes still living today. We also find the name Ch'iang in Chinese texts written after 500 B.C. that are still preserved. The oracular bone inscriptions have given us proof that these historical texts are by and large quite reliable for the Shang time.

On the assumption that the relatively late texts are reliable, we can proceed in a different way. We can take all references to people who were different from the writers—that is, not Chinese—found in texts of our first period (1500? to about 1050 B.C.) and try to establish the place where they lived. Chinese historians spoke of "the barbarians of the four directions." And we find, indeed, references to tribes all around the focal point of Chinese civilization during the first period. The map we can construct shows that, at best, only a tiny area is not inhabited by "barbarians" and is, therefore, "Chinese."

Ecological and Economic Symbiosis

Cases in which two groups share one geographical area, the one living in the plains while the other lives on the hills, are well-known from other parts of Asia and from China (Yünnan Province) down to the present time. As we discussed in Chapter 1, there is usually a kind of symbiosis between them. For instance, the Ch'iang, peoples of Tibetan stock, lived right in the center of China even after the end of the Shang. What does this mean? First of all, there seems to be a clear indication that the central area of Chinese culture was inhabited by more than one ethnic group. As Tibetans in later periods are normally sheep breeders who prefer to live on mountains rather than on plains, we can assume that the Ch'iang, as a subgroup of Tibetans, at early times also already lived on the mountains, while the valleys and plains were inhabited by "Chinese" who practiced wheat farming and perhaps, even at this early date, rice cultivation. The Ch'iang are mentioned here only as one example to clarify the hypothesis: Chinese and Ch'iang settled in the same area, each group exploiting its own ecological niche.

Symbiosis does not exclude occasional fights, and the numerous wars against the Ch'iang by the Shang rulers may indicate one or several things. It is quite possible that the Shang expanded and took some hilly areas occupied by Ch'iang away from them; equally possible is that the Ch'iang descended occasionally from their hills and let their sheep eat the green grain in the fields on the plains. Or perhaps the Shang rulers needed human bodies to perform the numerous sacrifices by which they implored their deities to help them. We know from later histories that the Chinese preferred mutton to beef and that down to late historical periods the sheep were imported from areas inhabited by relatives or descendants of the Ch'iang. The Chinese usually did not raise sheep, probably because of the difficulty of keeping them away from the fields and the necessity to graze them on hills where farming was not possible.

We also know that the Shang had cattle, horses, and pigs. Horses were essential for their war chariots. Cattle were used as harness animals, more often for wagons than for ploughs. Beef as meat was not much appreciated in China down to the mid-twentieth century. Horses, which were used for the Shang war chariots, do not flourish in the climate of China. Until recent times horses were imported from the people north of China—Mongols or Turks—or from the Ch'iang in the west. Tibetan horses are a different breed from Mongolian horses. The Shang also kept pigs. All through Chinese history pigs and dogs were the garbage and human waste collectors around the house; the garbage was recycled into meat, which again fed the humans. Pigs flourish in almost every climate, but best in wooded and not too hot places. The white pig seems to have been typical of North and East China and to be connected with a special ethnic group of the Northeast; the black pig, on the other hand, seems to be typical of West China and linked to the original inhabitants of the present province of Szu-ch'uan.

Rice, now the typical grain for the south and center of China but marginal in the areas inhabited by the Shang—that is, the southern part of Hopei, the western part of Shensi, and east of Honan—was and still is always linked to Thai people. It is still unknown whether rice cultivation was developed on the soil of today's China or in Thailand. However, this question is, in a sense, wrongly put because, as we shall see later, long before a Thai state developed, Thai tribes lived in parts of China.

North China has been wheat and millet country down to the present time. Many scholars think that millet was cultivated first in East Africa and from there spread all over Asia; wheat was cultivated first in the Near East (eastern Turkey, Iran, Iraq) and then brought to China. This may be so, and it seems that wheat came later than millet. But the assertion has also been made that both plants were independently cultivated in the Far and the Near East. Both are well suited to the dry climate of North China and the adjacent steppes. The Shang seem to have had both grains, in addition to numerous vegetables, the distribution of which has not yet been studied.

The time before the first period, then, was a time in which tribes of different cultures (as shown by the different domesticated animals and plants) coexisted and began to coalesce. The focal point was in the area of southern Hopei, western Shantung, and eastern Honan. This process came to a preliminary end around 250 B.C. Until that time we find non-Chinese tribes right in the center of the area that was inhabited by "Chinese." The Chinese fought against these tribes and pushed forth into the areas where the tribes still lived. Both groups, the people who already regarded themselves as a distinct group—as Chinese—and the non-Chinese, soon called barbarians, melded together, each one assimilating some elements of the other in a slow process that may have been peaceful at times and warlike at others. In the end, a highly specialized, ecologically well suited, unified culture and society emerged—the early Chinese culture. But in it we can detect—often still in our time—many of the elements of a tribal past.

The Minorities of the Northeast and the North

THE MANCHUS

Beginnings

We shall first consider a group of tribes that lived in the area that is now Manchuria (Chinese at present use the term *Northeast province*) and apparently also in parts of North Korea. Reports of these people in Chinese sources begin in the middle Chou period (about 500 B.C.) and end sometime before A.D. 600. Earlier texts described the tribes as fairly primitive, subsisting mainly by hunting with bow and arrow. Down to the third century A.D. their arrows were made of a special wood and had an arrowhead made of stone. Chinese in North China used the same wood even later than that, but replaced the stone arrowhead with a metal one. These tribal people had armor made of bone plates, a technique the Chinese also used before they made metal-plate armor, at the latest in the third century B.C.

In addition to hunting some groups practiced farming, cultivating wheat and millet as well as some vegetables, using a plough that had to be drawn by two people. Their main animal was the pig. The forests with mixed trees, among them oaks, are the natural environment of pigs but do not provide good food for cattle or horses. It is reported that they had horses but did not ride them, using them only for pulling carts. Cattle seem to have been quite rare. The pigs supplied them with leather, the main element of their clothing, and lard, which they used as a skin cream to protect them from the harshness of the winter climate. They used human urine to wash their heads, a custom widely reported among modern Siberian tribes but also occurring in parts of North China.

Most peculiar was their housing: Their houses were pits, sunken into the ground and lined with lumber. They could be entered either from the top by a ladder or from the side by a gangway leading down. Such subterranean or partly subterranean houses are still found in modern Siberia. But more important is that the earliest houses excavated in China proper also were of this kind. This form of house apparently was used in winter, at a time when there was no rain, only snow. In summer they lived in what the texts describe as "tree nests." We think that this means wooden buildings on posts, most practical when the ground is wet or inundated.

Map 1   The minorities of the Northeast and North

We do not know exactly what larger group these tribes belonged to, mainly because they disappear from the texts and new names come up, perhaps indicating new tribes. It seems certain that all were the ancestors of the present-day Tungus tribes. It is also almost certain that tribes of this type were among the ancestors of the Koreans; they certainly inhabited an area that included at least the northern part of Korea. It seems likely that Korean society and culture developed not long before the beginning of our era from a fusion of several ethnic elements. Many scholars assume that the Korean language is largely based upon a Tungusic root, and the Tungusic languages are believed to be related to Turkic and Mongolic languages, the so-called Altaic languages.

Old texts report the legend of the origin of the first "state" in this area:

When in ancient times, the ruler of So-li[1] went out, his handmaid got pregnant during his absence. When the ruler came home, he wanted to kill her, but the handmaid said: "Before this, I saw a vapor in the sky, as large as the egg of a chicken. This vapor

[1]Not identifiable; Fu-yü, mentioned later, is in the area of Kirin in Manchuria.

descended upon me and impregnated me." The ruler incarcerated her. Later, when she gave birth to a boy, the ruler let him be put into the pigsty, but the pigs blew on him with their mouths and so he did not die. Then he let him be put into the horse stable, but the horses did the same. Now the ruler thought he was a supernatural being, and let his mother raise him. He gave him the name Tung-ming [Light from the East]. When Tung-ming was grown up, he was an excellent sharpshooter. The ruler was angered by his fierce [temperament] and again planned to kill him. But Tung-ming fled and went south to the Yen-szu River.[2] Using his bow, he struck the water and the fish and turtles came together and floated on the surface. Tung-ming used them and crossed over. He then came to Fu-yü and ruled over Fu-yü as king. (*Hou Han shu*, 115, p. 2a)

THE JURCHENS

The name Su-shen was given to the most typical and most often mentioned tribe of this larger group. About the culture of the Su-shen we know almost nothing. One text mentions that they still used stone arrowheads, when the Chinese had for centuries used metal arrowheads. They kept pigs and probably also other animals. For many centuries we hear nothing about the Su-shen; contacts of the Chinese with them seem to have stopped. Then, the name Ju-chen begins to appear. Ju-chen corresponds with the modern term *Djurdchen* or *Jurchen*. The Jurchens began to play a political role only in the late eleventh century A.D. At this time they had formed a confederation of tribes, and had accepted much of the culture of the Liao (Khitan), another federation of tribes that lived south of them and controlled the Jurchen tribes before they had formed a unit. Soon the Jurchens created their own dynasty (1115) and destroyed the Liao (Khitan) (see p. 38) state (1125). Immediately thereafter (1126), they conquered large parts of North China including the capital of the Northern Sung dynasty. They even took the emperor prisoner. They advanced further and reached the Yang-tse River. This was their maximum extension, and soon a slow retreat began, characterized by constant fights between them and the Chinese, who by then had reformed into the Southern Sung dynasty with a capital at the modern city of Hang-chou.

The Jurchens, whose ruling dynasty was called the Chin or "Golden People," were clearly a federation of Tungus tribes. When we speak here and later of federations characterized by a certain language, we do not mean to say that all tribes spoke the same or even a closely related language. The leading tribe spoke that language, but each of the federations of which we hear also included tribes that spoke different languages and were not forced to accept the language of the leaders. Many elements of the old Su-shen culture are still visible in the Jurchen culture, though Jurchen culture was more advanced. Their state now was an imitation of the Liao (see p. 37) and, ultimately, of the Chinese state because the Liao had formed their state according to the Chinese model. There were military and civil bureaucrats, solid houses and palaces, a modern army with a fine cavalry; the use of iron, steel, and copper was widespread; and the life of their upper class was not too different from the life of well-to-do Chinese.

The Jurchens were the first people of the Tungus group who were able to conquer large parts of China and to rule over the Chinese. Some of their tribes had earlier been subjects of other federations in the North (which we will mention below), but as a federation they had never been subjects of China. When the

[2]This may be the present Kai-sze River in Korea.

Chinese subjugated parts of Korea for a short period in Han times and early T'ang times, some of the tribes must have come temporarily under Chinese control.

In 1139 one of the tribes in the Jurchen federation revolted and began to create a new federation; this tribe was not a close relative of the Jurchens' ruling tribe, and, it seems, spoke a different language. In 1147, with other tribes, some related to this tribe and some not, the leader of this tribe formed a federation called the Mongols and assumed the title of emperor. This quickly expanding federation annihilated the Jurchen empire in 1234. Many of the Jurchen tribes retreated into Manchuria, their old home. Thus, what we call the Mongol Empire was led by men from the dominant tribe and early followers, who spoke a language closely related to the modern Mongolian language; but it also included tribes of other origins, such as the Jurchens.

Soon, Manchuria and Korea came under Mongol domination; the Mongols even tried twice to conquer Japan, but both attempts ended in total failure and a great loss of men and ships. When the armies of the new Chinese Ming dynasty (1368–1644) drove the Mongols out of China, the Ming rulers gained some control over Manchuria and even over Korea, which was then attacked by the Japanese, a development the Ming rulers wanted to prevent. Therefore, they founded military posts in southern Manchuria to prevent the tribes from threatening Chinese lines of communication with Korea. For this purpose the Chinese also used soldiers recruited from among the tribes of the area. These soldiers learned Chinese ways of warfare and organization; they also learned Chinese technology, which allowed them to make their own weapons. In time, the various detachments of Tungus began to unite and establish their leaders in one tribe, which called itself Manchu.

The Manchu Dynasty

Time had not stood still: The stone arrowheads of the Su-shen became iron heads. The old tribal societies changed more and more into societies with a military organization that had learned from the Chinese military. Their economy became more diversified, and farming as well as trade increased. They delivered furs and skins to Chinese traders and received Chinese products, including advanced weapons. But perhaps the most important change was the development of script systems of their own. First the Khitan from the tenth century and then the Chin developed scripts modeled after the Chinese script (at least it looked similar to Chinese script; the decoding of these two systems is not yet completed). But then the Mongols learned from the Uygurs of Sinkiang a system that fit their language better, and the Manchus adopted this Mongol script with some changes relevant to the structure of their own language. The Mongols have kept their script until the present day; Manchu script is today as good as extinguished. The use of a script of their own enabled the Manchus to create a bureaucracy and thus set up a more efficient political and economic organization than would be possible without script.

The more the power of the Ming dynasty declined in the sixteenth century as a consequence of poor administration and numerous serious uprisings, the greater was the opportunity for the Manchu federation to gain power. When finally the emperor of the Ming, threatened in his own palace in Peking, committed suicide and the rebel Li Tzu-ch'eng set himself up as ruler of China, the chance of the Manchus had come. A Chinese imperial general, Wu San-kuei, was opposed to the rebel emperor—and perhaps interested in making himself emperor. As his own Chinese troops, stationed in Manchuria, were not strong enough for this task, he asked the Manchus, who in the meantime had become independent of Chinese control, to help him in the reconquest of China. This plan succeeded—the rebel Li had to flee and was later killed—but the Manchus made it clear that they and not General Wu would rule. They established the Ch'ing or Manchu dynasty in 1644 and ruled as the last imperial dynasty of China until the end of 1911. Wu San-kuei helped the Manchus in their conquest of South and Southwest China but then again tried to establish a Chinese state under his own leadership. He was able to defend himself against the Manchus until his death, but his son was defeated by Manchu armies. This was the end of Chinese resistance against the foreign rulers.

Conquerors have often been a minority in the countries they conquered—just think of Pizarro or Cortes in the Americas. In such cases we do not use the term *minority* but rather speak of colonial rule. In the case of the Manchu dynasty neither the Chinese themselves nor the Western nations regarded the Manchu as a colonial power but as a regular, legitimate Chinese dynasty. This changed only in the last period of Manchu rule, when Chinese politicians began to speak of the foreign rule of the Manchus that should be ended and replaced by Chinese rule.

The Manchus themselves were conscious of their foreign origin and their minority status and tried by all means to fortify and protect their rule. We do not know how large the Manchu group was, but, around 1700, among some 300 million Chinese, they constituted probably less than 2 percent of the population. They tried and, we may say, succeeded well in consolidating their rule by two different processes.

One concerns the person of the emperor and his family. From the beginnings of the dynasty on, the imperial family tried to learn the Chinese language and literature. In fact, they did so well that the young princes forgot their own Manchu language, and some Jesuits who had learned Manchu were engaged to teach the princes their native tongue. From the great emperor of the K'ang-hsi period (1662–1722) on, the emperors were scholars of Chinese, fully educated like Chinese of the upper class. Some of them were able not only to write in good style but also to compose Chinese poems. They mastered the classical literature and were familiar with Chinese history. In no way were they inferior to Chinese emperors of earlier times.

Though they performed the state sacrifices and official ceremonies exactly as they had been performed traditionally, the Manchu emperors also continued, among themselves, to perform some old Manchu ceremonies and cults that we may characterize as shamanistic. They kept their old marriage system alive, and no Manchu emperor could marry other than a Manchu woman from one of the leading families of the leading tribes. Even their concubines had to be of Manchu stock. At a time when most Chinese women of the upper and even lower classes walked around with tiny, bound, crippled feet, Manchu women were not allowed to adopt this fashion. Manchu men and women also kept their specific style of clothing, which was different from the contemporary Chinese style. Even after the end of the Manchu dynasty Manchu men could be recognized by their way of greeting one another. And although most Manchus had lost their own language and spoke fluent Chinese without an accent, they remained conscious of their origin as Manchu.

On the other hand, the Manchu emperors, outwardly "Chinese" emperors, set up a system of rule we would today call racist, although the Manchus were not racially different from the Chinese. Manchu soldiers were stationed in all provinces of China, where they lived in garrisons. They were usually not active, as there were few revolts against Manchu rule. Each of the more important positions in the civil and military administration had to be filled by a Manchu, who was assisted by a Chinese. The latter was subordinate to the Manchu, at least in theory, although often he was better qualified than his Manchu boss. Normally, a Chinese could enter the bureaucracy only by passing the state examinations. There was a *numerus clausus*, that is, each year only a certain number of people could pass, so many qualified applicants failed because the quota was filled. Manchus also had to pass examinations. However, there were many slots for them, and, furthermore, their examinations were much easier than those for the Chinese. Some vacancies in the central government were open only for Manchus, as were some governorships. There were, of course, many capable and active Manchu officials, but more often than not the actual work was done by the Chinese assistant and then approved by the Manchu official, if he did not overrule it.

The military contingents of the Manchus were organized in the form of detachments called *banners* (*ch'i*). This form of military organization was first created by Mongols and later taken over by the Manchus. There were eight such banners; some were purely Manchu, but some were also Chinese, manned primarily by Chinese who had surrendered to the Manchus very early. A Chinese banner could have either Manchu or Chinese leaders, but a Manchu banner could not have Chinese leaders. There was a special jurisdiction for the Manchu banners; Chinese officials could punish only Chinese, not Manchu, bannermen.

Manchus were better paid and received higher rewards than Chinese. Manchus received land inside China and, in addition, their military pay and military food allotments were paid by the Chinese. Only after 1728 were Manchu civilians subject to the same laws as Chinese.

In spite of all this discrimination the system worked quite well during the first 150 years. The emperor of the Chi'en-lung period (1736–1796) brought China to a peak of glory and wealth hardly ever experienced before; certainly, China reached its greatest expansion at this time, greater than even today. China's population increased rapidly. Modern historians point out the roots of decay in the eighteenth century, but it is important to note that there were no rebellions against the foreign rulers during this period. The Manchus were "Chinese" emperors, in spite of their discriminatory administrative system.

The reasons for this acceptance of what was essentially a colonial regime seem to be multiple, different for the upper class and for the commoners. The Manchus made it clear that they admired Chinese culture by learning Chinese and accepting a largely Chinese style of life. They drew Chinese scholars to their court and honored them; they collected objects of Chinese art—the so-called Palace Museum in Peking (parts of the collection are now in Taiwan) was the collection of the Chi'en-lung emperor—and some Manchus were poets who expressed themselves in beautiful classical Chinese. The educated Chinese upper class had career possibilities, as they had had before under the Chinese Ming dynasty, and the limitations set for their ambitions were not really serious. There was no aristocracy in China and therefore no class of people who lost their privileges after the conquest. The Manchus did not expropriate the property of the rich landowners from whose families many of the scholars came; they made a new land survey but no land reform that could have impoverished the landlords.

The common people in China traditionally had never had contact with the emperor. The emperor could not see his citizens. He lived far from them in his palaces. When the emperor traveled, people had to put their heads on the ground so that they could not see anything. The emperor's only contact with the people was the local magistrate, comparable to a county administrator. The emperor feared the magistrate and avoided contact with him as far as he could, though he had to see this official when he was called to court or when he sued somebody, and that was a dangerous business in any case. The magistrate remained the same as before the Manchu conquest: He was a Chinese. The only difference was that the early Manchu regime controlled the local officials better and corruption was less common. What really mattered for the common people was peace—and the Manchus established peace in the interior of China. The many wars they conducted were in areas largely populated by non-Chinese, far away from the land in which the Chinese peasants lived. Moreover, the Manchu garrisons in early times controlled bandits, the other great danger for the life and welfare of the peasants. So, why should anyone rebel against the colonial regime?

The Fall of the Manchus

The first massive reaction against the Manchus began in the nineteenth century. It grew quickly after the first military defeats of the Chinese by European attackers and the apparent inability of the emperors to drive the foreigners out and reclaim all the territorial and other privileges they had wrested from the imperial government. It is not important whether the blame was really with the Manchu court and its officials or whether the Chinese in the administration were equally at fault. Chinese nationalism, at least in part fostered by Western literature on nationalism and democracy, began to grow among the intellectual leaders of China, and this nationalism turned against the Manchus as "foreigners," an occupation power. In the seventeenth century the Manchus had forced all male Chinese to change their hair style and wear a "pigtail" as a sign of submission. Original opposition to it was short-lived. At the end of the nineteenth and the beginning of the twentieth centuries, however, the pigtail suddenly became an unacceptable symbol of submission. One of the first acts of the Chinese revolutionaries was to cut it off as a sign of liberation.

In February 1912 the Manchu emperor finally had to abdicate, and a purely Chinese republican system, shaped somewhat after the Western European and American models, was created. What happened to the Manchus? They could not return to their old homeland, Manchuria. Almost all Manchus had left Manchuria and had settled inside China proper. For a fairly long time the Manchus had tried to keep Chinese out of Manchuria, but after a period of secret influx from the northern provinces of China immigration into Manchuria was officially allowed. Settlers flooded the country, opened up land that had been forest or pasturage, and set up villages and towns. Manchuria became a Chinese country, and three new provinces were opened in the Northeast, as Manchuria was soon called. Even though many settlers had arrived as tenants of absentee Manchu landlords, the landlords could not return because they could not force the Chinese settlers to go back or to continue to pay rent, as they were now protected by a Chinese republican administration. Other Manchus had acquired property inside China, had established themselves in business or trade, had concluded marriages with Chinese families and adopted Chinese family names. In short, they had become assimilated.

In the 1920s ethnographers could still find in Manchuria some small Tungus tribes such as the Solons—tribes who had not been members of the Manchu tribal and military federation, who were still able to speak their own language, and who continued to live as hunters in their old ways. A group of a few dozen people is today recognized as a minority—which could make these people China's smallest minority—but, in general, the Tungus tribes in Northeast China disappeared by becoming Chinese. When the Japanese occupied Manchuria during World War II, they set up a shadow government called Manchu-kuo (in Japanese, Manchukoku), which lasted until 1945, ruled nominally by the last Manchu emperor, the Hsüan-t'ung emperor. But this "Country of the Manchu" was populated by Chinese. A Manchu revival or renaissance did not take place, nor was this intended by the Japanese. After 1945 the Hsüan-t'ung emperor became a subject of the Communist regime, where he lived a pitiful life until his death in 1968. Hence, we do not find a Manchu minority in China today. The Manchus are the only colonial rulers of China who were not killed or exterminated when their rule ended, but who also did not return to their old home country and did not try to reform into a new unit under their own rulers. They simply became Chinese.

THE MONGOLS

Let us now move farther to the west, into the area directly north and west of Peking. This is the old territory of Mongol tribes, that is, tribes that spoke a "Mongol" language. Mongol is related to languages farther west, the Turkic and Altaic languages. There are apparently some connections between Mongol and Tungus languages, but we are not yet clear whether these connections indicate an original common root or whether they are the result of cultural contacts. Racially the Mongols are today very little different from Tungus and Northern Chinese, so that they cannot easily be identified when all are dressed the same way.

Early History

The earliest history of the Mongols is still unclear. The first tribes of this area mentioned in historical sources were called Tung-hu. This term simply means eastern hu; *hu* was a term used by the Chinese as a general name for all tribes north and northwest of China proper. Some scholars point to the similarity of Tung-hu with *tongus*, which means pig, and with Tungus, the tribal group discussed above. As we saw, keeping pigs was for a time characteristic of Tungus tribes. Today, we reject such identifications and regard the Tung-hu as a group of tribes that may have been Mongol. The name Tung-hu disappears around the beginning of our era and we find instead new names that seem to indicate not so much individual tribes as tribal federations.

The first new group are the Wu-huan, who fought the Chinese as sometimes quite dangerous enemies between the beginning of the common era and the end of the third century A.D. The Wu-huan are described as good hunters who lived in tents that opened toward the east and the rising sun. They dressed in woolen cloth and drank *kumys*, a drink made of fermented mare's milk, slightly intoxicating and somewhat comparable to a light beer. The use of wool indicates that they kept sheep, and the use of kumys that they had horses. Chinese sources say that they had no script and used notched sticks to keep records, a custom that was widely known all around China in early times. What astonished the chroniclers most was the structure of their families. A man abducted the woman he wanted to have, but after that he had to give gifts in the form of cattle to his wife's family. He moved in with his in-laws and worked for them instead of for his own family, as Chinese would do. The texts also indicate that women had a say in political questions, another custom unheard of in China. When a Wu-huan died, there was a funeral with dancing and singing. A horse and a dog were sacrificed in honor of the dead, the dog to guide the soul to the Red Mountain. The Wu-huan venerated the deities of mountains and rivers, heaven and earth, sun and moon. The belief that the dead live on top of a holy mountain has parallels in the old Chinese religion.

At almost the same time the Wu-huan appear in early chronicles another and more powerful tribal federation is mentioned—the Hsien-pi. Chinese sources say that their language and culture is identical with that of the Wu-huan, though nothing is said about the role of women in their society. The Hsien-pi language, of which only a few words are reported in Chinese sources, has been said to be a mixture of Mongol and Tungus languages.

The Hsien-pi appear as a political unit, more powerful than the Wu-huan. When the Wu-huan slowly faded out and disappeared, the Hsien-pi succeeded in occupying parts of Northern China and created a number of dynasties, all of which were short-lived but often wielded great power. There is an Earlier Yen dynasty (352–370) under the leadership of the Mu-jung tribe, a Later Yen dynasty (384–409), a Western Yen dynasty (384–394), a Western Ch'in dynasty (385–431), and a Southern Liang dynasty (379–414). All these dynasties were military regimes that had no time, and perhaps no real interest, to build up a system of government in which the foreign masters and their subjects could live in peace.

In fact, we do not know how the Chinese fared; almost all of our information concerns the military rulers and their fights among themselves and with other pretenders.

Power and Organization

The inability to establish more permanent states seems to have two roots. First, neither the Hsien-pi nor the Wu-huan had an aristocracy: There was no tribe among them that had, for some historical reasons, higher prestige than the others and which, therefore, had a traditional right to lead and to rule, as was true later among the Hsiung-nu tribes. Thus, their federations were always unstable. Tribes joined in a federation and conquered land, but when the leader of the federation was incompetent, they left the first federation and joined another one. So there was no continuity of rule.

Secondly, there seems to be a typical development among tribes that form federations when no aristocracy exists. The chief of such a federation could never be sure of the loyalty of the tribes other than his own. To assure himself of loyalty, such a ruler, again and again in history, tried the same policy—separating the tribal leader from his tribe. This could be done by brute force, by murdering the leader and his family. A better and safer way, however, was to make the leader of a tribe commander of a group that was larger, and therefore more powerful, but which was not his own group. The man felt himself honored and eager to assume more power but usually forgot that in his new position his power was based solely upon his personal qualities rather than heredity; he could not count on the automatic loyalty his own tribe had given him. The next step was then to see that he was deprived of his power and replaced by a relative of the chief of the federation.

The relative would be loyal, it was hoped, as long as the chief lived, but there was no guarantee for the next generation.

Along with this strategy of power, a clever chief would try to split up the tribes by adopting a kind of military organization comparable to that of the Chinese, that is, one based upon the military qualifications of single men and small groups. Thus, a tribal organization was slowly transformed into a military one, in which men were able to rise above the level of other tribesmen but in which they served in units composed of men of different origins. This process, when it goes on for some time, breaks down the tribes: Tribes simply disappear from history, or else the remaining elements of the tribe move away, often hundreds of miles, and begin a new tribal life. But in time the new military formations had a tendency to merge and to reform themselves as a new kind of tribe, as such often assuming a new name. In such cases we speak of a *secondary tribe*. History books may suddenly present us with "new" tribes, but these were in fact newly formed groups composed of different factions of former tribes. The secondary tribe may take on the name of an old one because its newly established leaders came from the old tribe. In this case we find two tribes in different areas both with the same name and, in part, the same history. To make things even more complicated, one of these tribes may later join a new federation, while the other joins a totally different federation in a different area. Thus, we later have tribes with the same name in Afghanistan and in Mongolia belonging to different federations and often even speaking different languages.

In sum, we can say the cause of the political weakness of Hsien-pi federations was their lack of an aristocracy and their attempts to transform the members of the federation from tribes into military units, a process that was never quite accomplished.

The Shih-wei

The Hsien-pi dynasties disappeared shortly after A.D. 400. We know that several of their tribes joined the Toba federation (which we will study in the next chapter); others reappear as tribes of the Shih-wei. The Shih-wei leaders were clearly Mongols. Their homeland historically was north of the Hsien-pi and Wu-huan, in the transitional zone from the wooded country of southern Siberia to the steppe and desert. They seem to have migrated slowly out of their forests into the steppes, which apparently involved a decrease in the importance of hunting—it became more of a sport than a way to get food—and an increased emphasis on cattle breeding. Chinese sources mention many Shih-wei tribes with different cultures according to the area in which they lived. The southern tribes moved from the south, where they lived in the winter, to the north in the summer, as genuine nomads who had to find pasturage for their cattle. They lived in their carts so as to be easily mobile. Their northern brothers lived in tents covered with the bark of birch trees. We have reports that some of them lived in caves during the winter. The sources mention that there were many deer; we believe this meant reindeer. Even the use of skis or snowshoes is reported. The dead of these northern tribes were buried on a platform in trees. These and other traits continued among the Siberian tribes as late as the 1930s, and they may still exist today.

As the majority of the Shih-wei tribes lived far from the borders of what was China between A.D. 400 and 700, they had little direct contact and no wars with Chinese. Another group of these Mongols were the Qai (in Chinese sources, Hsi), who lived farther west and were known not only to the Chinese but also to the people of the Near East.

Tribal Federation and the Khitans

Most important among early settlers in Mongolia, who probably spoke a language related to Mongol, were the Khitans (Chinese, Ch'i-tan), who gave their name to China in Russian sources (Kitay), from which is derived the English Cathay. They are first mentioned in the latter half of the fourth century A.D. Chinese sources say directly that they were like the Shih-wei, and descriptions of their culture confirm this. The only peculiar trait noted is their use of a human skull for sorcery, a custom they retained for a long time, even when they ruled over North China.

Like most of the tribes of the north, the Khitans had an origin myth according to which a young man on a white horse and a young maiden in a cart drawn by a black ox met at the confluence of two rivers. They married, and their children became the ancestors of the original eight tribes of the Khitans. This myth indicates that the tribal federation of the Khitans was structured in a way we find in several other federations. There was a dominant tribe, in which there was a dominant family, out of which came the traditional leader. Though tribes usually consisted of several or even many separate families, the people believed that all of them were related to one another and had a common ancestor. The founder of a federation was a man with special leadership abilities; these made him the head of his tribe if he was not a descendant of the tribal leader's family. Typically, such a leader induced a number of related tribes to join him, under his leadership. This could be a voluntary act of the tribes—for instance, the result of a political marriage of the leader with women of one or several tribes. It could also be half-voluntary, when the other tribes became weaker (which could easily happen as the result of a harsh winter in which the tribe lost most of its animals, for instance) and joined the leader in order to avoid being conquered. Thus, we start with an original federation of eight tribes, the "inner circle" of privileged tribes. Traditionally, the chief of the federation took his main wife from one of these tribes of the inner circle; the latter tribe was then often called the "uncle of the state's tribe," as the father of the "empress" is by marriage an uncle of the "emperor." (We do not know whether the Khitans used terms like *state*, *emperor*, and *empress* at this time, but we do know that a preferential marriage system for the ruler existed from the time the federation came into existence.)

Led by its chief's drive for power, the small federation could attempt to conquer other tribes. If this enterprise was a failure, the federation was finished and disappeared from the map. When it was a success, more tribes were by force added to the federation. Fifty or even a hundred tribes could be added in this way as "outer tribes." They owed loyalty to the chief, supplied him with soldiers in war, and benefited from even later conquests. But some of them might have been in a state of servitude: Their sons would have had to serve the ruler, and they themselves might have been obliged to produce certain objects, such as arrows and other weapons or cloth, as a yearly tribute. In some cases whole tribes were degraded to slave tribes, with individuals becoming slaves of the ruler, the ruling tribe, tribes of the inner circle, or individual leaders of inner tribes. At this point the society had become highly structured and aristocratic.

The economic question now becomes important. We will discuss parts of this problem in the next chapter. However, we should note here that a large federation needs to keep a fairly large army. Military preparedness reduced the Khitans' productivity: There were not enough men available to take care of the cattle and sheep that were their source of food. Their agrarian neighbors—China—had much desirable food, especially grain, which can be stored, while animal products spoil easily. Thus, the temptation to attack the agrarian neighbor was great, especially given the riches and luxuries of that neighbor. The Khitans launched an attack on China at a time when China was rife with internal revolts and therefore weak.

In 916 the leader of the Khitan federation declared himself "emperor," a title that indicates he wanted to become ruler of China. In 937 he adopted Liao as the official name of his dynasty, and that term is used thereafter in Chinese political sources. In 947 the Khitan emperor declared himself emperor of the Khitans and the Chinese, ruling over large parts of North China, parts of Manchuria, where the Jurchens were subjugated, and parts of North Korea; however, the conquest of the whole of China did not succeed. The Khitan emperor lived in the city we have called Peking. He and his entourage enjoyed all the luxuries of a developed country, especially after a victory that forced the Chinese Sung dynasty to make regular large payments of tribute to the Khitans. Sung policy at this time was that, in recognition of their military weakness, it was cheaper to make a large annual payment to the enemy than to organize, train, and supply large armies with the risk of another defeat by the Khitans and even more loss of territory.

As with most payments of what today we call reparations, the victorious receiver lost in the long run compared to the defeated payer: The luxuries of the court in Peking decreased the interest of the Khitan rulers in wars. Moreover, not all tribes and not all the members of a tribe lived in or close to the capital. Many remained in the old home in the north, and did not participate in the luxury of those close to the court. Nevertheless, they had to protect the dynasty from attacks from other northern tribes. Tensions developed. The result was that a group of tribes of the "outer circle" broke away and formed their own federation, the Jurchens, whom we mentioned earlier. This was the end of the Khitan federation (1124). Some of their tribes were forced to serve the Jurchens; others moved far away into the land we have called Western Turkestan (now a part of Russian Central Asia) and reformed themselves as a new small federation called Kara-Khitai (Black Khitans), which continued to exist until 1203. Still other tribes retreated into Mongolia.

The Rise of Mongol Power

In Mongolia some of the tribes seem to have joined a federation that called itself Ta-tan, a name from which our Tartar comes. In the T'ang period a tribe began to appear among them under the name Meng-wu, a name that later was changed into Meng-ku and forms the basis of our word *Mongol*. The Jurchens (Chin) tried to put down rebellions (as they called them) among the members of their federation, but could not defeat one of the rebellious groups. Out of this group rose a man who became known and feared all over the world, Chinggis Khan (Genghis Khan). In 1206 Chinggis Khan assumed the title of emperor of the Great Mongol Empire.

Fortunately, we have a unique document from which we can see clearly the rise of the Mongols to world power, the so-called *Secret History of the Mongols*, written in Chinese characters but in the Mongol language. Only a few decades ago, scholars succeeded in reconstructing the original Mongol text from the Chinese transcriptions; before that we had to use a translation into Chinese, which was not completely accurate. The *Secret History* is the first document of a non-Chinese ethnic group in the Far East, which, written in their own language (though probably in Uygur script), describes their history as they saw it; all earlier and most later reports are written by their enemies, the Chinese. The Mongols soon developed their own script, which was derived from the Uygur script (which will be discussed further later) and became the model on which the Manchus developed their script. Mongolian script is still used in Mongolia, while Manchu is the script of a dead language.

Following the same pattern as the Khitans (Liao) described above, Chinggis Khan began to attack the Jurchens (Chin) in 1210, but it was his son Ögödei who finally conquered them in 1234. Another federation, the Hsi-hsia, whose state west of the Chin state had been a constant worry of the Chin, was subdued by the Mongols in 1227. As usual, many Chin and Liao joined the Mongol federation and from then on may be regarded as "Mongol' tribes. Others retreated into Manchuria or farther north. The death of Chinggis Khan (1227) and problems in the succession gave China's Sung dynasty some reprieve from attacks by the Mongols.

Succession is always one of the intractable problems of a monarchy; no fully satisfactory solution has ever been found. Among nomadic tribes there is usually no primogeniture. Some tribes prefer ultimogeniture; that is, the older sons receive a part of their future inheritance when they come of age and move away from their parents, establishing their own households. The youngest son remains with his parents and, after the death of the father, inherits the rest of his property and takes care of his widowed mother. Naturally, he inherits more than the older brothers who could use their shares immediately and make profits; the youngest son, so to speak, gets his share plus the interest accumulated over the years. Similarly, the daughters' dowry is regarded as their share of the inheritance. However, they do not get animals, which are the main investments of nomads.

The other form of succession among nomads is that the best son becomes the successor of his father. As it is not clear to everybody which son is the best, two solutions are possible. According to one, chosen by the Ottoman emperors of Turkey who followed the old traditions of Central Asia, the old ruler, on his deathbed, gives the name of the son who in his opinion is the best. All other sons are killed immediately so that no fights for the throne can occur. This system did not work well because the fathers apparently made poor choices several times. The solution adopted by the Mongols was to convene a tribal council, which made the final decision. This system naturally led to the formation of factions that fought one another by word or by weapon, but the choices were not bad. The council met following the death of Chinggis Khan far from the borders of North China and selected Ögödei (died 1241).

After him came two Khans, Küyük (or Kuyuk, died 1251) and Mongko (Möngke, died 1259), who enlarged the Mongol empire greatly, so that, with the exception of the Southern Sung state, which ruled only over South China, the whole Far East, large parts of Central Asia, and even parts of the Middle East were ruled by Mongols. But only under Khubilai (ruled from 1260 on) was all of China conquered and, for the first time in history, ruled by a non-Chinese. Before 1280 only North China had been, for longer or shorter periods, ruled by Northern tribal federations. In 1644 the Manchus would become the second foreign masters of all of China.

The Mongol Empire

Under Khubilai China was only a part of an empire that stretched over most of Asia. Khubilai tried to conquer Japan, but a storm destroyed his fleet twice. Japan was never conquered until 1945. However, Khubilai's other wars of conquest were more successful. In 1282 he began to fight Burma; in 1284 he conquered Annam (most of today's Vietnam) and Cambodia. In 1292 he tried to conquer Java; this attempt ended in failure, but on their way back his armies conquered most of Southeast Asia. Central Asia, the area that is now Russian Central Asia, large parts of Russia and Poland, Iran, and Afghanistan were all parts of the great Mongol Empire.

Like all tribal federations, the "Mongols" were not all Mongols. The federation was, as usual, a graded one, with those Mongol tribes that had joined it at the beginning at the top and other tribes that were conquered early under them. Even among these secondary tribes there were some who probably were not Mongols, that is, who did not speak the Mongol language. Then there were tribal groups the Mongols called "various tribes" (*sê-mu*). These "various" people included mainly communities that were not Mongols at all—for instance, Christian (Nestorian) tribes, Muslims, Tibetans, and Turkic tribes. Below these were the Northern Chinese, the former subjects of the Chin, and, at the very bottom, the Southern Chinese, former subjects of the Sung dynasty who were conquered very late. It is interesting to note that even Chinggis Khan was not a pure Mongol, but had Turkic blood (his mother was from a Turkic tribe) and seems to have spoken the Turkic language better than Mongol. In the whole empire the language of communication was not Mongol but Persian. If Marco Polo were really an official in the Mongol administration of China (we are not absolutely sure that he was ever in China), he clearly did not know Chinese but used Persian.

In spite of the fact that the empire stretched over most of East, Central, and West Asia, China was the heart of Khubilai's empire; certainly it was the most populous country (over 100 million inhabitants) and the richest of all countries of the empire. It was also the country in which Khubilai had his residence. Under his rule Peking, the capital, was built up. The Central and West Asian sections of the empire were comparatively independent under the rule of Khubilai's relatives. The states of Southeast Asia became tributary states; that is, they recognized the overlordship of the Mongol rulers of China and paid regular tribute by sending tributary missions to the court, but they were ruled by their kings more or less as they chose.

The Mongols were faced with the problem that bothers every colonial regime: They were only a tiny minority, probably at most 2 percent of the population of China. Before them the Liao had established a bipartite system of government: The affairs of the Khitans (Liao) were regulated by a "northern court" and the affairs of the Chinese subjects by a "southern court"—a system that sounds logical, but which soon proved unsatisfactory. Because the affairs of the Khitan minority were politically much less important than the affairs of the Chinese majority, the officials of the southern court were soon dominant, and their staff was predominantly Chinese not Khitan. The Mongols (whose ruling house was called the Yüan dynasty) were much stricter and developed a policy of segregation so that Mongols would remain the dominant group. Their troops were garrisoned in all strategically important cities of China. The local people had to feed them and supply them. Intermarriages of Chinese with Mongols were forbidden, though Mongols could take Chinese women as concubines. All important government positions were reserved for Mongols, and only the underlings were Chinese. This often had funny consequences as the Mongol high official frequently could neither read nor write Chinese and just put his stamp on the document his Chinese secretary wrote, without knowing what was in it.

Among other laws introduced by the Mongols was the prohibition against learning foreign languages: Chinese citizens were not allowed to learn Mongol or Persian. Moreover, Chinese were not allowed to travel to foreign countries. Consequently, it was virtually impossible for them to conduct business with central or western Asian businessmen. The trade with Asia was totally in the hands of Uygurs, Persians, and other foreigners, while the Mongol rulers were busy investing in caravan trade companies. Caravans started in China and went to central or western Asia, where they sold their merchandise and bought local high-value objects. They returned after one or, more often, two years, usually having made a profit of about 200 percent.

Such regulations bothered mainly the well-educated families, the upper-class Chinese. But the common people also suffered. As the Sung dynasty had had its capital in Hangchow (south of present-day Shanghai), the transport system was geared to the needs of the area. Now the court, greatly increased in number, resided in Peking and occasionally stayed for a time in Mongolia during the summers. It had to be supplied with food, mainly rice, which was brought from central and southeastern China, where it was produced, up to North China. A big fleet had to be created, and existing canals had to be broadened, deepened, and sometimes newly constructed as transportation by sea was dangerous and unreliable. The farmers had to furnish the labor—unpaid, of course. In addition, large tracts of land were taken away from the farmers and allotted to temples. The Mongols tolerated many religions in their empire—even Christian missionaries were active in Mongolia and China—though in general they favored Buddhism and its various sects. More land was given over to the military for production for the garrisons and the Mongolian horses they needed, and many high Mongol officials received large land grants. The land was taken away from Chinese landowners, and the farmers who lost their land had to become tenants of Mongol landlords.

Decline of the Mongols in China

Now, for the first time in Chinese history, there arose a feeling of nationalism and hatred for the colonial rulers. Collaborators were severely criticized by their friends and colleagues. Reaction against this harsh rule began in 1325, after more than forty years of relative internal peace, and did not stop until Chu Yüan-chang, one of the rebels, drove the Mongols out of China and established China's last indigenous dynasty, the Ming (1368–1644). The final battles were quick and decisive because the Mongol garrisons in the provinces were not experienced in fighting after the long period of peace; they were sons and grandsons of the conquering soldiers and, after 1325, had to fight only more or less localized uprisings.

What happened now? Not all the Mongols were as decadent as Chinese sources seem to indicate. The Mongol court and many garrison soldiers fought their way through to Mongolia; the Chinese pursuers were not inclined, or perhaps not able, to continue pursuit and eradicate the Mongols. These fugitives joined their original tribes in Mongolia and returned to the simpler life of nomadic breeders of cattle and horses. Soon new federations of tribes arose, and it was not long before the Chinese had to fight Mongols who tried to control the trade routes to western Asia by threatening the provinces of Kansu and the area of Sinkiang (Eastern Turkestan, as it was called until recently). The Mongols had capable leaders and once succeeded in taking a Chinese emperor who had set out to defeat them. They even threatened Peking. The policy of the more moderate rulers of the Ming dynasty was to leave the Mongols in Mongolia and to satisfy them by setting up markets where the Mongols could sell their horses and buy Chinese silk and other products. We will discuss this situation in detail in another chapter.

Recent research has shown that many Mongol families remained in China. Some individuals, apparently equally fluent in both Mongol and Chinese, got high positions in the Chinese foreign service: They were sent as ambassadors to the Mongol tribes, they received and guided Mongol embassies to China and controlled the hostels in which the ambassadorial missions lived, and some of them controlled the business contacts between Mongols and Chinese along the border markets and in Peking. All these Mongols, who were active in China and therefore mentioned in Chinese sources, had Chinese names (just as Westerners who are active in China even now must have a Chinese name). Hence it often is quite difficult to discover from the texts that they were originally Mongols.

Others apparently had a harder life. There are several reports, apparently reliable, that the women of common (not upper-class) Mongols who could not flee in time became hereditary prostitutes (that is, their daughters had to be prostitutes too, and so on) in Nanking, where they inhabited a special quarter of the city down to the end of the Ming dynasty or perhaps even later. They were, the reports indicate, completely sinicized, having given up their own language and customs. We do not know much about them—for instance, how many there were or whether such cases existed in other cities of China—but clearly we have an example of a caste of people with hereditary status, hereditary occupations, and (we would guess) some religious customs and beliefs of their own. We will later discuss other such tiny minorities in China.

The Mongols in Mongolia

Let us return to the Mongols in Mongolia. These Mongols established good relations with the Manchus at an early date. In 1594 five ambassadors from the Mongol Khalkha (Qalqa) federation were sent to the Manchus. In 1607 another Khalkha, who had already visited the Manchus in 1605, performed the kowtow (full prostration in front of the leader as a sign of subjection) before the Manchu leader Nurhaci and proclaimed him *qagan* (*haghan*, ruler). The Manchus used this term—the same as *khan*—as did the Mongols. When speaking of the Chinese emperor, they also called him khan, which indicates that they did not regard their own rulers as basically different from or lower than the emperor of China.

When the Manchus conquered China and ruled as the Ch'ing dynasty (1644–1911), the Mongols were their allies, and when the Manchu military system was set up in the form of a banner organization (military units which were distinguished from one another by banners of different colors), the Mongol tribes became banners in the Manchu armies. These Mongol banners were a military establishment higher in rank than the Chinese banners. The Chinese banners consisted partly of Chinese soldiers who had surrendered to the Manchus early, and partly of Chinese later taken into the armies and organized. Mongol cooperation with the Manchus was the free choice of the Mongols. They belonged to the privileged classes of the Manchu regime, and the Manchu government always treated Mongol "princes" with special courtesy, not interfering much with their inner tribal affairs. The Mongols, for their part, remained loyal to the Manchus.

For more than a thousand years Chinese merchants had ventured into Mongolia and had established trading posts in various places. A Chinese business company in Urga (capital of Outer Mongolia, now called Ulan Bator) prided itself on 300 years of uninterrupted business. But closer to the borders of China proper, in the area formerly called Inner Mongolia, a different process developed during this period of peace. Chinese farmers bought land from impoverished Mongol princes or lower rank leaders and began farming; other Chinese rented land from them. Catholic missions bought large tracts of land and established whole new villages in which they settled only converted Chinese farmers—a socially successful form of settlement for people who had cut themselves out of social life in their home villages by adopting a religion that did not allow mixing with other religions. More and more Chinese settlers immigrated into Inner Mongolia, and more and more tensions developed.

The Mongols in the Twentieth Century

The critical historical moment for both the Mongols and the Chinese is the abdication of the Manchu dynasty and the establishment of the Chinese Republic (1912). The situation that developed at that time still shapes international relations in the Far East.

When the Manchus abdicated, the Mongols of what is now Outer Mongolia (and the heart of the Mongol land) declared themselves independent (December 1, 1911) and made a "living Buddha" of their emperor. A living Buddha is believed to be an incarnation of an earlier Buddha or earlier living Buddha; as such, he was the highest religious leader among the Mongols at that time. The Mongols understood that they had always been allies and friends of the Manchus and not subjects of China, so with the end of the Manchu dynasty they had no obligation to be loyal to a Chinese regime. The situation looked very different from the Chinese side: The Manchus had been emperors of China, and Mongolia had become a part of China through the Manchus. Therefore, they should remain a part of China.

The early Republican regime was quite weak and could not assert control over many parts of China. So the Mongol "emperor" remained untroubled for eight years. However, in Inner Mongolia Chinese settlers already were in the majority, and the Mongols—both princes and commoners—were weak and often impoverished. The Repulican government changed the status of Inner Mongolia first by cutting it up into three "special" administrative areas—Jehol, Chahar, and Suiyüan. In 1928 these special areas were changed into regular Chinese provinces, in which the Mongols were an ethnic minority. Conditions in the late nineteenth and early twentieth centuries were chaotic. A foreign observer wrote at the end of the nineteenth century:

> Mongols under Chinese government seem to have no protection at all. A band of robbers has only to appear, and the country far and near is at their mercy. . . . The officers at the nearer military centers may bestir themselves as they like, the military organizations are such that no protective force can appear on the scene till long, perhaps months, after the country had been "eaten", and the inhabitants dispersed or slain. (Gilmour, pp. 366–367)

Outer Mongolia continued to live as before until 1919. On his flight before the Red armies of Soviet Russia, the White general von Ungern-Sternberg occupied Outer Mongolia and set up a regime of terror. He unilaterally declared total independence of China because, from 1915 on, the Chinese government had made diplomatic and military attempts to gain control over Outer Mongolia. These were the years right after the end of monarchy in China (1911), the years in which unstable and extremely weak Republican regimes were finally ready to grant Outer Mongolia autonomy, but within the framework of the government of China. Von Ungern-Sternberg's regime was soon ousted not by the Chinese but by the Red armies. Communist Russian pressure on Mongolia became so strong that the Mongols had to set up their own Communist regime in 1921. At that point Outer Mongolia (now called Mongolia) became the first satellite of Soviet Russia and began expropriation of land, expropriation of all Buddhist monasteries, defrocking of monks, suppression of religion, and all the killings that accompany such processes. Mongolia has been able to remain an independent state by playing the Russians and the Chinese off against one another and maneuvering cleverly, while modernizing the country and raising the standard of living. We can leave the topic here because Mongolia no longer counts itself as a part of China or its people as a minority in China. Nevertheless, both Chiang Kai-shek and Mao Tse-tung regarded Mongolia as an integral part of China. We might mention that, in the ironic way discrimination breeds counterdiscrimination, after the attainment of independence Chinese businessmen resident in Outer Mongolia had a hard time. For example, a Chinese visitor describes one situation:

> Another grievance [of the Chinese in Outer Mongolia] has to do with the theatre that is set up in every banner. For this a contribution of 10 dollars is exacted from each Chinese firm. Then the theatre shows plays depicting the oppression of the Mongols by Chinese officials like Ch'en I. The Chinese merchants are forced to attend; if they fail to do so, each one is fined 60 dollars, and if they leave after seeing half of the play, they are also fined. (Ma Ho-t'ien, p. 20)

The situation in Inner Mongolia developed differently. The Chinese Nationalist Party (KMT), under temporary Soviet influence (1923), began to speak of the self-determination of peoples and autonomy (1924). The central government should help only the weak and small racial groups and guide them toward self-determination and self-government. These lofty ideas were given up when, in 1928, the administration of the former Inner Mongolia was changed by including the three new provinces into the administration system of China without any special minority rights.

With the Japanese invasion of Manchuria (March 1, 1932) came the creation of the puppet state of Manchukuo (see page 34). This Manchukuo (-*kuo* means *state*) controlled, with the help of Japanese armies, the old homeland of the Manchus—in which, however, practically no Manchus lived anymore. The majority of the population were Chinese immigrants from Shantung and other North Chinese provinces. The Japanese clearly saw this new state as a building block for their planned control of all of China. The symbol for this was the creation of a new monarchy under the rule of the last emperor of China, who had lost the throne of China in 1911. The Japanese government obviously hoped that, after Japanese conquest of at least North China, many Chinese would more readily accept their old emperor as ruler than a Japanese. History, however, took a different course. In this Manchukuo a special "minority" district, Hsing-an, was created as an autonomous area of Mongols living in the country. A prince from Inner Mongolia, called

Prince Tê (Tê-wang), was made its head. This was a clear Japanese attempt to gain the trust of Mongols in Inner, and perhaps even Outer, Mongolia, to put a wedge between Russia and China, so as to facilitate the conquest of China and to forestall an attack by Russia. These plans came to a sudden end with the defeat of Japan (1945) and the subsequent occupation of Manchuria by Russian troops. The Russians had to take into consideration that the Communist fight for power in China, ending in a victory in 1948, was a promising event for the Communist movement, and that Mao Tse-tung, while staying in Yen-an close to the provinces of Inner Mongolia, had already established contacts with some Communists in that area. In 1945, Inner Mongolia's leaders were still undecided what to do, whether to join the Communists of Yen-an or the KMT in Nanking. Finally, their own communists declared the areas to be "autonomous regions," but troops of the Soviet Union disarmed them (1945–1946). Prince Tê, the traditionally recognized leader, too, was oscillating in his intentions, but was captured in 1949 (and "pardoned" in 1963) by the Communists. There was a short period of independence, when the Inner Mongols were strengthened by a KMT general who had surrendered to them (late 1949), but from then on Inner Mongolia has been a part of the People's Republic of China.

Minorities of the Northwest and the West

We now move still farther west, to an area that includes the northwestern section of the province of Shensi, the area of Ninghsia, and the province of Kansu and adjacent areas to the north. Ancient texts mention many tribes that seem to have lived in the area, but it is difficult to identify them, and we hear next to nothing about their culture. It is possible that among these tribes were some of Turkic, some of Tibetan, and probably some of Indo-European stock. These tribes had some contacts with the feudal statelets of the Chou dynasty, perhaps even with statelets controlled by the previous Shang dynasty. In combination with Chinese statelets they attacked the political capital of the Chou rulers and forced them to retreat to their secondary, sacred, capital near present-day Lo-yang (770 B.C.). We should not forget that, at that time, many of these tribes still lived free among areas the Chinese already regarded as their own territory.

In 770 B.C. the tribes seem not yet to have been organized in a tribal federation. Apparently, they also did not yet use cavalry—which the Chinese did not yet use, either. The technique of employing cavalry came to China some 250 to 300 years later from tribes that lived in the area we are considering, and the Chinese adopted it quickly. The use of horses in warfare necessitates not only a knowledge of riding but, most notably, the ability to use long-distance weapons, such as a bow shot from horseback, especially against an enemy who pursues the rider. This technique apparently spread to all animal-breeding societies to the north of China and to China itself at some time between 500 and 400 B.C., and it soon resulted in the obsolescence of the war chariot, which had been the main weapon of the Chinese since about 1400 B.C.

THE HSIUNG-NU

Early Tribal Federation

The situation in our area changed drastically a short time before 200 B.C., when the first tribal federation in the Far East arose. Suddenly we hear of the Hsiung-nu, a name that was not known before, and we learn that they were a very

Map 2   China and its northern neighbors (A.D. 220–280)

powerful group. The Chinese were obviously surprised by these people, and it took them a good hundred years until they found that the Hsiung-nu state was basically different from their state, representing a federation of tribes and not a bureaucratic-military, unified government. They knew that the Hsiung-nu were under a leader whose title was *shan-yü*, comparable to later titles like khan and khaghan (qagan). What Chinese sources tell us about the first, great leader Mao-tun is clearly information told them by Hsiung-nu, and most probably a fragment of a Hsiung-nu epic tale: In the beginning the Hsiung-nu were subject to the Yüeh-chih, another tribal federation, which included tribes of Indo-European stock. Maotun was a hostage among the Yüeh-chih but succeeded in running away and gathering a number of men around himself. These, according to the tradition, he trained to automatic, unthinking obedience; whoever did not do what he was told to do was killed. He tested their obedience first by asking them to shoot his own beloved wife, and, when they proved themselves, he had them kill his father. Thus, he made himself leader of the Hsiung-nu federation.

We do not know why now, for the first time, the tribes united into a federation. It is likely that the process was something like this: There is, as we have seen, a large area in North China and places farther north that can be characterized as a marginal area, in which farming of wheat and millet normally is possible, but which is at least equally suitable for cattle or sheep raising. We assume, on the basis of data from other areas of Asia, that people living here had a mixed economy, based partly on farming, partly on animal breeding. As the animal breeders had to move around in order to find good pasturage and water, some specialization probably began early on. When, in the south of this area, an organized state emerged that made demands of its subjects in the form of taxes and forced labor, the animal breeders may have moved farther to the north to evade the controls. They still had some agriculture, but their livelihood was now based mainly on the products of the animals: meat, fat, milk, skins, furs, and wool. As animal products are more perishable than grain, these new nomads had to try to sell their surplus to farmers who wanted to have meat, fat, and wool. Nomads try to slaughter weaker animals in the fall season, and farmers harvest in the fall; fall was thus the ideal season for exchange. A kind of symbiosis may have developed, centuries before the emergence of the Hsiung-nu. Such symbiosis is, however, a labile condition and can easily be destroyed.

First, the farmers or their business agents could withdraw their grain until the nomadic partner, who could not wait long, was willing to pay a higher price than usual. Moreover, animals do not give much, if any, milk in the winter and little during the spring, when they calve, so the animal breeder needs to have some staple food for the winter and for emergencies. Second, an organized agrarian state may, and often does, try to prevent nomads from coming into the area it claims as its own territory. Nomads, however, like to move to the south in the winter to avoid the harsh climate and the snow. They like to graze their animals on the harvested fields, where new weeds grow up and where remnants of straw and grains of wheat are ideal for their animals.

There was a third element, unique to our specific case: Shortly before the Hsiung-nu emerged as a power the state of Ch'in had conquered all former feudal states of China, dethroned the Chou dynasty, and established the first centralized, bureaucratic, nonaristocratic government in China. One of the first great works of the powerful new government was the erection of a long wall along what they regarded as the northern frontiers of their state, the first "Great Wall" of China.[1] The wall cut right through the Ordos Steppe area (in today's Shensi Province), exactly that marginal land in which farming and animal raising are equally possible, but also an area quite close to the capital of the Ch'in and therefore exposed to sudden, quick attacks by horsemen who could move through thinly inhabited land without immediately being detected. The wall severed the two empires: in the south the state of Ch'in; in the north the federation of the Hsiung-nu.

When the farmers or their business agents tried to exploit the nomads by raising their prices, or tried to keep the nomads out of their fields to force them to pay in cash or goods for the use of the fields, the nomads had to adjust. They

---

[1]Today's great wall is not the same as this first one; it has been rebuilt several times up to the recent past. Nor is the great wall of the Ch'in the first one. Centuries before the Ch'in several feudal states had built walls, often quite long ones, to protect their territory against other states or against tribes.

learned quickly that they could easily get what they wanted when they made an attack upon a village in the fall, right after the harvest. The granaries were full and the farmers were not militarily organized, while the nomads were good fighters because of their hunting expeditions and raids against other nomads. Consequently, almost every fall the nomads made an attack against some villages and got what they needed without paying for it. The next step in this development was that villages built walls around their settlements, usually made of dry clay or adobe bricks. They could defend themselves against a surprise attack and knew very well that cavalry cannot engage in a long siege because of supply problems. The third step was an attack by a larger force, consisting of members of more than one tribe. But this step was answered by more effective military protection or by the building of defensive long walls, which closed a whole area for the attackers. Concomitant with these three changes was a shift from a nomadic lifestyle with supplementary farming to a full nomadic and warlike lifestyle; we see the emergence of warrior-nomads, whose food supply came mainly from raids on farming communities. This process can be seen to have developed among the Hsiung-nu who still practiced farming in the early years of their federation, but who more and more turned toward the warrior-nomad style.

The First Period: Consolidation and Expansion

The first period of the Hsiung-nu federation's life can be called a period of consolidation and expansion among the nomads of Central Asia. The decisive first change came around 200 B.C. in the first years of the newly established Western Han Dynasty (209–206 B.C.). The first emperor, after his death called Kao-tsu, still had powerful pretenders to fight, and he was afraid that one of these would make a treaty with the Hsiung-nu because their army was strong enough to defeat Kao-tsu. Kao-tsu saw this danger and moved toward Mao-tun, but was soon encircled and threatened with annihilation. The Chinese sources give us different accounts as to what Kao-tsu did. Some say that he succeeded in arousing the jealousy of Mao-tun's principal wife by enticing him with other, beautiful girls, with the result that the queen advised her husband to give up the siege of Kao-tsu. More likely, however, is another version, according to which Kao-tsu succeeded in making Mao-tun believe that a large rescue army was on its way. In any case, Mao-tun left, and Kao-tsu was saved.

The sources also tell us that, in their opinion, Mao-tun was toying with the idea of making himself emperor of the Chinese. However, an advisor told him: "Chinese are different from the Hsiung-nu. They live in a hot, sticky climate and toil the soil; we live in nature and freedom. Our people would not like to live in China, not even as rulers." Whether this report is genuine or was invented by Chinese, it is the first time in Far Eastern history that the basic problem of nomadic rulers is discussed; that is: We could conquer China (or, we have conquered it). But then, what can we do with it, and what is the cost? In this case, the simplest answer is given: There is no use to conquer China, as our people do not want to live there. Later on, other answers were given.

The events of 200 B.C. were of worldwide importance for another reason. The Chinese had to make a treaty with the Hsiung-nu, the first foreign treaty ever made in the Far East. Many treaties between feudal states inside China had been made, centuries before this event. But people outside China had never been regarded as "states"—they were just "barbarians," who should be driven out of China or annihilated. Now the Chinese had to send the Hsiung-nu silk and foodstuffs regularly, and the peace treaty had to be sealed by an exchange of daughters: The shan-yü of the Hsiung-nu sent a daughter to become one of the wives of the Chinese emperor, and the Chinese emperor had to reciprocate. Whenever one of the rulers died, his country had to notify the other country, and with the succession of the new ruler, a new treaty and a new exchange of daughters had to be made. We do not know much about the Hsiung-nu "princesses," but it is clearly indicated that none of the Chinese "princesses" was a daughter of the emperor. Normally, she was the daughter of some distant relative of the emperor.

The treaty contained still another important feature. In the style of European diplomacy one ruler had to use the correct address when writing to the other ruler. There were no established rules of etiquette yet, as the whole treaty business was new, but the diplomats agreed that the Chinese emperor should speak of himself as the "older brother" and the Hsiung-nu leader as the "younger brother." The two partners seem to have understood this terminology quite differently. For the Chinese it meant that the Chinese emperor was superior to the Hsiung-nu shan-yü and had the right to control him, as any Chinese older brother could do with his younger sibling. But for the Hsiung-nu it may have meant that the Hsiung-nu were superior because the younger son is the true successor of his father. In any case, for the Hsiung-nu the older brother had no rights over the younger one. This misinterpretation had consequences some 400 years later.

For a Chinese a treaty meant a document on special paper, of a specific size and color, nicely written in classical, courteous, and flowery style. The Hsiung-nu could not write at this time. In order to be able to write and to read diplomatic correspondence, they had to have Chinese assistants with sufficient education. And they had to set up a more or less permanent office building and formulate some rules of bureaucracy. We do not know exactly when the Hsiung-nu government began to build something like a capital city with office buildings and other structures, but we may assume it was not long after 200 B.C. Such buildings had to be built also for the Chinese princesses and their staff, although in their letters home the princesses wrote that they had to live in a cold, smelly tent. Probably they did live in tents when their husbands were engaged in warfare or extensive hunting trips, but certainly the main body of their personal entourage stayed in permanent dwellings.

Recent excavations give the impression that such a city was indeed something like a Chinese enclave, filled with Chinese in the court's employment, including craftsmen and other service people. One of these numerous Chinese expatriates is well known. He left because of a grudge against the Chinese government and became very important among the Hsiung-nu because he organized their whole bureaucracy and the forms of the state ceremonial. It was this man who advised the Hsiung-nu shan-yü to use paper of a size larger than that used by the Chinese emperor in order to indicate that he felt himself socially and politically higher than the Chinese ruler. It was this man who saw that Chinese ambassadors were treated as the Hsiung-nu wanted to treat them, not according to Chinese customs or wishes. The presence of upper-class Chinese in the princesses' court and other Chinese personnel required suitable food—that is, Chinese food—as Chinese hated to eat chunks of raw meat with the knife and the hands. So Chinese food and other luxury objects, including yeasts to make Chinese wine, were imported. All this created a kind of double administration among the Hsiung-nu: As head of the federation, the ruler ruled like a feudal lord, counting on the loyalty of those tribes who formed his federation. But in his personal court he saw a bureaucratic administration grow up. This process had parallels some centuries earlier in China proper and centuries later in Europe.

Shifting Aggression and Control

The peace treaty did not establish peace. Hsiung-nu raids continued, and often they were quite serious. After the death of Kao-tsu struggles for the succession occurred in China; the next efficient emperor, Wen-ti (179–164 B.C.) pursued a policy of strengthening the structure of the Chinese Empire by numerous reforms, but he did not change the foreign relations of his country. Only under one of China's most powerful emperors, Wu-ti (140–87 B.C.), did China begin a policy of aggression and become the most powerful state in the Far East. The time of contact between China and the Hsiung-nu may be divided into the following periods:

200–133 B.C.	Hsiung-nu aggressive
133–89 B.C.	Chinese aggressive (Wu-ti)
89–51 B.C.	recovery of Hsiung-nu and Chinese; stalemate
51 B.C.–A.D. 1	peace and dynastic change in both countries
A.D. 1–25	Chinese aggressive, but failing
A.D. 25–73	Hsiung-nu aggressive
A.D. 73–92	Chinese aggressive
A.D. 92–200	stalemate and dynastic changes

(According to Fairbank, pp. 186–187)

It is not necessary to narrate all the events of these more than 400 years, but a few important details should be mentioned. The aggressive Chinese policy under Wu-ti became possible because the Chinese had learned the typical strategy of the Hsiung-nu, who, when faced with an enemy, retreated as if beaten but then quickly turned, encircled their pursuers, and often annihilated them. Wu-ti's generals were careful in the pursuit of fleeing Hsiung-nu horsemen and followed the strategy of weakening them by taking their herds away instead of capturing their soldiers. The military aim of Wu-ti was not so much to protect the frontiers as to secure the road to Turkestan, where the trade routes from Western Asia ended. Many cultivated plants and animals (especially Arabian horses), and many luxury articles could easily be obtained by the power that could control the trade routes.

Already in the earlier part of Wu-ti's expeditions, some tribal units of the Hsiung-nu had to surrender with all their men to the Chinese because without their herds they could not continue to live. One of the leaders, who surrendered when he was still a young man, entered the service of the emperor, rose to high rank in a short time, and, when the emperor died leaving a minor child as heir to the throne, became one of the regents who protected the young emperor. He is the first known non-Chinese official at the Chinese court. We do not know too well what happened to the many, many prisoners taken by the Chinese in this period. We assume that the women were enslaved and became servants and prostitutes in rich families, while the men were transported into districts in the interior, presumably as slaves. Nothing is known of their offspring, if they had any. Thus, the prisoners did not become the nucleus of a minority group.

The first important consequence of the third period, the period of peace, is a split in the Hsiung-nu federation, most likely as a result of the many wars with China: A large part of the tribal people left the Far East and migrated westward (around 50 B.C.). Some scholars think that they are the so-called Huns who later invaded Europe. It is probably safer to say that among the Huns were elements of former Hsiung-nu tribes. Another consequence of this period of peace may be development of an international diplomatic system. In 53, 33, and 25 B.C. the ruler of the remaining branch of the Hsiung-nu came to the Chinese court at New Year's time, and the emperor, in an elaborate ceremony, received not only the dignitaries of the realm but also the ambassadors of foreign countries. In the following periods Hsiung-nu ambassadors (though not rulers) came more or less regularly to the New Year's reception, brought "tribute," and sent hostages to the court. The tribute was, for the Chinese, officially a recognition of China's superiority over the tribute bringers. For the bearers it was a lucrative trade expedition because tribute missions consisted of many people who brought merchandise and sold much of it in China. They also received gifts of more or less the same value as the tribute. We shall discuss the function of tribute in more detail later. The "hostages" lived at the imperial court, received a Chinese education, and learned Chinese, so that upon return to their own land they had a much better knowledge of China than the Chinese had of their country.

In the latter half of the second century A.D.—that is, in the fourth period—there was a new development: The Hsiung-nu were weakened by the split, somehow "corrupted" by their now close relations with China on the one hand, and, on the other hand, wooed by the different parties within China that fought one another in a civil war of long duration. The Chinese sold weapons to the Hsiung-nu and tried to enroll their soldiers in Chinese armies.

When larger numbers of tribes, whose membership certainly numbered in the tens of thousands of men, together with their wives and children and animals, surrendered, the Chinese were faced with a new problem. Not all these people could be enslaved, nor could they be killed. The solution was to settle them in the northern provinces of China, close to the borders, where few Chinese farmers lived and where the Hsiung-nu could continue to live as animal breeders. Nineteen tribes are mentioned, and this is the first time we hear of the names of most Hsiung-nu tribes; before, only a very few names were known. Somehow controlled by the local Chinese administrators, the Hsiung-nu continued to live in their old lifestyle but were expected to strengthen the Chinese armies in case of serious conflicts with their free, independent brothers beyond the border. At this point, then, we have a Hsiung-nu minority living in China and controlled by Chinese.

A Minority Comes to Power

This experiment seems to have worked well until the period of the Three Kingdoms (A.D. 220–265). The Later Han dynasty had been replaced by the Wei, but in South and West China two contenders (Wu and Shu-Han) set themselves up as emperors, with the result that there was continual warfare for more then forty years. The Shu-Han dynasty in West China claimed to be legitimate because their emperor asserted that he was a member of the Liu family, the same as the family of the Han emperors. In order to defeat their competitors, all three (Wei in the North, Wu in the South, and Shu-Han in the West) tried to strengthen their armies by recruiting everybody they could, including non-Chinese. So the Wei recruited Hsiung-nu men from the nineteen tribes and armed them. The Wei dynasty was dethroned by the Chin dynasty (265), which finally (280) reunited the country under its rule.

One of the first acts of the Chin dynasty was a general demobilization and confiscation of weapons. It seems clear that the Hsiung-nu soldiers did not give up their weapons. In fact, it is likely that they even bought more weapons by giving some of their land inside China to Chinese farmers, who then became their tenants, and became full-time mercenaries of the Chinese warlords. Their great leader, Liu Yüan, emerged in 287 as a threatening power. Liu Yüan, however, was no longer culturally a Hsiung-nu. On the one hand, he was an accomplished general who commanded his troops and at first helped the Chin dynasty; on the other hand, he had a thorough Chinese education. He had studied, as an upper-class Chinese at the time did, under a famous Chinese teacher, had memorized the Chinese classics, and admired Chinese culture. He had many friends in government circles who accepted him as an equal. His name was a normal Chinese name, and his dress and his habits were Chinese, too. His family, we hear, had accepted the family name Liu 500 years earlier, at the time of Kao-tsu's first treaty with the Hsiung-nu. As the Han emperor's family name was Liu, the Hsiung-nu rulers, as "younger brothers" of the Chinese emperor, also took the name Liu as their family name. Their clan remained over many centuries the Hsiung-nu clan that supplied the rulers or chiefs of many federations; the tribe Tu-ku, to which they belonged, was a "leader tribe."[2]

In 220 the Chinese imperial family Liu lost the throne, and even its somewhat questionable successor, the Shu-Han dynasty, was dethroned. Liu Yüan claimed to be the legitimate successor and rose against the Chin (304). These are Liu Yüan's words:

> The Han dynasty ruled the realm for a long time and their glory was engraved in the hearts of its people. I am related to the Han family, like an older brother to a younger brother. When the older brother dies, can the younger one not take his place? Therefore, we can take the name "Han dynasty" and honor the last Han ruler posthumously and so fulfill the hopes of the people.

This was the first time in Chinese documented history that a minority rose and assumed power over the majority. In 311 Liu Yüan's son conquered the capital of China and captured the emperor. The Chin set up another prince as emperor, but he too was captured (316); this was the end of the Western Chin dynasty. One of their princes set himself up in Nanking as the first ruler of Eastern Chin, but from now on North China was ruled by different regimes, almost all of them of non-Chinese origin. Several of these dynasties were created by members of the old Hsiung-nu federation, which had ceased to exist; others were, as we have mentioned, of Hsien-pi origin. Still others were created by military leaders of tribes of Tibetan affiliation. Among all these foreign rulers of China only one was in power for a relatively long time—the Toba (T'o-pa: 385–550).

---

[2]The term *clan* is used here to define a group of people who believe that they all are descendants of one *historical* ancestor. A *tribe* is a larger unit of people who may believe that they all are descendants of a *mythical* ancestor and who believe that they belong together. The next larger unit in these nomadic societies is the *tribal federation*, which brings a large number of tribes together under one leader.

THE TOBA

The Toba were a federation of a fairly large number of tribes, among them the former Hsiung-nu tribes. It seems possible that the leading tribe spoke a Turkic language, though some scholars assert that theirs was a Mongolian dialect. Doubtless, there were Mongol tribes in the federation, as well as Indo-European, probably Tibetan, and perhaps still other tribes.

For our purpose the most important point about the Toba is the end of their rule. During the 165 years of their rule a slow, disintegrating process began. Their first capital was in the north of the present-day province of Shansi. This was an area in which, since the middle of the first century A.D., tribes of the Hsiung-nu had been settled as subjects of China, an area with much pasture and not many Chinese farmers. However, from the beginning of their dynasty the Toba had to employ many educated Chinese from East and Central China as administrators and officials in order to collect taxes from the Chinese population. When the Toba conquered large parts of North China, supplying their growing administration with food became very costly, so they decided to move the capital into the center of production of wheat and rice, to Lo-yang (493–494). At this point, the civil administration came almost totally into the hands of Chinese, while the Toba controlled the military. The Chinese, many from powerful land-owning families, voluntarily cooperated with the foreign masters because they could keep their estates or wealth. But the Toba themselves acculturated to such a degree that the emperor issued a law that all Toba must speak and write (if necessary) Chinese, and that they had to wear Chinese dress instead of their national dress; in other words, they had to become Chinese. We soon see numerous intermarriages between Toba and Chinese from high and powerful families.

The common Toba from the ordinary tribes still lived close to the borders and continued their nomadic life. In time, the gap between the sinicized ruling class of the Toba and the commoners became so large that the empire split (550). The two halves represented the two parties, until both were replaced by a military Chinese family (581) that was tied by marriage to the Tu-ku clan of the Toba rulers.

For several centuries we now find in the high ranks of the Chinese government people with Toba family names, people who openly admitted their Toba ancestry but who were in all ways Chinese. Thus, between 600 and 900 the Chinese upper class included many families of foreign origin—a minority that was not regarded as a minority, and which did not want to be seen as such.

TURKS AND UYGURS

We said that there were tribes in the Toba federation that possibly spoke a Turkic language and therefore could be regarded as Turks. During the Toba period new federations were created in Central Asia, two of which are important for us.

One was the T'u-chüeh (Turks or Köktürks), who created a strong empire that lasted, with some interruptions and reformations, from 553–840. Naturally, their federation was also an ethnic mix, with Toba and other tribes among them. The Turks were the first Far Eastern group outside China, Japan, and Korea to develop a script of their own, a runic script with symbols that have been deciphered by Danish and other scholars. They, too, threatened China, and at one time their rulers claimed to be higher in rank than the emperor of China by assuming a title that implied this.

Among the closely related Turkic tribes were the Uygurs, who, at the end of the seventh century, became independent of the T'u-chüeh; they officially created their own dynasty in 744. The Uygurs helped the Chinese emperor against a rebel and entered the capital of Ch'ang-an in 757 and again in 762. Although they were allies, the Chinese complained bitterly about them because they robbed and plundered the capital. Moreover, a great number of Uygurs settled permanently in the capital and a few other cities as big businessmen with good connections to Central and West Asia. The Uygurs had a more practical script, developed from a Syrian syllabic alphabet, and for a while Uygur became the commercial language in Asia. Many documents in their script have been found that show their language was closely related to other Turkic languages. The Uygurs seem to have been Buddhists until another religion of Near Eastern origin, Manicheism, was introduced among them, and Manicheans created a number of colonies in Chinese cities. Traces of their religion existed in Chinese secret religions for many centuries. When, shortly after their great victories, the Uygur state broke up and only small Uygur statelets continued to exist in Central Asia, their language and script remained dominant in these oasis cities; even at the time of Mongol rule much official correspondence was written by Uygur scribes in Uygur script.

Numerous Turks and Uygurs became permanent settlers in China; some even lived in compact ghettos in large cities of central China. They disappear from the texts most likely because they so thoroughly assimilated that they were no longer noted as a minority. To the present time there is a population of Turkic type in some parts of the present province of Kansu and adjacent areas, but the largest group is now in Sinkiang.

SINKIANG AND OTHER MUSLIM AREAS

The center of Turkic population within the political borders of today's China is Sinkiang ("The New Frontier"). It received this name when it was integrated into China as a province in the nineteenth century, after long and bloody wars in the eighteenth and early nineteenth centuries. In Western sources we find the name *Eastern Turkestan* in contrast to *Western Turkestan*, which is a part of the Soviet Union. *Turkestan*, meaning "land of Turkic people," indicates the ethnic make-up of the populations. It is not used any more. Let us briefly go through its history.

Early Expansion to the West

The expansion of China into the West began with the wars against the Hsiung-nu in the late second century B.C. At that time the northern parts of the older provinces of Shansi and Shensi were fully integrated, and most of the province of Kansu came slowly under Chinese rule. In all these areas there were, at the time of conquest, minorities of different ethnicities. In Kansu, besides the Hsiung-nu, who seem to have spoken a language related to either Turkic or Mongolian languages, there were also tribes of Tibetan stock, speaking a language related to the Tibetan language.

At the same time, at the instigation of emperor Wu the first Chinese expeditions went farther west. One of these was diplomatic. In 138 B.C. Chang Ch'ien, a general, was sent out to try to make an alliance with the Yüeh-chih, former enemies of the Hsiung-nu, against the latter. What Chang Ch'ien did not know was that the Yüeh-chih, a federation of tribes under the leadership of tribes of Indo-European origin, had been defeated by the Hsiung-nu and moved so far to the west that they had no inclination to collaborate with the Chinese to destroy the Hsiung-nu. Although from this point of view Chang Ch'ien's expedition was a failure that cost him many years of detainment by the Hsiung-nu, the knowledge he brought back to China was extremely exciting. We now know that there had been trade between China and the west of Asia probably centuries before Chang Ch'ien's time, but the Chinese court knew nothing about the political situation in Central Asia. We assume that the merchants from either side of Asia did not travel all the way across but met at certain places in between and exchanged their wares. Chang Ch'ien gave his emperor a detailed description of the numerous states, both small and large, in Eastern Turkestan (Sinkiang) and even in Western Turkestan (Russian Central Asia, now divided into several Soviet Socialist Republics), including some information about a great country in the Far West—the Roman Empire.

The conquest of Turkestan that followed was, it seems, motivated more by the desire to control the transcontinental trade than to check the power of the Hsiung-nu. Tradition tells us that many plants and, for example, trees came from the West to China, among them the grape vine and one variety of the peach, which later played an important role in Chinese myth and symbolism. More important to the Chinese were the new acquisitions of Arabian horses, which they called "blood-sweating horses" and which were superior to the Mongolian or Tibetan horses they had before. These horses became a luxury for the emperor and his court rather than an instrument for warfare. After the return of Chang Ch'ien the Chinese armies conquered numerous small states up to the borders of Western Turkestan and left small garrisons in them. The rulers of these states remained in power or were replaced by persons acceptable to the Chinese; the Chinese garrisons lived in part by doing some farming so that they did not depend upon supplies from far-away China.

Early Central Asia

At the time of Chang Ch'ien's return (about 125 B.C.) Central Asia was inhabited by numerous tribes and tribal federations. Some of these were Tocharians, an ethnic group of Indo-European stock; others were of Turkic stock; still others may have been of Tibetan type; and some cannot yet be surely identified. The states centered around oases, while the tribes inhabited the steppe and desert land outside the oases. The inhabitants of the oases lived in cities with permanent houses and farmed the land as far as there was water. The water often was brought from the mountains in subterranean canals and fertilized the soil, which produced famous melons and fruits. The tribes lived in tents and migrated farther to the north in summer and to the south in winter. They formed their own federations, though many tribes were for a time included in the Hsiung-nu federation. Their wealth consisted of animals. The main livelihood of the ruling classes in these cities was derived from trade.

There are some indications that, already at emperor Wu-ti's time, Buddhism had reached Central Asia; monks may have accompanied the merchants from India or Iran. Although Chinese tradition says that Buddhism did not come to China until the first century A.D., it seems likely that it actually reached China more than a century earlier, though it became a power there only at the end of the second century A.D. There is no doubt that it came to China from Central Asia. Only in later times did monks also arrive in Vietnam and in South China by ship from India. For a long while the monks were all foreigners from India or from Central Asia; as Buddhist monks did not marry, they did not become a self-propagating ethnic minority in China. Their religion began to interest Chinese of all classes. The Indian philosophy they introduced in China, as well as the Indian astronomy, geography, and medicine, was exciting for Chinese thinkers. The common people found in the teachings of the Buddha some explanation for those eternal questions for which the ancient Chinese religion had only vague answers.

We have seen that the power of the Hsiung-nu declined after the conquests of Wu-ti. China, too, was weakened by the long wars. Its power in Central Asia declined, and the small states became more and more independent. In the last quarter of the first century A.D. after the advocates of peace had been influential, the war party in China got into power again, and China regained control for a time over Central Asia. But with the breakdown and end of the Later Han dynasty (A.D. 25–220) Central Asia regained its independence for centuries. The Hsiung-nu disappeared and new federations arose; the Indo-European tribes moved slowly to the west and southwest, and Turkic tribes gained more and more importance. In the centuries between 200 and 600 the various rulers of North and South China retained some contacts with Central Asia, trade connections continued, and monks—now also Chinese monks—traveled in both directions, until the early seventh century when, as we have seen, Turkic federations became a threat to China. By 640 the armies of the T'ang dynasty had conquered most of Central Asia, though they were able to hold it for only a short period.

The Penetration of New Religions

Trade contacts continued unbroken, and in the later part of the T'ang dynasty (618–906) the merchants who now could come to the Chinese capital brought with them missionaries of new religions. Already before the T'ang, Mazdaism, a Persian religion probably created around 500 B.C. by Zoroaster, and Manicheism had reached China. In T'ang times, Nestorian Christians and some Muslims settled in China.

The first Jews seem to have reached South China in the ninth century, and Central China a century later. All these immigrants from Western Asia seem to have engaged in long-distance trade. There seems to be some indication that the early Jews were connected with cotton trade. Later (probably in the twelfth century) the city of K'ai-feng became their center. When the first Jesuit missionaries came to China in the sixteenth century, they heard about the Jews and found them in K'ai-feng. They still practiced their religion, and their rabbis could read Hebrew, but the community was small and clearly was ethnically mixed. In the nineteenth century visitors from Europe and the United States reported that the Jewish community had more and more assimilated with the Chinese and that not many of their Hebrew books had been preserved. From then on we hear no more about the Jews in China. Their names, originally biblical names, had become completely Chinese names, and physically they were just like all other Chinese. This seems to be the only case in which a Jewish minority was totally absorbed and disappeared without having been subjected to discrimination and persecution. We assume that most of the Jewish merchants who settled in China came without wives, married Chinese women, perhaps adopted Chinese orphans too, and, in the course of more than a thousand years of close contacts with other Chinese, lost their identity.

The Nestorians seem to have disappeared after a relatively short time, though traces of Nestorianism were found in Mongolia until fairly recent times. In Europe a legend of a Christian state in the Far East seems to refer to these remnants of Nestorian Christianity.

Muslims in China

Muslims ("people of Islam," as opposed to *Mohammedans*, or "followers of Mohammed," the founder of Islam; Chinese: Hui-hui or, briefly, Hui) first came to China mainly by ship as traders from the Persian Gulf. It may well be that they were ethnically not Arabians but Persians (Iranians) converted to Islam because there had been a strong Persian trade connection with South China for centuries. These early Muslims, like the Jews, adopted Chinese family names. They settled in South and Southwest China, apparently in ghettos. They are now physically Chinese, also as a consequence of marriages with Chinese women.

From the later tenth century on Islam began to penetrate into West Turkestan, and in the following centuries Buddhism and all the other religions in Central Asia gave way to Islam. Until 1948 all inhabitants of Sinkiang were Muslim, with the exception of the Chinese who recently immigrated into the province or were forced to settle there. The original population is now (with the exception of some tiny fragments of other groups) called Uygur, although their culture and language are no longer the same as the old Uygurs (see p. 55). Muslims who live farther east, in the provinces of Kansu and Shensi, and who are probably Chinese converted to Islam, are now a special minority called Hui, which refers to their religion not their physical traits. In earlier sources they were often called Dungan.

When the Mongol Empire established its rule over most of Asia and many Central Asians got high posts in the Mongol administration, even in China, another group of Muslims, also of Central Asia origin, settled in China in its southwestern province of Yünnan, where they are still found. They, too, did not differ much from the local population, which was also mixed (as we shall see later), but remained a distinct religious minority there. We do not hear much of them until the nineteenth century, when tensions between the Muslims and the Chinese administration arose. The Yünnan Muslims revolted in 1818–1819 and again in 1834. There was unrest among them again from 1856 on, and they found a capable leader in Tu Wen-hsiu, who called himself Sultan Suleiman. He was finally captured in 1873 and committed suicide. This ended some sixty years of rebellions of the Muslims in Yünnan, rebellions characterized by massacres that decimated this minority people. Not too many details of these years are available: Chinese sources do not like to give details of such "local" events, and few foreigners lived in Yünnan at the time, mainly Catholic missionaries from whom we have some information. One estimate, which may be too high, is that, even after the massacres, 25 percent of the population of Yünnan was still Muslim.

In spite of the importance of Muslims as good warriors, often fighting for independence, only in modern times have the Chinese attempted to get a better understanding of Islam. The following extract from an eighteenth-century manuscript that describes Islam and Islamic customs shows how little was known or how little interest Chinese scholars had in Islam, despite the fact that they ruled over millions of Muslims.

> Their holy book in one volume is called Ko-erh-han [Qoran]. It has 30 sections. What is said in the book teaches believers to honor heaven, accumulate luck and do good [works] and so on. It forbids Muslims to wear red. They say when one wears red, then the calamity of war will follow. Men all wear black, women white. They say fire overcomes metal, and water overcomes fire. They also say that the people of the sunrise [country] have white faces, full eyes, small noses, little beard. They are good riders and shooters. Their dresses are very long. Those who come to Buhara all belong to them. The priests worship every morning, then go on a high place and wake up the people and [all] start working. In the evening they go to a high place and make music and send the sun home. They have no statues or paintings. Those who believe and spread the teachings are called Ahun. They accept no office, do not go to war, do not drink wine or smoke. They only recite the book, explain the rites, admonish the people to do good [works]. The Muslims all honor them, venerate them. (*Hsin-chiang sheng hu-ching chih*, Manuscript of Ch'ien-lung's time, Ch'eng-wen reprint, 1968, pp. 45–46)

> In Sinkiang from Hami to the west, all is Muslim. Their religion and customs are not like those of the inner land [i.e., China], and also different from Mongols, South barbarians, Miao, Man and I. They have no family names. Within three generations they all say "we are one clan." Men and women have only first names. Apart from honoring their own grandparents and parents, they also honor their stepmothers and uncles. The sons and daughters of the brothers of their parents marry one another. When they meet one another after three generations, they have no ties anymore. They seat people according to age [i.e., not according to relationship]. One man has two or three wives. Their children are all called "close relatives." If one woman has two or three husbands one after the other, her children are all called "offspring of the same womb." Recently, because they became more civilized they were annexed by and incorporated into China. They also link up and like Chinese customs and slowly turn to ritual and righteousness [of Chinese type]. (Ibid., pp. 54–56)

Muslim Uprisings

Let us return to Sinkiang, which regained its independence from China when the Mongol Empire broke up. Sinkiang's independence became a threat for China when another great conqueror, Timur, who had created a great empire in West Asia, planned an invasion of China in the first years of the fifteenth century. Fortunately for China, Timur died before he could begin his campaign (1404). China's last Chinese dynasty, the Ming (1368–1644), weakened by a dynastic fight, was in no position to repel Timur. The Ming established trade and diplomatic relations with the states in Central Asia but did not try to rule over them because the remnants of the defeated Mongols had founded new federations and, especially in the early sixteenth century, became a very dangerous enemy again. The Manchu dynasty had already established its relations with Central Asia two years after the conquest of China and the end of the Ming dynasty: In 1646 the city-state of Turfan sent a tributary embassy to their court. But a series of wars followed, and fighting in Central Asia ended only in 1755, when the Manchu armies captured the capital of the Mongolian Oirat. These wars against federations of Mongols and Turks, who were also called Dzungars (Zunghars) by the Chinese, were costly and difficult. Even the Manchu emperor went out in person to fight. The emperor celebrated his victory by writing a rather flowery memorial, which was carved in stone and erected in the Ili area. Dated 1755, it contains a report of his activities and a characterization of his enemies. Let me quote a few sentences here:

The Dsungars are nothing but pitiable Mongols who separated and are lonely and solitary. Through several generations they turned their back to civilization and did nothing but murder, rob, and plunder. Why did they regard the totality [of Chinese people] as enemy? Dawaci [their leader] was especially recalcitrant. Continually he committed cruelties in drunken condition. The mind of the trembling masses was scared; it was as if the grain on the fields got worms. They shrank back as if they were bitten by a snake. Unanimously they opened their mouth, and, in common aversion, they come [to me] to ask [for help]. How could one remain indifferent in the face of their request? I thought about how to liberate you, how to save you in the quickest possible way. After I had seen your grief, I was deeply moved. Therefore I sighed full of commiseration and wished to save you as quickly as I could. [translated from the Manchu language original]

One group of the Mongols evaded the attackers by moving into the Ili region, where they established a new home after defeating the local Kazak (Kazakhs) and other Turkish tribes. Some of the Kazaks had left earlier and had migrated still farther west, surrendering to the Russians, who were at that time extending their colonial empire in Western Turkestan. The Russians settled them near the new town of Orenburg in what was then the western part of the Kazak settlement. Other tribes, mainly the Turgut, a Kalmuk group, had moved to the lower Volga River in 1630 and settled there. The Manchus entered into relations with them (from 1714 on) and persuaded them to return into Manchu territory (1771) to repopulate the old Kalmuk territory, which was almost unpopulated after the horrors of the long wars. The Ili area, into which the Kalmuk finally had retreated, now became Manchu territory until the Russians, after long disputes, finally took it over in 1881. The Chinese governments of the twentieth century still regarded it as a part of China that should be returned.

In the oasis states of Central Asia a different development had begun. Muslim leaders called *khoja* (teacher) had established themselves, mainly in Kashgar. Forcing tribute from Kashgar and other small states, the Manchus gained a kind of control over Central Asia during a period of peace from 1759 to 1820.

In the nineteenth century sixty-five years of more or less constant fighting began. The Manchu dynasty's power had begun to weaken around the middle of the previous century. One of the trouble signs was a revolt inside China by the White Lotus sect, a secret religious-political society. Some of their teachings were derived from Buddhism, so they gave themselves this name to pretend to be just a branch of Buddhism. The revolt continued until 1802 and cost many lives. In 1813 another secret religious society succeeded in actually infiltrating the palace, threatening the person of the emperor. The population of China had grown to almost 400 million. The European powers, Russia as well as England, began to exert pressure at various points along the borders. In Central Asia, too, new sectarian religious movements developed within the Muslim communities and challenged the Manchu supremacy, with varying degrees of success. Again and again, smaller or larger "insurrections" occurred.

Finally, the Manchu dynasty became involved in the greatest and most dangerous uprising, the T'ai-p'ing rebellion, which began in 1848 and spread all over South, Central, and East China, at one point threatening the very existence of the dynasty. The Manchus could not control the trouble spots in the West and Northwest, where another new sect, which had originated in the mid-eighteenth century, spread in Central Asia and in the two provinces of Kansu and Shensi. This sect, founded by Ma Ming-hsin (executed probably in 1784), was more orthodox and conservative than its parent Shi'a group of Central Asia. The Shi'a is one of the two main branches of Islam and is, to this day, the dominant religion in Iran and in Soviet Central Asia. It is possible that the sect's fanaticism became the stimulus for conflicts with non-Muslim Chinese. The uprising in the 1860s was especially severe among the Salars around Hsün-hua, an area in the modern province of Ch'ing-hai, close to the Kansu border. Salars are documented beginning in 1371, but they themselves assert that they existed some 500 years earlier. They are Muslim, and some of them speak a Tibetan dialect, others Chinese. It seems that originally they were Uygurs (of the Sari, or Yellow, Uygurs). Their name seems to point to a Persian word, *sâlâr*, "chief." The center of their settlement was in Hochou (Kansu). Like the Dungans, who will soon be mentioned, they seem to be an ethnically mixed group that accepted Chinese culture to a considerable degree, and gave up their language for Chinese (in the case of the Salars either Chinese or Tibetan).

At the same time, an even larger uprising began among the Muslims in Shensi Province. It began with several small local incidents and grew in scope with the harsh reactions of Chinese officials. The Shensi revolt threatened Hsi-an, the capital of Shensi (1862–1863), until the Chinese local armies succeeded in pushing the Muslims into Kansu province (1865–1866).

Also at this same time a new leader, Khoja Buzurg, rose to power in Central Asia, returning to Kashgar, the traditional seat of Khoja regimes. When he began to consolidate his forces, he was joined by a man who soon took over and became ruler over most of Central Asia—Yaqub Beg. He took over Kucha (1864), Urumchi (1865; present name Ti-hua), and the Ili area (1866). He established diplomatic relations with the Ottoman Empire (Turkey) and contacted Russia and England. Because of the uprisings in Shensi, Kansu, and Ch'ing-hai, the connection of the Manchus with Central Asia was cut off. Discussion in Peking revolved around the point that a reconquest of Central Asia would be very expensive and not really worthwhile, and it was proposed to give up Sinkiang. However, because of the possibility that this might lead to greater losses and a general "Turkic" uprising, sponsored by the Ottomans, the Chinese government finally decided to regain Turkestan.

Their first act was the appointment of a military commander, Tso Tsung-t'ang. Tso was the first Chinese general who had taken command in Sinkiang; all of his predecessors had been Manchus, a sign that Sinkiang was regarded as an area directly under the Manchu regime, not a part of China, down to 1874. Before his new appointment Tso had been sent to Shensi (1867) to fight the "rebels" there. He had then fought the Muslims in Kansu (1869) and resettled those who remained alive after their defeat in another, easily controllable area (1873). Now, with his new appointment, he could fight his way into Turkestan and finally destroy Yaqub Beg and his men (1878). The outcome of the reconquest of Central Asia was that this whole area became a Chinese province with the name Sinkiang (1884), controlled by a Chinese governor. In other words, the area ceased to be simply a part of Manchu territory.

Muslims in Twentieth-Century China

The troubles in Central Asia and adjacent Kansu were not yet ended, however. Again and again, we hear of revolts (1895, and again in 1928 in Kansu). Increasingly, the area became involved in the quarrels of the so-called Chinese warlords, whom the KMT—the Nationalist Party of Sun Yat-sen, then led by

Chiang Kai-shek—tried to upset and to bring under Nationalist rule. Several of the warlords of the Northwest and Sinkiang were local Muslims, mostly with the family name Ma, indicating the Muslim religion. Ma Ti-t'ai, for instance, was in the 1920s governor-general of Sinkiang and crushed a movement against himself in 1924 with the help of the Turgut tribes in the north. In Ch'ing-hai Province, the province just west of Kansu, Ma Hung-kui was governor; in Ning-hsia (north of Kansu) Ma Pu-fang ruled. In 1934 a Chinese leader, Sheng Shih-ts'ai, asked the Russians to help him against Ma Chung-ying, a Dungan who threatened Urumchi, the capital of Sinkiang. Dungans are Muslims who probably came mainly from Turkic stock but who are now totally Chinese in language and customs. Sheng then turned against the Russians and pro-Russian local people. Yet between 1938 and 1943 Russian influence in Sinkiang was so overwhelming that some observers predicted Sinkiang would soon be integrated into the Soviet republics. However, the configurations of powers during the Second World War influenced the policy of the Soviet Union, which withdrew from Sinkiang in 1943. For the first time a Nationalist Party representative became governor of Sinkiang (Wu Chung-hsin, 1944). But the western sections of Sinkiang made themselves independent of China (1944). With the rise of the Chinese Communists, even the local Turkic Muslim governor of Sinkiang turned toward the Communists.

The Problems of Sinkiang

After this lengthy, complicated political survey we can ask: What are the real problems of Sinkiang; why these constant "rebellions"? The main reason for mentioning the constant conflicts was to show that Sinkiang is a country of numerous ethnic groups, mostly non-Chinese. One estimate is that, before the Communists took over, 94 percent of the population was Muslim and non-Chinese. In spite of almost 2,000 years of contact China had never really ruled Sinkiang; it had occupied it for some time, had brought parts of it into "tributary relations," had driven out some local rulers who were unfriendly and replaced them with collaborators, but all of this had only temporary effects. We saw that even the Manchus had only loose ties with Sinkiang for over 200 years. Only in 1884 was Sinkiang forcefully integrated into China, as Russia had integrated Russian Central Asia.

In our terminology Sinkiang was a colony. It is, therefore, understandable that, whenever there seemed to be a chance to regain freedom, the people of Sinkiang tried to cut themselves off from China. Unfortunately, the people of Sinkiang have had no way to publicize their condition or requests for support. Very little news has come out of Sinkiang to the West, either in the past or in the present. What we hear comes mainly from Chinese sources, and the Chinese regard Sinkiang as an integral part of their country. A part of the political dilemma stems from the fact that Sinkiang is totally landlocked. It has no direct access to the sea, and all contacts have to go through other countries that may or may not give the right of passage to diplomatic missions or individuals.

Another problem is the geographical condition of Sinkiang. It consists of a large depression surrounded on three sides by high mountain ranges. Only from the Chinese province of Kansu is there a relatively easy access. The mountains catch rain, which feeds into rivers, all of which end in more or less salty lakes or marshes in the depression. Here there are oases that allow agriculture and arboriculture, but each oasis is separated from the next one by long stretches of desert without any water, extremely hot in summer and cold in winter. This situation favors small city-states in oases and nomadic tribes in the desert and steppes around them. So Sinkiang was never a unified country, except under colonial rule. Such rule was hard to maintain and economically unprofitable. Statistics are not available even now, but we get the impression that, since the beginning of the Christian era, the population has not increased much and the area available for agriculture has remained more or less the same. An estimate of 1911 states that only 1.6 million acres of land were under cultivation, 10 percent less than in 1759. A 1943 estimate gives 3.6 million acres. The Communist regime has developed new farm land by using the Tarim River, the largest in Sinkiang, for irrigation, and by improving other, older canals that bring water to the oases. In 1961 the government claimed that now 7.9 million acres are under cultivation. This great increase is not intended for the native population but mainly for the supply of the Chinese occupation army and the masses of Chinese settlers who are brought, more or less voluntarily, into Sinkiang. It is questionable whether the agricultural surface can be extended any further because a consequence of irrigation is increasing salinization, which after about twenty to fifty years takes much land out of production.

Chinese garrisons had lived in Central Asia over the last 2,000 years. They lived, of course, in military compounds, physically separated from the local population yet often mixing with them and intermarrying. In the last centuries before the integration of Sinkiang into the Chinese Empire many Chinese merchants settled in the oasis cities. An example of the interrelation of the Chinese and the indigenous population can be seen in the description given by a Turk of the small town of Lükcün. There was an old town, in which the local Dungans and the Chinese lived, and a new town, in which Turks lived. The Chinese operated ten shops, the Dungans three, the Turks four. The Chinese had only one temple, but the Muslim population (Dungans and Turks) had eight mosques, one religious seminar, and two schools. The Turks seemed to feel that the presence of Chinese merchants was responsible for the flourishing prostitution, lesbianism, and bestiality in the area.

The reason for the settlement of many Chinese in Sinkiang was in part to change the proportion of Chinese in the local population, an attempt to make a majority into a minority. This may be achieved by now, and, if so, Sinkiang may truly become a "Chinese" province.

In the last twenty years we have heard of numerous cases of local Turkic people who fled into adjacent Soviet Central Asia, where they still have relatives who speak their language. Clearly, Soviet Central Asia has a much higher standard of living, and even a little bit more freedom, than Sinkiang. We also hear that Soviet Russia has trained some of these refugees and sent them back as agitators. The effect is that China has felt compelled to keep a large and well-supplied army in Sinkiang at high cost, while on the other side of the border Russia keeps its own forces. Russia may be interested not so much in Sinkiang itself as in the oil and minerals that have been discovered in the eastern parts of Sinkiang. There are also Chinese atomic installations and testing grounds, which Russia may be interested in should relations between the two countries further deteriorate.

So the geographical position of Sinkiang between two great powers and its ecological problems are two reasons for the instability in Sinkiang over the centuries. Another important reason is the ethnic situation. As we have seen, over time numerous city- or oases-states have arisen and decayed in Sinkiang; many tribal federations have formed, uniting tribes of different languages and races, and disappeared again. The main stock in recent centuries is Turkic, that is, people speaking a language closely related to Turkish. The Chinese now call these people Uygurs, connecting them with the Uygurs of the T'ang time. They are physically different from the Chinese, closer to the people of Russian Central Asia, but as a result of conquests and contacts most of them have some Mongol physical traits.

The real problem, however, is not race but religion. The people of Sinkiang adhere to the Hui-chiao (Muslim religion), which is, like Christianity, not compatible with Chinese religion. Islam demands faith in the one and only God, Allah; there is no place for any other god. Thus, Muslims cannot worship with their Chinese neighbors in a community temple in which different deities are worshiped; they cannot worship their ancestors as all Chinese do. Muslims stand outside the community of Chinese and live in their own community. Muslims cannot participate in Chinese social life. They are not allowed to drink alcoholic beverages or to smoke opium, a social custom widely practiced until very recently. In Chinese cuisine the meat is predominantly pork and the cooking fat is pork grease, and Muslims are not allowed to eat pork. The typical meat of Muslims is mutton or sometimes beef, but many Chinese do not eat beef because they regard it as ungrateful to kill and eat the animal that, through its labor, provided the farmer with grain. There may also be an influence of Indian worship of the cow, which came with Buddhism. Anti-Muslim Chinese say that Muslims do not eat pork because their ancestor was a pig. When this story was published in a booklet in the early 1930s, the author was mobbed by irate Muslims. Anti-Muslim Chinese also sometimes forbade the slaughter of cows in Muslim Central Asia, which angered the Muslim population. Further anti-Muslim sentiment can be seen in the rumors circulating again and again among the Chinese that the Muslims abduct or buy Chinese children, circumcise them, and thus make them Muslims—rumors that, of course, cannot be verified.

Other factors also work against Muslim–Chinese integration. The Muslims did not want to become members of the Chinese communities in their neighborhoods but established their own tightly organized communities according to Islamic beliefs and rules. Such a Muslim community (called *umma*) has a religious leader (*imam*) who is a scholar insofar as he must have learned Arabic in order to be able to read the Qoran, the holy book of Islam. At the same time, he is a teacher and keeps a religious school in the mosque for the children. He also often has to act as a judge, solving problems between members of the community or mediating conflicts. There is usually also a *muezzin*, a man with a good voice who calls the believers to the prayers, five times a day. Every Muslim is expected to pray his five daily prayers, possibly at least once in the mosque, and under all circumstances to pray in the mosque the big prayer on Friday. A Muslim is expected to give alms to the poor and give to religious foundations, if he does not set up a foundation of his own. Every child that is born is introduced into the religion, and when a boy is a few years old, he must be circumcised. The imam has to be present for the funeral of a believer and to see that the burial is performed in the right way. Every Muslim receives a Muslim name. All of this practice is in complete opposition to Chinese religious customs. In China many temples do not have a priest, and priests do not have to have a special education and often do not have prestige in the community. A Chinese community is based much more on alliances of families and on neighborhoods. An Islamic community is based on religion and is, therefore, not only a local community like a Chinese one. When Muslims travel to another town, they are at home there in the local group of Muslims. All Muslims try, when they have the means, to make the pilgrimage to the holy place, Mecca in Arabia, once in their life. When they return, they have acquired a new status, the highest status in their community, as a *haci*, a pilgrim.

This all gives the Muslim group strength: Messages can be transmitted by any Muslim from one town to the other, and communities will try to act in common if there is danger. By the institution of the pilgrimage the communities also have ties to foreign countries, which may have political importance. Even at the height of World War II at least one group of Muslims from China proper and from Sinkiang passed through Turkey and other Near Eastern countries on their way to Mecca and brought news from China; it is possible that they also reported back home about the situation in the Far West. There was no great language difficulty: The so-called Uygurs from Sinkiang could understand the Turks of Turkey and, when necessary, could also use their Arabic, though it was classical and not the modern Arabic of Arab countries.

Thus, the Muslim communities, especially in Sinkiang where the majority of the inhabitants are Muslim, are a block against sinification because of their religious organization. There is a rule that any non-Muslim woman who marries a Muslim has to convert to Islam and, therefore, to separate from her own family. The community tries hard to prevent marriages between a Muslim woman and a non-Muslim man. Consequently, intermarriage is uncommon and thus has not aided in assimilation.

Because of their strict religious practices the Muslims in general resisted assimilation into Chinese culture. However, because neighboring Soviet Central Asia has a population with close ties to the people of Sinkiang, this area is now a zone of danger. Therefore, the Chinese have brought not only Chinese soldiers but also masses of Chinese settlers into Sinkiang. One can forsee that the majority of the population of Sinkiang will soon be Chinese.

TIBETANS

Turning now from the Northwest to the West of China, we shall discuss the Tibetan people. These can be clearly divided into two great groups. The more northern group had contacts with the Chinese since very early times, while the southern group had contact with Indian states and only relatively late with China. We shall treat each group separately until about A.D. 600. Both groups speak a Tibetan language that is in some ways related to Chinese but probably even closer to Burmese, so that we often speak of Tibeto-Burman and of Sino-Thai languages as two separate language families. The Tibetans are commonly included in the Mongol race if we still accept the four great branches of humanity as races. Some scholars have pointed out that some North American Indians look like some tribes of Tibetan stock, though others have denied it. It is impossible to know whether such similarity, if it truly exists, indicates a relationship; it may simply mean that some Tibetan tribes look slightly different from the Chinese of the North.

Habitat and Livelihood

The habitat of all Tibetans is highlands with a cold dry climate. The northern part of Tibet, mainly the present Chinese province of Ch'ing-hai (Köke nor; "blue sea") was at the dawn of history inhabited by Ch'iang tribes. We have mentioned above that Ch'iang tribes lived far to the east, inside the earliest settlements of Chinese, on the mountains and hills, keeping their sheep and goats, and continuously in conflict with the emerging Chinese states. They survived until the Han dynasty (206 B.C. to A.D. 220), but from then on Ch'iang inside the borders of China were almost extinct, and fights with Ch'iang took place mainly in the western borderlands of the Chinese state. In other words, the Chinese pressed them farther and farther west into the high mountains. We hear about a number of individual tribes, but military conflicts were mainly between federations of tribes and the Chinese. Tribal organization seems never to have been as tight among the Tibetans as among Turks and Mongols. The tribal chiefs, too, seem not to have had as much power as in their nomadic neighbor tribes. There also was no aristocracy among them as among Turkish tribes. They usually lived in tents made of wool and did not develop the complex round tents the Mongols and Turks had. Their religion, about which the early sources do not speak, was a kind of shamanistic belief in numerous deities, often local ones who were believed to exist in caves or heaps of rocks. This can be seen in the origin myth of the first ruler of one of these tribes. This man, Yüan Chien, who supposedly lived in the early part of the fifth century B.C.,

> was once captured by the Ch'in [a Chinese state in Northwest China at that time] and became a slave. Nobody knew from which group of the barbarians Yüan came. Later, he succeeded in running away, and when the Ch'in pursued him, he hid in a cave. When the Ch'in wanted to force him out by smoke, there was a shadow like a tiger who covered the fire, so that Yüan did not die. When he got out, he met in the wilderness a woman whose nose had been cut off [as punishment for some crime]. They became a couple and, because she was ashamed of her condition, she covered her face with her hair. Therefore, the Ch'iang [tribes] have this custom [of covering their face]. Then they moved into the area between three rivers. When the Ch'iang saw that Yüan had not been killed when the smoke came close, they admired his supernatural abilities, feared him and served him, making him their chieftain. Between the Huang-ho and the Hsi-ning Rivers there was little grain and many birds and animals. Hunting was the main occupation. Yüan Chien taught them agriculture and animal husbandry. (*Hou Han shu*, 117, pp. 2b-3a)

The Tibetans' main livelihood came from their sheep and goats, though there was some, apparently simple, agriculture. Buckwheat and barley were their typical crops because they can grow buckwheat in the difficult climatic conditions in which the Tibetans live. As they lived in the mountains that had forests if the altitude were not too high, they also were woodcutters who sold lumber to the Chinese, or they collected herbs and animals that became the bases of many medicines the Chinese appreciated very much. Lumber and medicine remained the most important articles of exchange by which the Tibetans could get the more developed products of the Chinese. In addition, the Tibetans had bred a horse that was quite small but very tough and ideal for travel and transport in the mountains. Through all ages Tibetans of the north sold horses to China.

Tribal Conflicts and Movement

Troubles began around A.D. 200, when the Han dynasty was deposed and three pretenders fought for power. The state of Shu-Han in the West (province of Szu-ch'uan) recruited among the Tibetan tribes because the northern state of Wei hired foreign soldiers from the North. When finally, as we have seen above, the

North of China fell to the northern tribes, some of the Tibetan military leaders also tried to set themselves up as rulers over North and West China. One of them created his own dynasty, the Earlier Ch'in dynasty (351–394), which gained power over many other pretenders and, under Fu Chien (357–385), ruled over all of North China. He even tried to conquer the South—the first foreigner to make this attempt—but ended in failure. The reason for the failure is not clear because Fu Chien's armies were large and well organized, while the South was weak. However, the fact that his organization was purely military and not based on tribal traditions may have been responsible for his downfall. The military organization was relatively new, based upon cavalry and modeled after Chinese military organizations, so that when the first difficulties in the conflict with South China (Eastern Chin dynasty) began, the loyalty of the individual detachments was questionable and impeded unified operations. When defeated, Fu Chien's armies simply disappeared; each little group acted independently under its own military officers. Men who had remained in the capital set up a dynasty of their own, the Later Ch'in dynasty (384–417) and killed Fu Chien and all the members of his family. There were still other dynasties, usually equally short-lived, in West China until the whole of the North and West came under Toba rule.

In this period, between the late fourth and the fifth century, fragments of defeated Hsien-pi tribes fled from North China into the mountains in the West, so that we begin to see in the territory of the present province of Ch'ing-hai a great mixture of camp settlements by tribes of the Hsien-pi and tribes of Ch'iang Tibetans. Their coexistence in this area continued down to the present century, alongside the newly arriving Chinese settlers. There are villages in which people speak Mongolian dialects, while nearby people speak a northern Tibetan dialect, and, in still another place, only Chinese is spoken.

There was also a hybridization at the federation level between Hsien-pi and Ch'iang, resulting in the T'u-yü-hun federation. The T'u-yü-hun were attacked around A.D. 600 by the Chinese, who were afraid that this federation could threaten the Central Asian policy of China by allying themselves with the Turkish tribes. After their defeat a new federation of similar composition arose, the T'u-fan. The T'u-fan allied themselves with the Turks at the moment when China was extremely weak because of the revolt of An Lu-shan (755). When the emperor fled the capital, the T'u-fan and the Turks entered the capital of Ch'ang-an as "saviors" of China, but in fact they plundered the capital, and some parts of Kansu remained for a long time under Tibetan rule. We should mention very briefly a small minority group in the Ch'iang territory, which by the sixth century had already disappeared: The "Little Yüeh-chih" were that part of the Yüeh-chih tribes that had not migrated into Central and later South Asia but had fled into the northern Tibetan mountains. They, too, mixed with local Tibetans and reappeared in history for a short time as Ti tribes. No trace of them seems to have survived.

When the T'u-fan dissolved, the Tanguts created a new federation, which benefited from the disorders of the tenth century, during which China broke up into a number of small states (906–960), and the Sung dynasty (after 960) did not succeed in reconquering North and Northwest China. Here, then, the Tanguts set up their own Hsi-hsia dynasty (1038–1227). The Tanguts of that time were basically northern Tibetans with Hsien-pi and other Turkic and Mongolian tribal elements. Like the Khitan, the Hsi-hsia developed a script of their own, modeled on the Chinese script. (Until the 1960s this script, which had long since fallen into disuse, had not yet been deciphered.) The Hsi-hsia balanced cleverly and successfully between the Chinese in the South and the Khitan in the North until finally the Mongols destroyed them. By destruction we mean the disappearance of a unified political regime; the tribes again reverted to their old way of life.

Some of the tribes seem to have migrated farther south and southeast. At the time of Mongol conquest and down to Manchu times the Tibetan state in the South, of which we shall speak below, controlled the Tangut tribes to some degree, and in the last century more and more Chinese settlers moved into their country. The Manchus conquered their territory early in their conquests and organized the area under twenty-nine banners, with a center in Hsi-ning, a city in Kansu province. In 1928 Hsi-ning and some surrounding territory was divided from Kansu and made into the separate province of Ch'ing-hai. We mentioned above that there are still minorities in Ch'ing-hai, not only Muslim groups like the Salar but also northern Tibetans. Ch'ing-hai Tibetans had, at an early period, accepted Buddhism in its northern form of Lamaism. They remained culturally close to Tibet proper, on the one hand, and also to the Mongol neighbors with whom they had such close ties of blood and tradition. Some of their monasteries were, until the twentieth century, visited by many pilgrims from Mongolia.

The Country and Culture of Tibet

What we normally understand when we speak of Tibet is the southern part of the great highland of Central Asia, the Himalayan mountain area and its northern slopes—the country that has Lhasa as its capital. This country came into the light of history only relatively late because of its inaccessibility, and it has remained until today a country closed to Western scholars, with a few exceptions. We have to rely on recent Chinese reports, which, like all publications about areas that were subjected to occupation and radical changes, have to be taken with caution. We are best informed about Tibetan history and religion, but only a very few anthropological or sociological studies were made before the Communist takeover in the 1950s.

Located between the two great civilizations of Asia, India and China, Tibet's geographical position is crucial for its development. We have the impression that Indian influences were felt earlier than Chinese and that the most important early relations were of a religious character. The mountains of Tibet were regarded as the center of the world. The Indian Kailasa Mountain was thought to be somewhere in the north of India; the Chinese K'un-lun Mountain, equally regarded as the center of the world, was west of China but more to the north than the Kailasa. Indian monks retreated into these mountains and tried to achieve perfection by meditation. They seem to have spread early Buddhism into Nepal and Tibet, where they found another religion, later named Bon, a cult of demons and deities, some of them female, many fearful to look at and often dangerous to men. In all of East and North Asia shamanism was common—cults in which men or women reached a trance, during which they could send their souls far away to meet deities or dead persons and talk with them; or they could ask souls to enter their body and speak out of the mouth of the shaman. Shamanism appears in different forms in this area, but it is never an organized religion and is always practiced by individuals. In Tibet, however, much of shamanism was integrated into the Bon religious ceremonies. It may well be that the specific forms of Buddhism in Tibet—Lamaism and Tantrism—developed inside Tibet under the stimulus of Bon practices and beliefs.

By Lamaism we understand the monastically organized church and its doctrines; Tantrism refers to a specific form of Buddhism that has integrated into it not only a cult of fearful deities but also ways of attaining enlightenment through sexual practices. Many of the Tantric teachings were secret and transmitted only to advanced students. Tantrism entered China in T'ang times and gained more influence during the Mongol period, but it was never a dominant form of Buddhism in China. Buddhists also introduced into Tibet their Indian script, which became the basis of the Tibetan script.

The character of the Himalayan range dictated that movements from India to the north of the range would circumvent the direct approach. The trade routes went to the northwest of India and passed through either Afghanistan or the passes of Gilgit to the western edge of Sinkiang and only then turned east toward China. Tibet proper was thus avoided. The same was true of the Chinese contacts: Chinese went from Northwest China through Ch'ing-hai into the northern Tibetan area of which we have spoken above and generally stopped there. China knew of India before it knew of Tibet; it also knew Nepal much better and earlier than Tibet. Buddhist pilgrims going to and from India used the route through Sinkiang and northwest India, and all states and statelets along this route were well known to Chinese, but Tibet itself was not traversed. Chinese learned about it not much before the late sixth century A.D.

What Chinese sources report is, in general, very similar to their descriptions of the culture of the northern Tibetan tribes. Two cultural traits astonished the Chinese particularly: the influence of women and the custom of polyandry. In the very earliest reports on Tibet we hear of a "Country of Women" (Nü-kuo or Tung-nü), in which women ruled and men were politically subordinated to the queen and the assistant queen. The queen, it was said, lived in a stone house with nine stories. (Most of the houses in the country were built of stones, not of mud, the material of many houses in North China, and not of wood, like houses in South China.) Polyandry, an institution in which one woman has more than one husband, was a custom the Chinese found abominable. Both polyandry and matriarchy (the political rule of women) fit well in a society in which the men were often away from the women and children for long periods. Tibet is large and barren. Much of the food had to be purchased in areas far away, and so many Tibetan men traveled around in caravans selling their animal products and medicinal herbs, while buying the products of their agricultural neighbors. In the absence of the husbands the women took over the control of the house and property. They often also took a second husband, normally a brother of the first husband; conflicts were avoided because one of the husbands was away when the other one was at home. Many men also were temporarily or for long periods in monasteries as monks; a second husband could take the place of such an absent man.

Tibetans were warlike and often fought with their neighbors. Hunting was important in Tibet, and not much agriculture was possible. Their clothing was made of felt or wool, and the reports stress the fact that the Tibetans were very dirty. To what degree this is true is hard to say, but in a country with snow and ice over many months of the year, and little firewood because trees are scarce, one cannot expect that people would wash themselves very often, and the felt cloth of earlier times was not easy to clean. The main animal of the Tibetans was always the yak, a sturdy large animal that could stand the climate, provided milk and wool, and was the mainstay of the transportation system. Horses demand a better climate, and they were more typical of the northern and eastern Tibetans. The reports mentioned the use of what foreign observers have often called rancid butter. Yak milk was made into butter, which was then clarified and preserved; this butter was pure fat and had a particular smell and taste. Besides using it in their food, Tibetans put it, together with flour or animal blood and salt, into their tea. They also used it for cosmetic purposes on their faces and as a hair tonic.

The Development of States and Buddhist Influence

Beginning about A.D. 600, the same time that Buddhism was introduced, states developed in Tibet proper. The impetus for the formation of states seems to have come from the north, from tribes such as the T'u-fan mentioned above, while Buddhism came from the south. The first, and most famous, indigenous ruler was Srong-btsan-sgam-po whose reign, according to tradition, began in 629 and who sent an embassy with gifts to China in 634. It is said a Chinese embassy went to Tibet soon afterward. The Tibetan ruler had heard that the rulers of the tribal federations had asked for Chinese princesses as wives and had received them, so he, too, requested a Chinese princess. He finally received one in 641, though he had to pay "gifts" valued at 5,000 ounces of gold for her. Srong-btsan-sgam-po also received a princess of Nepal as wife, thus balancing between the two powers to the south and east of him. The custom of giving a princess to a foreign ruler in order to establish peaceful relations was very common in T'ang times.

Both wives of Srong-btsan-sgam-po, according to the legends, were Buddhists and introduced the new religion together with the culture of their homelands. They propagated Chinese dress for the men and women of the ruling class; invited Chinese teachers to come and teach the sons of the nobility; imported silk worms, and therefore the production of silk, and technicians who could make paper and Chinese ink. All these reports in Chinese sources may not be absolutely factual, but there is no doubt that the main elements of Chinese and Indian (and to some degree also Nepalese) culture penetrated into Tibet from the mid-seventh century. Among the Buddhists in Tibet a competition began between the Indian and the Chinese sects. A struggle also developed with the indigenous Bon religion and its priests, which persuaded the ruler (around 741) to invite a famous Indian Buddhist, Padmasambhava to drive the demons and enemies out of Tibet and to introduce the "correct" Buddhism. Padmasambhava indeed brought some powerful *dharani*, or magic formulae, to Tibet. He also started, with a host of translators, a translation of masses of Buddhist texts into the Tibetan language. With him began the Tibetan form of Buddhism, into which, it seems, some Iranian concepts were incorporated along with Indian and Chinese ideas. At about the same time as the Chinese emperor initiated a short-lived persecution of Buddhists in China (ninth century), a Tibetan ruler observed the expulsion of Buddhist monks and the destruction of monasteries. A reaction began about a hundred years later, and from then on the wordly power of the ruler diminished and the Lamaist church took over. The individual tribes of Tibet, which had been temporarily amalgamated, separated again under the rule of their "feudal" tribal chiefs.

After this we hear almost nothing about Tibet because the tenth century was a period of the break-up of China into independent smaller states. When the Sung dynasty (beginning in 960) slowly regained power over Central and South, but not North, China, access to Tibet was closed by the non-Chinese states in the Northwest and by another non-Chinese state in Southwest China.

The Rule of the Lamas

The Mongols under Ögödei conquered Tibet in the thirteenth century, initiating some very important developments. In 1253 a scholarly young Tibetan monk, 'Phags-pa, a cousin of the famous Lama Sa-skya Pandita, was introduced to Khubilai (who was not yet personally in control of China) and impressed him very much. 'Phags-pa participated in religious discussions between Buddhists and Taoists in Mongolia at the Mongol capital (1254 and 1258), and it is through his influence that Lamaism became the dominant and soon the only form of Buddhism practiced in Mongolia. Since then Tibetan culture, especially its literature, has been a determining influence upon Mongol spiritual life. In 1260 'Phags-pa was raised by the emperor to the rank of "teacher of the country," which made him at least formally the head of Buddhism in the Mongol Empire of the East. In 1269 he was asked to develop a national Mongol script to replace the Uygur script used until then. This 'Phags-pa script, as it was called, was rather clumsy in comparison to the elegant and speedy Uygur script and was never popular in spite of Kubilai's orders to use it in all official correspondence. In 1274 'Phags-pa went back to Tibet, where he became the nation's spiritual and political head.

With the end of Mongol rule the lamas continued to rule Tibet. The next important development came with Tsong-kha-pa (1356–1419), who succeeded in creating a new, more conservative, orthodox sect and church, called the Yellow church because of the yellow headdress of the priests. The earlier Red church continued to exist but became less and less important. The priests of the Red church were allowed to marry—for any conservative Buddhist a very serious violation of the law—and thus they formed whole dynasties of religious leaders. In the Yellow church of Tsong-kha-pa the leaders had to be incarnations of the Bodhisattva Avalokiteśvara and the Buddha Amitabha. The Dalai Lama who ruled in Lhasa was an incarnation of Avalokiteśvara, and the Tashi Lama who resided in Shigatse was an incarnation of Amitabha. The latter was more a religious leader, while the Dalai Lama in time became the highest political leader. When one of these leaders died, emissaries were sent to all parts of the country to find a baby who had been born at or about the time the old lama had died and who also had a number of unusual physical and mental traits. That baby or youngster then became the next leader. The fact that it often took many years to discover the new Dalai Lama and that he always was very young meant that, in between rulers, the court, consisting of the powerful families of Lhasa, actually ruled the country even when a new Dalai Lama was set up as ruler. From the reforms of Tsong-kha-pa until the Communist revolution Tibet was in fact ruled by the Dalai Lama, and there were temples of the Yellow church in China, especially a famous one in Peking that is still in use. Within the country feudal lords ruled over their tribes or over several tribes almost fully independent of Lhasa, with the exception of more or less ceremonial "tribute" payments to Lhasa.

Tibet under the Manchus

The Manchus had established relations with Tibet even before they became rulers of China (1644), and in 1652 the fifth Dalai Lama arrived as a guest in Peking. He was a visitor, not a vassal, which indicates that Tibet was free but bound by "family ties" to China and thus, in a family way, subordinated to China. The Manchus also enforced a new rule intended to limit the power of the aristocracy—namely, that the new Dalai Lama could not be found among the members of powerful families (though it was possible, of course, that the poor family's son would be in some direct or indirect way dependent upon a powerful family). The Manchus conquered Tibet only much later. This was a necessary consequence of events in the early eighteenth century. In 1717 the chief of the Oirat federation moved against Tibet, intending to control the lamas of Tibet and thus to gain control over the Mongols, who were by that time fervent Lamaists. An alliance of the Oirat with the Tibetans, and perhaps the Mongols, would have threatened the Manchu Empire, and so the Manchus felt forced to move against Tibet, after winning a victory over the Oirat (1720). The conquest was relatively easy and resulted in no more than the settling of a Manchu garrison in Tibet, a garrison that got smaller and smaller over time and could hardly have kept the Tibetans under control had the Tibetans wanted to get rid of the Manchus. Tibet was also required to send a formal tribute to Peking.

In 1788–1789 and again in 1791–1792 Nepal tried to invade Tibet, and the Manchus had to send an expedition against Nepal (1792). The situation of Nepal after that time is unclear. Was the country a vassal of China or not? The Manchus did not seem to be too eager to control Nepal, although we may not yet be fully informed about what went on because the diplomatic correspondence between the Manchu court and Nepal is still in the archives in Kathmandu and has not been studied by scholars. Nepal sent tribute until 1908, but, as in other cases, this was not regarded as a sign that the country was a vassal. The question became acute when, at the beginning of the nineteenth century, England began to be interested in Nepal and wanted to integrate it into India. Nepal hoped for aid from Peking, but the Manchus did not help. Probably they could not help because, from about 1792 on, Manchu power in general and especially power over Tibet began to weaken rapidly.

In 1846 the British government discussed Tibet with the Manchus; this was, for England, an ideal moment, shortly after they had defeated China in the Opium War. On the other hand, in 1848 the great uprising of the T'ai-p'ing began in South China and threatened the Manchu regime, while the T'ai-p'ing's special type of Christianity seemed to offer to England a chance to control all of China or at least the southern parts of it. But the T'ai-p'ing were defeated, and the imperial government gained control over China proper. However, at the same time, unrest in Chinese Central Asia flared up and diverted England's interest in Tibet, so the Manchus retained their control over Tibet.

Tibet remained as it was—it did not change or modernize—but the world around it changed. Britain became more and more worried about Russian plans and tried to gain control of Tibet, which was to serve as a buffer. The first step was to persuade the Manchu government to agree to a trade pact (1893), which would have allowed some merchants and diplomats to take up residence in Lhasa. Tibet refused to honor this agreement, in whose negotiation it had no part. When England tried to contact the Dalai Lama's government directly, Tibet refused under the pretext that the Manchus would not allow them to deal with a foreign power. The only remaining option was a British military expedition against Tibet. The weak and antiquated Tibetan army was defeated (1904), and the Dalai Lama fled Lhasa. The Manchus declared the Lama deposed. The Tibetans were angry that the Manchus had not only not helped them, in spite of keeping a garrison in Lhasa, but that they had also violated their religious feelings: A lama, as an incarnation of a God, cannot be deposed by a worldly power. So, in the end, Tibet began to soften its line against Britain, English advisors were admitted, and trade with England via India grew. In order to stop English involvement in Tibet, the Manchus sent an army into the country (1910), which further aroused Tibetan feelings because they slaughtered many Tibetans and burned holy texts in one of the main monasteries, but Lhasa was not taken. It is thus understandable that the Tibetans were happy when the 1911 revolution broke out in China and the Manchus were deposed.

Tibet in Modern Times

Very much like the Mongols, the Tibetans felt that they were vassals or subordinates of the Manchus but not of the Chinese. The Chinese Republicans, however, did not see the situation in this light; they regarded Tibet as a part of China. In 1914 a large part of eastern Tibet was cut off and put under a separate military administration. The Tibetans did not agree to this and did not ratify the treaty until 1939, but the actual situation was not affected by this refusal. When warlords were fighting one another during the first fifteen years of the Republic, Tibet proper remained fairly quiet and protected, the more so because England and Russia were both involved in World War I and could not pay much attention to Tibet. Even when Chiang Kai-shek began to set up a regime that controlled large areas of China directly (1927) and which slowly began to eliminate one warlord after the other as well as to drive the Chinese Communists out of their stronghold between the provinces of Kiangsi and Hunan, his power did not yet extend to Tibet. The full-scale invasion of China by Japan (1937) ended the Nationalist government's attempt to establish full control over the country and forced it to retreat into the western parts, while the Communists used the opportunity to secure their stronghold in Yen-an against Chiang Kai-shek and to do guerrilla work behind the Japanese lines. Meanwhile, in 1940, the fourteenth Dalai Lama was officially installed, the last of his line.

When the People's Republic was established in Peking in 1949, Tibet did not feel much change. In 1922, shortly after its official creation, the Communist Party had promised to regard Tibet as an autonomous country, but by 1951 this policy had been changed: The so-called autonomous country became first an autonomous area, then an autonomous province, and no longer had the right to secede. Propagandists began to enter Tibet, some Tibetans trained in Yen-an and some Chinese. Mao Tse-tung promised that no revolutionary reforms would be made at least within the next six years. Only in 1956 were the first seven Tibetans accepted as members of the Communist Party. The promise of 1951 was not kept very long. The Chinese military moved into Tibet and, with it, work crews who built roads, partly as means to penetrate and to control Tibet, partly as an answer to the threats of interference by India. The presence of soldiers and cadres in the country produced friction: The cadres forced the Tibetans to abolish corvée (forced labor services for an overlord) and soon moved toward liberation of serfs, farmers who were bound to a landlord and had only the right to work on the land, but could not move away and had to pay rent to their lord.

Tibet had never been a wholly unified country. The Dalai Lama was the recognized ruler, but some of his "subjects" were feudal lords in the narrow sense of the word *feudal*: They ruled a certain territory like local lords, and, though they agreed to accept the overlordship of the Dalai Lama, they could not be forced by the Dalai Lama to obey orders that interfered with their control of their land. In

such a situation subversion was easy. One lord could be incited to act against another, and the people dominated by a lord could be incited to rise against him. In
addition, the Chinese military set up radio stations for broadcasting propaganda,
desecrated temples, and violated customs of the country. Here and there, smaller
or larger rebellions occurred, but the Tibetan government did not take decisive
steps against them. In addition, Tibetans from the border areas, especially Hsi-
k'ang, flooded back into Tibet and increased the ranks of the dissatisfied. In 1958
a large-scale revolt against the Chinese began in Tibet. The Dalai Lama felt
threatened and fled, together with an estimated 60,000 Tibetans, into India. The
uprising failed, mainly because of poor planning and coordination of the Tibetans,
but also because the superior equipment of the Chinese.

In March 1959 the Tibetan government was dissolved, and a communist-
style local government was created, the official head of which was the Panchen
Lama, who became "acting chairman." The Panchen Lama was the second-highest
religious leader of Tibetan Lamaism, whose traditional seat was near the city of
Shigatse in the northern part of Tibet, province of Ch'ing-hai (Amdo). This region
had already been controlled for some time by China. The tenth Panchen Lama was
installed by the Chinese before the Communist takeover; like his predecessor, he
was unfriendly toward the Dalai Lama. Thus, from the Chinese perspective, he
was a good choice: a man with high religious prestige and one likely to be more
responsive to the Chinese than to the people in Lhasa who had lived under his
opponent, the Dalai Lama. He, too, was eventually dismissed in 1964. The politically important figure was Ngajo Ngawang Jigme, a collaborator with the new
regime. Still, for a time, most members of his shadow government were members
of the old upper class.

By 1961 Tibet was still regarded as a country that had had its "democratic,"
but not yet its "socialist," revolution. This meant that land reforms had been carried out, feudal prerogatives abolished, and the first attempts to create collective
farms made. When the Cultural Revolution began, the so-called Red Guards appeared in Tibet, too. Fighting occurred mainly between the followers of the Liu
Shao-ch'i faction and the guards, who regarded themselves as Maoists. It is estimated that not more than 1 percent of the Tibetan population became involved in
this internal fight of the Chinese. The end of the Red Guard period (1968) saw
Tibet governed by a body of twelve Party members, so-called vice-chairmen, of
whom only four were Tibetans; the rest were Chinese.

Minorities of the South

With the exception of Sinkiang, all the areas we have discussed thus far did not belong to "China proper"—that is, the eighteen provinces of China existing at the end of the Manchu dynasty (1911), and even the status of Sinkiang was not the same as that of the other old provinces. All through history the various areas were inhabited by non-Chinese people under their own governments. In time Chinese settlers moved in and administrators followed, so that their governments were only the shadow of what they had been. When China became a republic, they, one after the other, became regular provinces, which did not have the right to independence or to secession. In all of them except for Tibet the original inhabitants are now a minority that is forced to accept what Peking wants them to do.

When we move further south or southeast, we meet ethnic groups that, for centuries, have lived inside the eighteen provinces and have been directly under Chinese control. While the outer areas were of interest to foreign powers like England and Russia because they once hoped to be able to separate them from Chinese rule, nobody outside of China was interested in the inner minorities; only a few scholars even knew of them. The generally accepted opinion was, and still seems to be, that there are no minorities inside China; in fact, not many even recall that the outer minorities once hoped for an independent existence.

EASTERN TIBETANS

The languages of the Eastern Tibetans are related to the other Tibetan languages, but as the people are divided into numerous, usually small, groups, there are numerous dialects. They even have other relatives further south, the Burmese. All these languages are put together by some linguists as a language family, the Tibeto-Burman languages. The Eastern Tibetans may have been close relatives of the Ch'iang, who have been discussed earlier. But the Ch'iang, who before 1000 B.C. still lived in the mountains of the heart of present-day China (Shensi, Shansi, and Honan), later amalgamated with numerous fragments of Hsien-pi, that is, Mongolian, tribes and others. The Eastern Tibetans, by contrast, may have lived originally in the provinces of Szu-ch'uan, Hupei, Hunan, Kueichou, Yünnan, and even Kuanghsi, though we cannot prove this because we have no documentation for these areas until about a century or two before the common era. It is also possible that they lived only in Szu-ch'uan, next to the Ch'iang proper, as close relatives of the Northern Tibetans, and moved into the mountains of the South when the pressure of Chinese settlers and armies became too strong. There are numbers of migration myths among the tribes of Kuei-chou saying that their ancestors once moved down from Kansu into their present homes.

Tribal Groupings and Life

Like the original Ch'iang (see page 65), the Eastern Tibetans did not form states. They seem not even to have had a strong tribal organization; at least the Chinese sources give us tribal names only for relatively late periods. Because the area of their distribution covers several climatic zones, from cold Tibetan mountains to hot Kuanghsi, their culture is not always the same. But still typical for all of them is their love of living in the mountains. Though for most endangered small ethnic groups a retreat to the mountains is a necessity, the Eastern Tibetans really seem to love the mountains. Their economy is adjusted to high altitudes. They are basically nomads whose main animals are sheep and goats. Like almost all nomads, they cultivate some plants, such as buckwheat, which can stand the climate and the usually poor soil, just as their northern brothers did. In addition, they supply lumber and firewood to other tribes and the Chinese living in the fertile valleys, and also herbs and medicines.

These tribes of Tibetan type are often known to the Chinese by a name that, in their own language simply means *man*, but in a number of cases is transcribed by the Chinese in a way that is offensive to them. The name Lolo, for example, was used for some of these tribes though it meant something like "bandit." It has only recently been replaced by another, nondiscriminatory name, Yi. The latter name, however, includes tribes in addition to those who were originally called Lolo. Another old designation of these tribes is Wu-man, the "black barbarians," perhaps in contrast to other tribes that had been called "white barbarians."

The exact position of the language of these Wu-man is not yet clear. Because it is assumed that Tibetan and Burmese languages in general are closely related, the Eastern and Southern tribes that live between the "real"—that is, Northern and Western—Tibetans and the Burmese speak languages that stand between both languages and are therefore called Tibeto-Burman. Most of these Wu-man tribes lived, or still live, in Yünnan. This southernmost province is the most complex ethnic area of China. The sources mention far more than 150 tribes but have very little to say about them, probably because they do not know much about their cultures. We can therefore identify only some 90 tribes or tribal groups as Wu-man, but there may be others.

The sources characterize the Wu-man as fierce, wild, and dangerous; often they were regarded as bandits or robbers. The "white barbarians," in contrast, were peaceful, it is said. We believe that the situation in the Southwest of China is similar to those other minority areas where nomadic and farming societies come together. Here, in a mountainous area, the fertile, often narrow valleys are occupied by groups who farm the land, but who desire some materials the mountains produce, such as those we have mentioned before: herbal medicines, firewood, lumber, and animal products like meat, fat, and wool. The mountain people are relatively poor, and the temptation to get rice, wheat, fruit, and other products of the valley people by force is great, though fights and attacks could be avoided by symbiotic arrangements. Perhaps there was such a symbiosis between the valley and the mountain people once, but when the valleys became increasingly settled by Chinese farmers who assimilated or drove out the original settlers, the situation changed. The shift to aggression and fighting may have occurred because behind the Chinese settlers stood the empire, but behind the mountain tribes, nobody; however, there may be another explanation.

Early States in Southwest China

Chinese sources of Han times, describing conditions probably of the second century B.C., mention several states in southwest China, and later sources again and again mention the existence of states at a time when the Chinese Empire began to penetrate with soldiers and settlers into the provinces of Kuanghsi and Yünnan. The earliest of these states to appear in the sources is Yeh-lang, which seems to have had its center in the present province of Kuanghsi. We hear that they were the largest unit of "Southern barbarians"; the Chinese sent an embassy to them, an indication that the Yeh-lang had considerable power, and we also hear that the Yeh-lang had asked the Chinese for silk. The origin myth of the Yeh-lang tells us:

> Among the Yeh-lang in the beginning, there was a girl who took a bath in the T'un river. [When she was bathing,] a piece of bamboo, about three bamboo knots large, floated between her legs. She heard sounds in it, broke the bamboo and, when she looked, she found [in it] a boy. She went home and raised this boy. When he was grown up, he was able and aggressive. He made himself king of Yeh-lang and took the family name Chu (Bamboo). (*Hou Han shu*, 116, p. 6b)

Social Organization

The fact that Yeh-lang had a king, and the silk was obviously for the ruler's official garments, is a sign that there was an upper, ruling class. We hear also that they had a number of famous families, another sign that there was an upper class. They were able to mobilize an army, which, in the late second century B.C., helped the Chinese armies in their fight with natives in the area of present-day Canton. A little later the sources mention a society west of Yeh-lang called Tsang-ko, which also seems to have been a state, because a ruling class is mentioned. While the Yeh-lang, according to the texts, had real towns, the Tsang-ko seem to have had settlements that were more like Chinese villages, that is, without real city walls, protected only by low mud (perhaps) walls. Still farther west we hear centuries later of a society named Nan-chao, already centered in Yünnan. It is said that this state, which seems to have been formed early in the seventh century A.D., is the result of the fusion of six Chao tribes and two other tribes that were later destroyed. Nan-chao—that is, South Chao—developed into a real state, powerful enough to cause the Chinese much trouble.

When we look at the social organization of these states, we see a class structure. But when we study what is reported about their culture, we see typical elements of nomadic Wu-man, Tibeto-Burman, and of rice-farming Thai cultures. This reveals a form of "superstratification," in which one ethnic group was subjected to the rule of another ethnic group. The two groups were economically different—the typical form of states evolving on the basis of a former tribal society. From the scarce reports, we get the impression that in Yeh-lang and Tsang-ko the majority were Thai-speaking tribes, ruled by a Wu-man class. In Nan-chao, however, the rulers seem to have spoken a Thai language; this may mean that the Wu-man were the lower class. However, in this latter case it seems more likely that the Thai were the subjected majority, and the rulers had, at the time for which we have extensive reports—about 200 years after the founding of Nan-chao—already adopted a Thai language.

Contact Development

For at least one of the Wu-man groups, the Ts'uan, some Chinese sources mention another way by which states may have developed. They say that the Ts'uan really were not "barbarians" in the beginning, that they were Chinese who left the state of Ch'u (the present province of Hunan) and settled in the Kuanghsi/Kueichou area. Chinese sources mention that such emigrants or emigrant colonies were founders of states in several parts of present-day Vietnam, especially in societies in which women have considerable status, as was the case with most Tibetan and Tibeto-Burman tribes. The leader of the emigrants first succeeded in marrying the daughter of the chieftain, and then he or his son took over control of the society. We do not doubt that such cases actually did happen, but there is no way to know whether the Ts'uan society came into existence by the direct influence of Chinese settlers.

However, the cultures of all the states we are discussing have some peculiar traits. The existence of family names similar to Chinese family names is unusual among tribes of the West and South; the existence of cities even more so. There are reports, from a somewhat later time, that several Lolo groups had a script of their own, whereas before they had only notched sticks as a form of recording. In recent years many texts written by the Nakhi, a Lolo tribe, have been published and translated. Their content is largely religious, and their religion is influenced by Buddhism, though there are also resemblances to Chinese Taoism. It may be mentioned that other tribes in this area also have developed scripts of their own.

What we see here is, in my opinion, a *contact feature*. Examples of such contact features or contact developments can be found in many parts of the world, even in the early history of Europe. When a tribal society or an early state is adjacent to a state at a more complex, or "higher," stage of development, one or both of the following developments may occur: The less advanced society may imitate elements of the higher society, consciously or unconsciously wanting to achieve equal status at least in social structure. Or the more advanced neighbor may, again consciously or unconsciously, introduce some cultural elements into the culturally lower state. *High* and *low* here always refer to what the people themselves feel and express.

For instance, let us first consider script. Examples of societies that have taken over the script developed by a neighboring society are numerous. We need mention only the Koreans and Japanese in Eastern Asia. Both for a long time used the Chinese script to express concepts but pronounced the words differently because their language was different. Later each created a different script, which did not express concepts by pictorial symbols but saved the sounds of the words. It seems clear that the idea of doing this came from the many societies of Asia that had phonetic scripts. Other East Asian societies, such as the Jurchens and the Hsihsia, created a script of their own, which looks like Chinese script though no Chinese can read it.

The Wu-man developed a kind of pictorial script, which expresses ideas in the form of pictures. (Of course, these pictures are often not easily identified, just as the original pictures of the Chinese script are identifiable only after special study.) The Wu-man pictures are totally different from the Chinese pictures, but for the transmission of script it is not necessary that the borrower accepts the script of the other; it is sufficient that he has gotten the idea of a script. In the case of the

Wu-man, historical arguments are compelling for Chinese influence rather than for independent invention.

A similar explanation can be given for the existence of family names and clans among the Wu-man. By contact with the Chinese they certainly would learn that every Chinese has a family name and, in general, also a long genealogy, and that the family name or the lineage name was essential for anybody who claimed to belong among the leaders of society. So leading Wu-man accepted Chinese family names by somehow transcribing the sound of their personal names so that they could be written in Chinese. This had another advantage: By having a "Chinese" family name, a Wu-man could claim to be originally Chinese and not "barbarian." We have cases from Kuangtung and Kuanghsi provinces in which non-Chinese who had adopted a Chinese family name succeeded in constructing genealogies that tied them directly to a Chinese family with the same family name; on the other hand, we also have cases where "barbarian" family names were translated into Chinese but where it is clearly indicated even today that the bearer's distant ancestors were not Chinese. As leading Chinese families are very proud of a long line of ancestors, their names and life histories were written down in a genealogy. Likewise, there are non-Chinese families in Kuichou who have genealogies that go back for six or more centuries and thus give them status among their own people and among Chinese.

In the field of social organization we find here a "marginal" or "frontier" feudalism. One typical result of superstratification by conquest is often what we may loosely call feudalism, a system in which the aristocracy—the conquerers—is stratified into hereditary ranks of different levels. Each rank has some obligations to the ruler at the top of society but also has some rights over land and the people living on that land. When such a society comes in contact with a "higher" society organized in the form of a bureaucratic, nonaristocratic system, there is a tendency to adjust to that society in form though not in content. Thus, it is said of the Black Lolo that they had nine "classes"; this shows that they identified ranks in their feudal society with the nine ranks of the Chinese bureaucracy. Otherwise there was no similarity with the Chinese system. Their society remained a feudal one, in which status or class was hereditary, while in China ranks were given to individuals for merit on the basis of state examinations. The process also operates from the other side. Chinese had to find forms of behavior suitable with persons of different rank and power in the "barbarian" societies they were in contact with. So they identified ranks in the barbarian society with ranks in Chinese society. Embassies to the barbarians typically brought as gifts Chinese silk dresses for persons of official rank, so that a barbarian man of rank looked as if he had a specific rank in Chinese society. Such a garment gave him status, if not among the Chinese, certainly among his own people.

Other such contact features between Chinese and the Wu-man could be shown. In fact, the Nan-chao state in the tenth and eleventh centuries looked organizationally quite similar to the Chinese state. But it is more difficult to see certain other contacts. Buddhism was strong in Nan-chao, and many of the Wu-man tribes were Buddhists. Did this Buddhism come to them directly from India, because Nan-chao and its predecessors were located on the road from India to China, which was open at least in the second century B.C., or did it come to them indirectly from China? Did Nan-chao or its predecessors invent the art of bronze making, or did bronze come to them from China? The finding of a very early bronze culture in Thailand suggests there is a possibility that bronze was invented or at least used very early by tribes like the Wu-man. Did they get the iron or steel for their famous swords from China, or was there an indigenous iron culture? We believe that China's iron age, which began around 400 B.C., depended on metal largely imported from the south.

There are many such questions that cannot be solved at the present time, because archaeological research has only recently begun. It seems certain, however, that some Wu-man tribes—in other words, Tibeto-Burmans—have remained to the present time small, individual tribal societies, while others in areas populated by predominantly Thai tribes developed quite early into states. Under Chinese pressure these states subsequently disintegrated and either regressed into tribal societies again or were totally absorbed into Chinese society.

South and Southwest China was also the home of a number of other societies that still exist. Some of these were organized in the form of tribes, that is, politically independent groups under a leader. The tribe often feels that its members all came from a common ancestor, though this can never be proved. It may consist of a number of families. In some cases Chinese sources give us the tribal names; in other cases they apparently did not care much about the organization of these groups and named them after the place where they lived or a particular item of their clothing or the color of their dress. They group the tribes in several large units—such as Miao, Yao, and the like—and in the course of history various tribes were put by some Chinese authors into one group and by others into another group. Because we do not have extensive dictionaries of the languages of all these tribes, we cannot yet identify them with certainty in accordance with the large linguistic categories Western scholars have constructed. So here we shall rely upon Chinese classifications and speak only of the large units, not of individual tribes.

YAO

Like the Wu-man above, the Yao seem to be called *man* in the earliest sources; the name Yao is used in later (eleventh century) and modern sources. Today they live widely dispersed between the present provinces of Kueichou and parts of Kuanghsi; remnants of them are found in the southern parts of Chêkiang (called Hsia-min); and they seem to have inhabited large parts of Hunan and Fukien, parts of Kuangtung, and even Kiangsi. Let me introduce the Yao by a Chinese description from the twelfth century:

> The Yao wear the pestle [coiffure], near to the forehead. They go barefoot and carry weapons. They are either naked or wear a dress made of rags, but sometimes they also wear dresses and pants made of cloth of different colors. Occasionally they wear head-turbans made of white cloth. Their leaders tie green turbans around the head and wear purple shirts. The women wear a shirt and, as underclothing, a skirt with a spectacularly colorful design. Only the upper garment has very fine stripes, because that corresponds to their taste.
>
> Their whole area has high mountains, so that whatever is produced faces a transportation problem. When they want to transport something and when it cannot be carried on their shoulders, they pack it into big sacks which are tied with long leather ties to their forehead and carried on the back. Even big pieces of lumber or rocks are thus carried on the back.

They live by agriculture on the mountains. Their main food is millet, beans and sweet potatoes. Rarely do they have rice fields. When their harvest is good, they live in their hideouts peacefully, but whenever there is a famine, they create revolts. (*Ling-wai tai-ta* 3, 11, pp. 51–52)

We can fill out this general description from other, earlier and later, sources. The earliest mention of the Yao refers to their myth of origin:

Formerly, in the time of Kao-hsin, there was banditry by the Ch'üan-jung [Dog Barbarians]. The emperor worried about their invasion and their cruelties and made an expedition against them, but he could not defeat them. So he searched for a man who could bring him the head of the general of the Ch'üan-jung. This man would be rewarded with 1,000 pieces of gold, enfeoffed with 10,000 families, and betrothed to the emperor's youngest daughter. At this time the emperor kept a dog with multicolored skin and the name P'an-hu. After the proclamation was made, P'an-hu came with a human head to the palace. The dignitaries wondered, checked it, and found it was really the head of general Mu. The emperor was very happy, but he thought that P'an-hu could not be married to a girl, and he also could not be enfeoffed. He wanted to reward him but did not know of an appropriate way. His daughter heard of this and knew that an emperor could not give an order and then not keep his promise. She therefore asked to go to P'an-hu. The emperor was thus forced to marry his daughter to P'an-hu. P'an-hu took the girl on his back and went into the southern mountains, where they stayed in a rock cave. The place was dangerous and remote and people did not go there. There, the girl took off her [Chinese] dress and made herself ugly clothes from simple materials. The emperor was grieved for her and sent ambassadors to search for her, but they always encountered wind, rain and darkness and could not find her. In three years she gave birth to twelve children, six boys and six girls. When P'an-hu died, these children married one another, made cloth from tree bark and dyed it with plant colors. They liked multicolored dresses and all their dresses are cut so that they seem to have a tail. . . . (*Hou Han shu*, 116; see Ruey, vol. 2, p. 544)

This myth has some important motifs. First, it is put into a period that is in the remotest antiquity; according to modern scholarship, no emperor of China, nor even a "China" itself, existed at the time this emperor is supposed to have lived. The war is against a tribe in the north of China, a tribe that occurs in later sources. The hero is a dog, and the Yao are the children of dogs, but also related to Chinese. In China the dog is a despised, dirty animal. We note, however, that most of the tribal names of South China are written with a compound character that contains the element *dog*, to indicate that these tribes are not really human. Only in the twentieth century has the element *dog* been replaced by the element *man*. Though formerly all Chinese and most of the non-Chinese tribes ate dog meat, the Yao even today do not eat dog. They regard the dog as their ancestor and still have a headdress they regard as symbolizing a dog's tail. We can be sure that the myth was an original Yao myth, to which the element of their relation to the Chinese emperor was added later to indicate that they, though different from Chinese, are descendants of a Chinese princess and a man who was more courageous than any Chinese. We shall later cite some further examples of attempts of tribes to "prove" their descent from Chinese. In any case, the Yao dog myth is still typical of the Yao and no other tribe.

Like the Eastern Tibetan tribes, the Yao like to live on high mountains, where they plant millet and beans and, in more recent times, sweet potatoes, but rarely rice. Dresses made of bark cloth, as well as clothes decorated with bird feathers, seem to have been given up and replaced by ordinary cloth. They still prefer to go barefoot, and they wear, if not the dog cap, a kind of turban. The "dog" dress also seems to have been given up. A later source describes it as a kind of blouse that hardly covered the navel in front but was longer in the rear. They live in reed huts with a fireplace in the center, around which they all sleep. Some are tattooed, and many women wear earrings. But most typical of them in all old and later sources is their love of singing. At any occasion boys and girls sing. They have special song festivals with competitions between different troupes. These festivals are occasions during which young men and young women become acquainted with one another, and the festivals often—to the horror of Chinese observers—end in secret assignations. Until the birth of a child, a girl lives at home; only afterwards does she move in with her husband.

Today, the Yao are a typical mountain folk who avoid the plains. But we have historical reports that there also were valley Yao. Thus, it is possible that they were pushed into the mountains by Chinese settlers. In any case, the sources abound with reports of military confrontations between Yao and Chinese since the late fourteenth century. The Yao, armed with strong crossbows and short swords, and sometimes protected by an armor made of bearskin, were dangerous enemies until about the eighteenth century.

MIAO

This minority is mentioned, though only once, in a very early source, where they are called San-Miao, the Three Miao. The mythical emperor Yao fights them, and his successor exiles them to a place called San-wei. Other sources put them in western Kansu and some later sources in the area of Hunan/Kiangsu. It is some 3,000 years later (if we are to believe the sources) that the Miao show up again in western Hunan and eastern Kueichou, where they still live today. On the basis of the earliest record some scholars think that the Miao originally lived in the northwest corner of China, an area in which Tibetan tribes lived before them, and that they later, under pressure of the Chinese, were forced southward until they finally settled in their present abode. Most scholars, however, deny any connection between the San-Miao and the present Miao.

Society and Culture

Like the Yao, some Miao claim descent from the Chinese, but they do not have the dog myth. Some Miao claim to be descendants of 600 soldiers of a Chinese general, others claim to be descendants of Chinese from a small ancient feudal state (Ts'ai) who were forcibly settled in their present area after the old feudal state of Ch'u defeated Ts'ai. Still others believe their ancestors were Chinese who left the old feudal state of Sung and intermarried in their new home with natives. All these events supposedly took place in the last half of the first millennium before Christ. We know that ethnic mixings did happen in the whole Southern area, but we prefer to regard the stories about their immigration from Central China as another attempt to prove that the Miao are not "barbarians," but real Chinese.

Their economy is slash-and-burn agriculture on mountain slopes and some hunting and collecting. They sometimes keep animals such as buffaloes or cows. They live more often in houses on piles than in houses on the ground with a central fireplace. The space under the piles is where their animals stay at night.

The culture of the Miao is very hard to define because sometimes the Yao are called Miao and because the Miao live surrounded by other tribes (soon to be discussed), so their culture has only a few unique traits. They are similar to the Yao in several regards: They love to sing and have festivals that may end in sexual orgies. They prefer to live in the mountains though not in such rough areas and such high mountains as the Yao. Almost nothing is reported about their religion, except that they produce the *ku-poison*, which, however, other tribes also produce. The preparation of this poison varies. Often several poisonous animals are put together in a jar, such as scorpions, centipedes, snakes, and geckos, and, as they are not fed, they devour one another. When the last surviving animal, which then contains the poison of the others, is dead, its pulverized body is the ku-poison. Beliefs about it differ, but, in general, it is believed that the poison can kill, for instance, an unfaithful lover or an enemy. It kills slowly, so that such a lover can be cured if he returns in time. Even Chinese in the South are afraid of this ku. In another form ku can produce dwarflike beings who keep the master's house clean and serve him or her in many ways, but he must give them a human being each year as payment for their services. When he does not do this, he himself will die. The belief in *ku* was known 2,000 years ago as characteristic of inhabitants of the South, and it is still widespread there today, not only among the Miao.

Military History

Like the Yao, the Miao are warlike (at least according to the Chinese), and the sources report numerous struggles in which they were engaged down to the twentieth century. The most violent battle took place in the eighteenth century, when not only local troops but also imperial armies were employed against them. The official chronicle of the province of Kueichou (*Kuei-chou t'ung-chih*) reports, for instance, that "Bandit Miao destroyed more than twenty forts and threatened the Chinese prefectural city of Chen-pien. At the time, the city did not yet have walls. So many Chinese were killed" (25, p. 1b). In nearby Ch'ing-chiang and in other towns more than 1,000 Chinese were killed. The Chinese were successful against them by treachery; they induced the Miao to surrender and, when they did, killed 600 of them. Now more military were brought into Kueichou from other provinces, and in the end (1124) 687 leaders and others of the Miao were killed and 5,539 captured. This led to the surrender of 126,217 Miao.

Even in the middle of the nineteenth century Miao still resisted Chinese domination, and a special book describing these fights, called *Plans to Pacify the Miao-Bandits* (*P'ing-ting Miao-fei fang-lüeh*) was published by imperial order. I give only one war report as an example:

> On the third day of the sixth [Chinese] month of 1855, more than one thousand bandits [i.e., Miao] burned the Chih-an fort down. This fort belongs to the district of Lung-li. The magistrate and others attacked them. They brought together three hundred soldiers, attacked the Miao and saved the Chinese. On the fifteenth day of the month several bandits surrounded and attacked a post-town.... The bandits became more and more numerous, came from every direction and cut the communications of the auxiliary troops. In the seventh month 1,300 soldiers came from Kuei-ting-tao via Ch'ing-p'ing to help [the Chinese] ... yet on the fourteenth day of the ninth month the city of Tan-chiang fell, because no food and no help could reach them. (1, p. 39–9)

Later it is said that 2,000 to 3,000 Miao were killed in this ninth month. Troops from four neighboring provinces were involved in this war.

Chinese Descriptions

It is significant that in these long and detailed war reports no tribal names nor any description of their culture is given. In some cases the family names of leaders are reported, but these names are already all Chinese names. Very often we do not know to which minority group an individual tribe belongs when a tribal name occurs in a text. Nevertheless, short data on a tribe can be very interesting, especially as these data are always colored by Chinese prejudices. Let me give a few examples from tribes in Kueichou Province. Of the Chung-chia tribe the official chronicle says:

> They begin the year with the twelfth month. They save the bones of cows, horses, chickens, and dogs, mix them with rice gruel and make an "unstrained alcoholic drink" of them. It is good, when it is sour and stinky. Their marriage [system] is by "illicit" intercourse: In the first month of spring they have a moon dance and make [for it] small balls of colored cloth which they call "flowery balls." When they see someone whom they like, they throw [the ball] and run away without restriction. As a wedding gift they use cattle. The number depends upon [the woman's] beauty; it can go up to thirty to fifty animals. . . .
>
> In case of death, they slaughter cows, call relatives and friends. They store wine in big jars and use cattle horns to drink until they are drunk, sometimes so much that they kill one another. The master [of ceremonies] does not eat meat, only fish and shrimps. For the funeral they use coffins and cover the tomb with an umbrella. After a year they cremate. (*Kuei-chou t'ung-chih*, 7, p. 10b)

I have doubts that one can really make wine by using bones of animals, but the description indicates that the wine of these Chung-chia does not suit the Chinese taste. The writer also clearly shows the Chinese attitude that the "free marriage"— that is, a marriage by self-selection of the partners, not by a go-between and parental order—is a barbaric custom.

Of another tribe, the Mu-lao, it is said:

> They live everywhere. They have the family names of Wang, Li, Chin, Wen. Among those who live in Kuei-ting and Tien-hsi the husband does not live together with his wife after marriage, before a child is born. In their sacrifices to demons [kuei] they use multicolored flags. At festivals they sing and dance for pleasure. They also have distinction between old and young. Those in Tu-chün and Ch'ing-p'ing wear clothes like the Chinese. People of the same family name do not marry [one another], those of different names do not eat dog [meat] together. When the parents die, they wear mourning clothes, but no hempen [mourning] gowns [as Chinese do]. The oldest son lives in the house for forty-nine days and does not wash himself and does not leave the house. At the end of the period they invite a shaman [wu] who prays and gives a name [to the dead one]. That is called "letting loose the demon [kuei]." After that [the son] can go out. When the oldest son is too poor to follow [the custom of staying in the house and not washing for forty-nine days], the oldest grandson or the second son replaces him. Their children also often engage a teacher and study. Many go to [Chinese] schools. (*Kuei-chou t'ung-chih*, 7, p. 20e)

Here again, the marriage system is indirectly criticized and, according to Chinese custom, the mourning ceremonies are incomplete and barbaric. Yet in the end some praise is given: The Mu-lao begin to study Chinese and may become "civilized." There are several almost "ethnological" descriptions often in albums that are illustrated. Most of the albums are from the nineteenth century, but we know that albums composed centuries earlier did exist. The descriptions are usually very brief, but some present important data, such as a report on cannibalism, on cou-

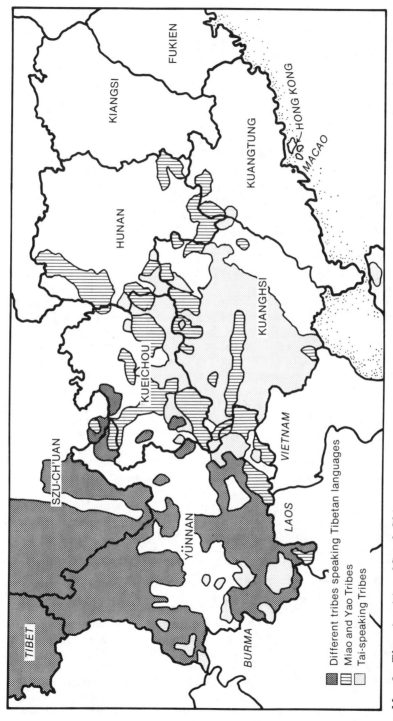

Map 3 The minorities of South China

Different tribes speaking Tibetan languages

Miao and Yao Tribes

Tai-speaking Tribes

vade, and on special types of burial. But often so little detail is given that we cannot decide whether a tribe belongs to the Miao or to another group such as the Yao. The reason for this may be that the Chinese writer did not have sufficient information at hand, or that the two cultures are very similar.

CHUANG

Today the most populous non-Chinese minority in the South are the Chuang. They speak a language that is related to the Thai language of Thailand. Sources mention twenty-five tribes. Some are a subgroup, the Chung-chia; others are the Lung-chia or Nung, and some are Tung or Sha; each of these subgroups is again subdivided into smaller units such as the White Chung-chia, the Black Nung, and so on, according to the color of their dress or other characteristics. Though they settled in several provinces, their center in recent centuries seems to be Kuanghsi. We also find them in Kuangtung, even near to the city of Canton. Some Chuang also live in Yünnan, Hunan, and Szu-ch'uan.

In contrast to the Yao and Miao, the Chuang prefer to live in plains and valleys; they move to the mountain slopes only when forced by Chinese settlers. But because their economy, centered upon rice cultivation, is in direct competition with the Chinese rice culture, the pressure of Chinese upon the Chuang is greater than upon the other groups. On the other hand, probably because they produced more and better food than the other groups, they were much more numerous. So they are today the largest Southern minority and one of the most acculturated. We can be sure (and will discuss this later) that many Chinese in South China are former Chuang who now are completely indistinguishable from Chinese.

We have reasons to assume that in early times people like the Chuang—that is, Thai-speaking tribes—lived far more in the North than now, occupying at least the provinces around the lower Yangtse and south of the lower Huang-ho. Because their present habitats, Kuanghsi and Kueichou, were integrated into China and settled densely by Chinese only in the last five centuries, reports about the Chuang begin quite late in history. The Chuang are farmers who also specialize in cattle and buffaloes, though these seem to have been more a symbol of wealth and a means of exchange than sources of meat. They were, of course, also used as draft animals for the plow. Like the other minorities, the Chuang are sexually less inhibited than the Chinese: Young women are free and move in with their husbands only after a child is born. During the time before the move a woman may have relations with several men, so that it is not the first-born child that has the preferential position, as in so many societies, but the second one. The Chuang believe that women can change into tigers and kill men, and they also use the ku-poison, perhaps even more often than the Miao. They know how to do batik and *ikatt* (a technique using threads that are individually dyed, so that each thread has several colors, and then woven into cloth). The women wear short straight-pleated skirts and the pestle hairstyle—the long hair is taken together on top of the head and formed into a knot. Tattooing was formerly common. They live in houses on piles, similar to the Thai and Burmese houses. One peculiar trait, mentioned in many early sources, is the custom of drinking with the help of a pipe or even of draining the liquid through the nose. And, in contrast to the other tribes we have mentioned, the Chuang are extremely fond of water and therefore very clean.

LIAO

In ancient times Liao were found in almost all provinces of the South; today, they seem to be almost extinct or assimilated into Chinese or other groups. We have reports about them from about A.D. 300, on, mainly from the border area between the provinces of Szu-ch'uan and Hupei, but also in southern Szu-ch'uan. At that time they seem to have been quite numerous, because one text mentions that the Chinese garrisoned 200,000 Liao families in an area in which the Chinese had built a fortress. In any case, constant wars with them continued to about A.D. 1000, and they are mentioned even until the recent period. They are described as very warlike and primitive; in fact, they seem to be the most primitive ethnic group that lived in historical times in the West and South of China. They have no real tribal organization; their best fighters are their leaders. They live in the mountains, as hunters and gatherers, in pile-supported dwellings we might call long houses inhabited by several families. Such houses are still common in parts of Southeast Asia.

Among the Liao's distinctive customs is the *couvade*, in which the husband pretends to be sick when his child is born; he stays in bed and is taken care of by his wife. This custom, incidentally, also occurred in other parts of the world, including Europe. The Liao have a kind of initiation ceremony for young boys: When they are fourteen or fifteen years old, two front teeth are filed down. Only after this painful operation are they allowed to marry. It is said that they believe that a person with all teeth intact can eat humans. Chinese assert that, not seldom, Liao sons, among others, may kill their own father. In such a case, they give their mother a dog as compensation. Whether or not this is true, they were undoubtedly very warlike and formerly practiced the custom of head-hunting. Their most valued victim was a bearded Chinese, which often meant a Chinese official or person of higher social standing. This head-hunting seems to have been a kind of fertility rite, with the heads put up in the fields. If so, we must assume that the Liao in early times had some kind of agriculture, which later sources mention only sporadically. Still another custom of the Liao frightened the Chinese. The Liao believed that a person can take off his head and send it by air to a house where that head may kill a person by biting him. The myth of the flying head is widespread in Southeast Asia today and is not limited to tribes in China.

I cannot explain why Chinese sources again and again assert that Liao women have a pregnancy period of only seven (lunar) months, whereas the "normal" period is ten (lunar) months.

YÜEH

Some Chinese texts regard the Liao as "Mountain Yüeh." Tribes with this name occur in early Chinese texts in several provinces south of the Yangtse. They are regarded as a branch of the Yüeh. We have better reports about the Yüeh than about the other groups we have discussed thus far. They appear before the middle of the first millennium B.C. as constituting a well-organized, civilized (according to Chinese concepts) state with its center in Kiangsi, Kiangsu, and parts of Chêkiang. In some periods their power extended north to the coastal section of Shantung. They were famous for their ships and often fought the Chinese of the North with fleets of large boats. Chinese regarded them as non-Chinese who were "civilized" by a man of royal blood who went to them and became their ruler. After the state of Yüeh was destroyed by the neighboring state of Wu, we do not hear of them for a couple of centuries.

In the Han period (206 B.C. to A.D. 200) two groups of Yüeh are mentioned by our sources. One of them lived along the coast of Chêkiang, which at this time was Chinese territory only in its northern and eastern parts. These Yüeh constituted small, independent states, which were destroyed during Han times when the whole province quickly became settled by Chinese (although some minorities—the Hsia-min, a Yao tribe [see pp. 80–82] are still living in Chêkiang today). The other Yüeh formed a state, too, in the area of Kuangtung province. Their ruler, Chao T'o, was perhaps a Chinese expatriate, but his state was, for a time in the early second century B.C., a real threat to the Chinese in South China. We now know that the Chinese built a great number of fortresses in the present province of Hunan, obviously to defend their settlers against the state of Nan-Yüeh (South Yüeh). Finally, Chao T'o's state was destroyed, and we do not hear much about the Yüeh after that.

It happens that the word *Yüeh* was always pronounced as *Viet*. The name Vietnam means not Yüeh from the South, but Southern Yüeh (in Chinese language Nan-Yüeh not Yüeh-nan), a term already in use 2,000 years ago, when most of these Yüeh still lived in today's Kuangtung province of China. We assume that the Yüeh were the original settlers of the area directly south of the lower Yangtse, extending north to Shantung. Due to Chinese pressure and the accessibility of the sea, some tribes became coastal people, specializing in trade and fishing, while other tribes sought refuge in the mountains. The "Mountain Yüeh" could not resist the Chinese and disappeared before A.D. 1000. The coastal Yüeh moved as a group when the pressure became too strong and finally settled in Vietnam. Some scholars believe that they may also be ancestors of the so-called Austronesians, the leading ethnic group in Indonesia and the Philippines. When the Yüeh settled in the northern parts of Vietnam, which formerly were called Tongking, they still remained under pressure from Chinese settlers. From about 200 B.C. on Tongking was for centuries regarded as a part of China. During the T'ang dynasty (618–906) it was controlled by China, and after 1258, when the Mongols conquered Tongking and Annam, both parts of Vietnam remained in various stages of dependency until the time of French colonial rule (1886). What our newspapers report today about tensions between Vietnam and China is only the latest in a development that has at least 2,000 years of history.

It seems certain that the Yüeh were the most developed of the minorities of the South. Possibly some of them settled in southern Korea and in Japan.

TANKA

Another coastal minority in South China, the Tanka (Tan-chia), are mentioned in early texts that describe ethnic groups that are not Chinese, often with pictures. The Tanka resent this name (which has the meaning of "egg people," but was written differently in the early texts) and pretend, like some other tribes, to be descended from a Chinese general's troops.

The Tanka are totally specialized in life on water. Their pile houses, when they have houses, are in the estuaries of coastal rivers, but most of them live all their lives on boats. They get their livelihood from fish, shellfish, and other products of the sea; any surplus is sold to Chinese. They also specialize in the fishing of oysters and sell the pearls to Chinese. Chinese sources assert that they can stay under water for three days and that they are descendants of water snakes. Not much else is said about them in Chinese sources, especially nothing about their language.

Today, Tanka in the Canton area speak the local Chinese dialect and maintain that they are Chinese whose profession is fishery. Like some other tribes, they have beautiful songs. Chinese often mention the love of singing among the tribes because few Chinese-educated people sing folksongs and because songs of natives were spread to China proper through singing girls and prostitutes and later transformed into Chinese songs with new texts. Several styles of Chinese music come from Southern non-Chinese.

I would be inclined to assume that the Tanka are close relatives of the Yüeh. There is "Chinese blood" in them as a result of sexual contacts through prostitution: Tanka operated so-called pleasure boats around Hong Kong and Canton. As a consequence of this intermingling, they lost their own language. Other scholars regard the Tanka as a branch of the so-called sea nomads—populations along the coasts from India to China who live like nomads on their boats, moving from one area to the other, never living for any long period on land.

OTHER TRIBES

There are still other small minorities in South China we should mention briefly.

The indigenous people of the island of Hainan seem to be the *Li*, although Yao and Liao also live there. The Li are famous in Chinese sources for being sorcerers. The well-known eighteenth-century writer Yüan Mei writes about them:

> Only half of the population of Hainan are Li. They are divided into civilized and uncivilized. The uncivilized live on the Five-Finger Mountain and are not subject to the Chinese government. The civilized obey the [Chinese] officials and when they come to one, they approach him kneeling.
>
> Among their women there are sorceresses who can cause the death of people. When they want to bewitch somebody, they take one of his beard-hairs or one of the betel nuts (the juice of which they have spat out) and put this into a bamboo pipe. Then they lie down naked at night on a mountain top and say incantations to the stars and the moon. Then that person dies within seven days. He has no wounds, but [his body] is like cotton. They are only able to bewitch Li not Chinese. When the harmed people can catch them and bring them to court, they put a long bamboo pipe under their neck and drag them [to court]. When they should come into physical contact with them, they are again bewitched. The women say: "When we do not bewitch others, then we ourselves have to die after a time." Among them are young prepubescent girls who have learned this from their ancestors. The incantations are very secret; they do not tell them, even when they are beaten to death. There are only female sorcerers, no males. The knowledge is given only to women not to men.
>
> For a wedding the Li do not use wagons or horses. On a lucky day the groom goes to his in-laws with a piece of red cloth, wraps the girl in it and carries her home. According to their customs, the groom visits the in-laws and lives together with the bride. This is called "entering the house." When before the wedding a child is born, they regard this as fine and the neighbors congratulate them. They bring several dol-

lars of their own kind of money, made of white paper, and throw it into a bamboo chest at the gate. The householder buys a big jar of wine and puts it in front of the gate with some thin bamboo pipes in the jar. The guests suck the wine with the pipes. There are no other [wedding] festivities. (Tse-pu-yü, 2, pp. 139–140)

The Li are also said to have used notched sticks as we use sale documents. And they, as well as some other tribes, believe that the human race was born of an egg that split and out of which came the ancestors of their race.

The *Ch'i-lao*, another small group, live in Kueichou, Kuangtung, and also in Hainan. They are sometimes regarded as a branch of the Li. Their typical clothing includes the poncho. They live not in pile houses but in rectangular houses on the ground. Chinese regard them as dirty, perhaps in contrast to the Chuang and Yüeh, who love to bathe. They also have an initiation of the young by removing several front teeth.

Like the Yüeh, the *Pa* are mentioned in very early sources as a relatively "civilized" ethnic group in the southeastern part of the province of Szu-ch'uan. Pa was an independent statelet in the first millennium B.C.; it was destroyed so early that we do not have much information about the culture. Typical of them is a myth about a goddess of the salt (Szu-ch'uan has famous salt wells that are still producing today), an origin of people from caves, and a lower and an upper class of people born at the same time.

Limited to the province of Yünnan are the *Pai-man* tribes ("white barbarians") who settled among the Wu-man ("black barbarians") mentioned earlier (pp. 76–80). Some scholars regard these Pai-man as remnants of Austroasiatic tribes that are also known from Burma and other parts of Southeast Asia. It seems likely, however, that at least some of these tribes are Thai, relatives of the Thai of Thailand. It is also very likely that some "whites" (according to the color of their dress, not the color of their skin) were descendants of Chinese who were taken prisoner by Wu-man and kept as slaves or agricultural serfs.

My lists contain another fifty-seven tribes that cannot be identified with any larger tribal group mainly because the data about them are insufficient. Even Chinese scholars of old or of today have not ventured to identify all of them. Many of these small tribes in the Southern and Southwestern provinces of China may be parts of the larger units which we have mentioned. When Fei Hsiao-t'ung, the dean of Chinese sociologists, was sent to South China to classify the non-Chinese minorities, he admitted that the data available to him were still not clear enough to allow him to find the right place for each small group in the few larger groups the government of the People's Republic wanted him to establish.

In any case, our discussions, brief as they must be, should have made clear that, on the one hand, we have not only a Chinese "march to the tropics" (as H. Wiens called it) but also expansion to the West and the North, a "march" that is not yet at its end. On the other hand, minority groups during many centuries, and still today, have found themselves forced to leave China and to move into Vietnam (where they are grouped together as Montagnards, such as Yao and Miao and the original Viet themselves. Recently Japanese scholars found in the hands of Miao in Thailand Taoist texts written in Chinese, which they had apparently brought with them during their migration from China. Until recently, they are known to have made pilgrimages to centers of Taoist cults in Central China (Kiangsi Province). Other tribes formerly occupied large areas that included modern Laos and Thailand or even Burma; some of them now are claimed by China as its subjects and citizens, while others are claimed by Burma, Laos, and Thailand. Because their distribution can at any time become a political issue for China, we have to understand some aspects of Chinese policy toward Burma, Thailand, Laos, Cambodia, and Vietnam in this light.

THE ABORIGINES OF TAIWAN

Taiwan was, since prehistoric times, inhabited by a number of tribes. As far as documents inform us, Chinese settlement of the area began not before the eleventh century A.D. and was, it seems, limited to some trading posts on the west coast of the island. Much earlier sources mention islands in the sea east of China, but it is unclear whether these references mean the Ryu-kyu (Liu-ch'iu) islands that now belong to Japan, or Taiwan, or both.

Immigration increased during the Ming period (1368–1644), and especially when the Manchus conquered China (1644) and masses of Southern Chinese fled and settled on Taiwan. The leader of the largest group, Cheng Ch'eng-kung (in Western sources, Coxinga), succeeded in forcing the Dutch as well as the Spaniards out of Taiwan. The Dutch had set up a colony with the center near the present town of Tainan in the South and had tried to "civilize" the aborigines, while the Spaniards had set foot on the northern end of the island, at the present town of Tan-shui (Tamsui). The Manchu emperors ruled the island after they had conquered it. But Taiwan remained the "forgotten island" until the end of the nineteenth century: Administrators sent to Taiwan did not really care for the Chinese and the native population, fights between both groups continued, and bandits were common. In spite of attempts of the government to limit Chinese immigration for many reasons, more and more people from the mainland, especially the province of Fukien, came to Taiwan, took the land from the natives, and set up new villages and towns.

Soon after the Japanese took over Taiwan (1898) as a consequence of their victory over China, they tried to find a solution for the conflicts between Chinese and the aborigines. The solution they adopted was differentiation between the "Plains Tribes" and the "Mountain Tribes." The tribes in the coastal plain had changed already under Dutch rule, had taken up farming with techniques similar to Chinese farm methods, had begun to dress more like Chinese, and some even had been converted to Christianity and taken Chinese family names. These early Christians seem to have disappeared; new missions were established only in the nineteenth century by Presbyterians. The assimilation of the Plains Tribes continued, and at the present time they do not exist as units. Some scholars have been able to discover remnants of their culture even today, as the former tribal people regard themselves as Chinese. On the other hand, some Chinese think they can identify such former non-Chinese by physical traits or by the Chinese names they have adopted.

The Japanese treated the Mountain Tribes quite differently. After prolonged fights they forced some of them, who had lived along the east coast, to resettle in the high mountains and then enclosed them in a special area to which Chinese had no access. The Japanese officials attempted to control them, increasing their pressure slowly. The closing of the frontiers prevented Chinese settlers from acquiring land in the mountains as well as from selling alcohol to the natives or supplying them with firearms. The Japanese policy was only partly successful; there were severe uprisings as late as the 1920s. During the period of Japanese colonial rule over Taiwan Japanese scholars studied the tribes. They left a great number of studies, which are now superseded by studies made by Chinese scholars but are important as documents of earlier stages of the culture of these tribes.

We can today enumerate nineteen tribes on the island. As far as we know, all the tribes speak languages that are closely related to the languages of the aborigines on the Philippines but are mutually ununderstandable. Even in their social structure there are important differences between the tribes. However, two characteristics are always mentioned in the early reports: the custom of head-hunting—and well-prepared skulls gathered not more than fifty years ago can still be seen—and the tattooing of women's faces. The tribes were hunters who also practiced slash-and-burn agriculture and planted various plants and millet on steep hills. Some reports describe the social structure of one tribe as feudal, though this is disputed by others.

Physically, all the tribes, with one exception, are like the natives of the Philippines but often indistinguishable from Chinese, and their languages seem to be related to the languages of the Philippine tribes. The exception are the A-mi on the east coast, who are said to have large, round eyes and a rather rosy skin color. Some scholars think they may have come from islands of Micronesia, such as Yap.

The total number of aborigines on Taiwan seems to be around 200,000 (Taiwan's population is now close to 18 million) and decreasing quickly. One factor contributing to the decrease is the common intermarriage of Chinese men with aboriginal women because the bridal price that has to be paid for these women is much lower than for Chinese women. Another factor is the migration of many men, and also of women, into the big cities, where they work as laborers. The Chinese government still continues some of the old methods to protect the tribes—trying to stop the sale of alcoholic drinks, or preventing Chinese from buying up the land of the aborigines or from cutting down their forests and selling the lumber to Chinese. There are schools in the area of the tribes, and missions are active among them. But the population pressure on Taiwan and the astonishingly quick and thorough industrialization foretells the end of the tribes as organized units and their assimilation into the majority of Chinese.

CASTES IN SOUTH CHINA

Minorities are often physically different from the majority in the midst of which they live, have (or at least had) their own languages and religion, and often have close connections with larger groups outside the country in which they live. What we call a *caste* is usually a group that is physically no different, or only minimally so, from the majority and which speaks the same language as the majority. But there is no intermarriage between the caste members and the majority; the caste often has to live in a separate location, not mixed with the others; it has different religious cults from those of the majority; and it is often specialized in a profession that is despised or regarded as unclean by the others. The classical case is the "untouchables" of India. And India, before modern legislation, was the only large nation in which all members belonged to a caste, high or low. Indologists have assumed that at least some present-day Indian castes are remnants of former minority tribes.

This seems to be the case in South China, too. Unfortunately, our data on these castes are very limited, mainly because they were regarded as "mean" people (*chien-min*). To this category belonged social groups such as actors in folk theatre troups, roving entertainers, and prostitutes—people almost as low in status as slaves. They lived separately, and intermarriage with them was almost always forbidden for Chinese. However, the groups we regard as castes differ from the chien-min, insofar as they were officially "liberated" in 1723 in documents that record their tribal names.

The best-known group are the To-min of Chêkiang Province. *To-min* means "the lazy ones." We hear of them since the fourteenth century, and from the reports we must assume that they were originally a tribe that specialized in keeping water buffaloes. When the Chinese population in their region increased more and more, they could not continue their tribal life as buffalo herdsmen. Instead, they turned to making Chinese lanterns of buffalo horns. (When thinly sliced, the horn is like a sheet of opaque plastic and was very suitable for lanterns before the use of glass.) The To-min also accompanied the marriage processions of upper-class families, their women helping the bride, especially with her hairdress. Chinese anthropologists have described them as a group of low-class professional people. The painter and man of letters Hsü Wei (1521–1593) reports on them:

> On the human body, there are tumors, and in folk life there are also tumors. Such tumors are the beggars. These are called beggar families. Nothing is known about their origin. According to tradition they are said to be descendants of criminals and prisoners of Sung times [960–1276]. Therefore people shun them. They are called To-min [lazy people]. Inside and outside the house they only do dirty and vulgar tasks, nothing useful. They are not allowed to do jobs of the [good] people. Whatever they do, others do not do and what others do not do, they do. Whatever citizens eat, they are not allowed to eat; what citizens wear, they are not allowed to wear, because people say, this is an official rule, to separate and to revile them. Therefore their activities and life to the present have not been assimilated. Only their dress has to some degree assimilated [to the Chinese way of dressing]. So people avoid them.
> But they have organized themselves in order to help one another in case of fights. They are slyer than citizens, because when an official hears of a fight, he helps the citizens. When, by chance, he does not hear [of a fight], the citizens often suffer. They regard this as a shameful thing, follow their old customs and defeat them, and then stop fighting. Therefore beggar gangs flourish more and more. Therefore, I say that these beggars are a tumor on the citizenry. . . .
> The beggars themselves say they are the soldiers of a general of the Sung, Chi Kuang-san, who deserted the Sung and went over to the Chin [Tartars]. Therefore, they were despised and got the name To-min. Whenever there is a wedding or a death or New Year, the men come in droves and ask for wine and food. The women are go-betweens and accompany the brides on their way to the husband's house. Or they are peddlers and like to steal. They are very good in mixing up truth and falsehood and thus divide the citizens. The men catch frogs and sell molasses. They make oxhead lamps of bamboo, in the shape of the head of an ox. They make clay figures of oxen and deities. They chase nightly foxes [ghosts] and thus chase away demons. The women make the hairdresses of women, comb their hair and make false pigtails. They stroll on streets and alleys in droves. (*Hsü Wen-ch'ang chi*, 18, pp. 7b–8a)

The other castes appear to be very similar. The Kai-hu (Beggar Families) also live in Chêkiang (district of Feng-hua), outside of the city, marry only among one another, have no contact with free citizens, and often receive food and clothing from Chinese officials. The women, the texts tell us, are prostitutes, descendants of criminals. In Nanking, which was the capital of China in the late fourteenth and early fifteenth centuries, the majority of the actors of the state theatre (*chiao-fang*) were from this group. Some of these same people are called T'un-t'o and also lived in Nanking, but they were not members of the theatre but rather were ordinary prostitutes. Both groups seem also to have been called Musician Families (Yüeh-hu). This term is a more general term and referred in ancient times to hereditary musician families, regarded as "mean" families. As such they are mentioned as attached to the armies in the fifth century in North China. In the early seventeenth century they were forced to leave Peking, and many of them went south to cities along the Yangtse (such as Yang-chou).

The most common story in the Chinese sources is that these Musician Families are descendants of the Mongols left in China after the Mongol dynasty was driven out (1368), and that their women specialized in making music and being prostitutes. It seems very questionable whether this story is true; it may be nothing more than an attempt to denigrate the Mongols when they were defeated, especially as professional musical families in China were mentioned long before the time of the Mongols. The sources mention only one single cultural trait as typical of them: When the music families have wives, the men are very jealous and do not allow any guests to see their wives. We know that the profession of musician was often close to professional prostitution, both being despised. We need only think of the treatment of gypsies in European history. In the case of the gypsies we know that they originally were a tribal group that, by slow migrations, came to Europe from Asia Minor in the medieval period and spread all over, including into the United States. It is possible, though we cannot prove it, that these Beggar Families (Kai-hu) and Musician Families (Yüeh-hu) were likewise descendants of originally autonomous tribes that were so engulfed by Chinese settlers they could not continue as independent groups, could not produce their own food, lost the land they had cultivated, and were forced to become a low-class sector of the Chinese population. The same happened to various Indian tribes.

Some sources also regard the Tan-hu, who have been mentioned above (p. 88), as a caste, though we have considered them as a minority. Chinese sources also mention a caste named Fisher Families (Yü-hu). They lived in the lower Yangtse area, close to where the To-min, Kai-hu, and Yüeh-hu lived, on boats like the Tan-hu. The sources say that they lived on boats, where their women were prostitutes. In this case they mention nine lineages (*hsing*) among them and say that they were descendants of followers of Ch'en Yu-liang. Ch'en was a rebel against the Mongols in the late fourteenth century but was defeated by Chu Yüan-chang, another rebel, who became founder of the Ming dynasty and drove the Mongols out of China. These Yü-hu were, like the others, liberated in 1723 and got the permission to change their hereditary profession after four generations.

All these reports are similar to one another and seem to indicate that there were indeed castes in South China down to the eighteenth century—in the case of the To-min to the twentieth century.

The Fate of the Minorities

Part Three

The Center of the World

In the preceding pages we have given in brief outline the history of China's minorities, from early beginnings to recent time. We looked at the changes that went on, with a certain intentional bias in favor of the minorities. In this part we will try to explain the attitudes of the Chinese toward their minorities, hoping that readers will see the parallels between China and numerous other countries who had or still have minority populations. We think here not only of the United States but also of countries like the Soviet Union or India, Pakistan, Burma, Thailand, and others. Our own record is nothing to be proud of, but neither is the record of the other countries, including China. Attitudes and policies toward minorities are changing in all countries, though no definitive answer has yet been found. Most of what will now be discussed belongs to the past, but what happened in the past—sometimes in the remote past—influences the present and the future.

THE SIZE OF CHINA'S MINORITIES

We may start with the question: What is the size of China's minorities? Are minorities a very serious, very important problem for China? It is impossible to give a figure that is anywhere near exact. The total population of China is estimated to be about one billion. This figure is based upon the so-called census of 1953, which was not really a census as we use the term but rather an estimate based on samples taken in different parts of the country and an extension of a population curve developed on the basis of earlier census results. None of the earlier censuses can be regarded as reliable, and the 1953 census is not reliable either. Revisions after 1953 were also made on the basis of spot checks. (Before we criticize China's census too severely, however, we should not forget that the latest American census seems to be wrong by some 10 percent even though the most modern methods were used.) Thus, the size of China's minorities is unknown; estimates oscillate between forty and sixty million, in other words, between 4 and 6 percent of the total population. The table below presents the latest data that could be found, broken down by language families.

To the linguistic groups listed on the table the Chinese add a few other groups not included here: Koreans, Russians, Vietnamese, and a tiny group of Tajiks (22,000) who live in Sinkiang. The linguistic groups cannot easily be compared with the ethnic groups. The ethnic groups we have discussed are those mentioned

	Estimated number (1953)
Speakers of Turkic languages	6,452,200
(Includes Uzbek, Kirgiz, Kazak, Salar, Uygur; the Uygur are the largest group in this family.)	
Speakers of Mongol languages	3,054,800
(Mongols are the largest group.)	
Speakers of Tungus languages	2,911,000
(Manchus are the largest group.)	
Speakers of Thai languages	16,716,000
(Chuang are the largest group.)	
Speakers of Tibeto-Burman languages	12,679,100
(Yi are the largest group.)	
Speakers of Yao and Miao languages	5,516,000
(Miao are the largest group.)	
Speakers of Austroasiatic languages	322,000
(Wa are the largest group.)	
Speakers of Austronesian languages	200,000
(The aborigines of Taiwan.)	
Chinese Muslims	6,490,000
	54,342,100

in Chinese sources, in some cases for over 2,000 years, in other cases for a century only. Linguists still do not agree to which linguistic groups these ethnic groups belong. For example, the Yi are not an ethnic group, and thus they do not occur in the texts. While most scholars would agree that the Wa (260,000 people) speak an Austroasiatic language, others would not put Miao and Yao into one group together, and so on. To set up Chinese Muslims as a special group is an irregularity in our system as their language is Chinese. However, counting people according to the language they speak is a doubtful way of determining minorities. If this criterion were used in the United States, Jews or Blacks could not be counted as minorities as they speak American English. When I spoke with census takers in Turkey, they admitted that they asked a person, in the Turkic language, whether he understood Turkish. If he said "yes," he was counted as a Turk and not as a member of a minority. We do not know how the census officials in China questioned the members of ethnic units, and we do not know to what degree the interviewed persons told the truth. Some may have identified themselves as Chinese if they spoke Chinese because they thought they might have better chances in life as Chinese than as minority members; others may have thought the opposite.

    Whatever the real size of China's minorities, they do not present a problem of dangerous proportions. But whether they are politically important or not, the minorities of China are a topic of interest as groups of people who make unique contributions to the larger society.

THE SELF-IMAGE OF THE CHINESE

We have mentioned that many early stratified societies use one term for themselves—a term often identical with the word we would use for man or human being—and another term for all other people. The latter term may be translated as *barbarians*, though we should be careful not to fall into the trap of believing that only the "men" are civilized and the others uncivilized "barbarians." Who is civilized and who not often depends on one's own standpoint.

The Country of the Middle

Chinese seem, from the time they conceived of themselves as a unit, to have believed that they were superior to their neighbors—as most other societies have done and as some still believe. They also believed that their country was located at the center of the world. They even tried to determine astronomically where the exact center of the world was and found it in a place near Lo-yang, an old capital of China; all astronomical calculations henceforth took this place as the starting point. Other societies, of course, have had similar beliefs: Once Jerusalem, once Rome was regarded as the center of the world. At only one time in China's ancient history was there disagreement with this position: A philosopher named Tsou Yen (late fourth century B.C.) stated that there were nine continents and that China was on the southeastern continent, not in the center of the world. His ideas, which possibly were influenced by early contacts with Indian thinkers, were strongly opposed by other Chinese philosophers and did not have a lasting influence. China remained the Country of the Middle (Chung-kuo) down to modern times, and this term is still the official name of China.

The focal point of civilization was in the capital of the country, actually in the emperor's palace, the place that was also the center of power. In a schematic form the classical book *Chou-li* (*Rituals of the Chou Dynasty*) outlines a picture of the world emanating from this focal point. First comes the capital of the country, which was surrounded by concentric squares (because the earth at that time was thought to be square, covered by a round heaven or sky)—first the province in which the capital city was located, then the inner provinces, the outer provinces, and so on to the end of the world. Square by square, the power of the emperor, and civilization in general, diminished. In the outside squares the inhabitants certainly did not know that they belonged to China and were under the (theoretical) rule of China's emperor, nor even of China's existence.

This means that the concept of a "border," as we have known it since the time of the Romans, did not exist. Even the Great Wall was not a border in our sense, although it had gates and battlements and was guarded by Chinese soldiers. This wall was comparable to the walls around a city—it was for the protection of some area that was often attacked by non-Chinese. Just as numerous citizens always lived outside the city gates but could, in case of danger, find security within the walls, so it was with the Great Wall and other fortifications. This understanding led to international conflicts in modern times when China claimed rights over certain countries, which had their own rulers ruling over what they regarded as their own territory—for example, Vietnam and parts of Burma. The situation along the

Himalayan range was similar and led to a war between India and China a few years ago. Of course, hard facts have shaken this picture of the world, and not only the Western expansionism of modern times. Even around 200 B.C. the Chinese were forced to recognize the territory of the Hsiung-nu as an independent country, not subject to China, by making the first "international treaty" between two countries. But, in general, a belief in what was called a *t'ien-hsia* ("all under heaven") remained as an ideal.

CHINESE ATTITUDES TOWARD MINORITIES

This perspective explains in part the pride of Chinese in their culture and their rejection of other cultures. As we have seen, what was not "Chinese" was regarded as inferior, as "barbarian." In the premodern descriptions of foreign countries we find only one country praised as "civilized," and this was the country farthest away from China, which we believe was the Roman Empire.

Even modern educated Chinese, though they may have lived among the minorities and may regard them with pity have little knowledge of these people. I quote from a writer of the 1920s:

> I lived in Kuei-chou five years and, because it was my duty to survey the land, I got to see every place. I had much opportunity to get in contact with the Miao, I paid attention to their culture and studied them, but (1) Chinese and Miao languages are totally different and I do not understand their language. I also did not fully understand the [Chinese] dialect of Kuei-chou, and though I tried, in details we did not communicate. (2) The line between Chinese and Miao is very sharp. They do not like one another and, when I asked them about their life, they often did not want to tell details. (3) Because the Chinese despise the Miao, they are ashamed to be Miao and are not at all ready to talk about their earlier history and present culture and customs. Therefore, my results are very limited in spite of a long stay.

He then characterizes these tribes:

> The Miao retain their old customs tenaciously; they drill wells and drink, they work the fields and eat (as a proverb says). Such a naive attitude is totally primitive; these are conditions of primitive men. In their social structure they still have conditions which make them appear exactly like a relic of primeval times. When one wants to study the society of primeval time and the traces of the beginning of human culture, they are the best material for study, better than fossil bones used to study animals, better than fragments of stone and metal.

Still, he has some sympathy:

> They [the Miao], since early times, fought with the Chinese. After their attrition, they retreated into the high mountains and steep cliffs of Kuei-chou and other provinces. There are many gaps in their history and little is known of their nature and culture. They are, among the five "nations" of the Chinese Republic, the Lo-lo. Though they are equal to the other races, the Chinese look down upon them, despise them, mistreat them to an extreme degree. To this it may be added that their condition of life does not suffice under the new demands. So, they decrease [in number] year by year and certainly, after a hundred years, they will be a people of the past. One really can deplore the fate of these displaced races. (*Tung-fang tsa-chih*, 20, pp. 73ff)

Such an attitude, however, also implies that China has a kind of duty to civilize the other countries, to make their people real "human beings." We can compare the belief of medieval Christians that all humans should, for their own benefit, become Christians and thus be included in "humanity," or the nineteenth-century belief in "the white man's burden." In none of these cases should we assume that the philosophy was simply a means to cover up brutal conquest, though these concepts did serve aggressors well as a justification for their own purposes.

The Chinese thus did not recognize that the cultures of their neighbors could have inherent values for these people. Only when aggression did not succeed did Chinese thinkers give consideration to some ecological factors. They would rationalize, for example, that the countries of the steppe and desert, in which agriculture is not possible, have their own kind of life and society, and the Chinese should let them have it. In a similar way non-Chinese people of the North pointed out that, for them, life in the moist, hot Chinese plains was not the right thing.

In general, we can say that Chinese did not try to understand the culture, attitudes, and beliefs of their neighbors. Let us consider a few of their descriptions of the cultures of non-Chinese peoples.

> The Hu [a general name for northern tribes] have no humanity; they are stubborn, cruel, and have no manners. They are not different from birds and wild animals. They also do not believe in emptiness and non-activity. Therefore Lao-tse crossed the frontier pass and taught them pictures in order to convert them. . . . The Hu are cruel and uncivilized, and in order to prevent them from producing worthless descendants, [Lao-tse] asked the men not to marry women and the women to remain unmarried. When the whole country accepts these rules, the Hu will by necessity be ruined. (*Hung ming chi*, 52, p. 50; quoted in Schmidt-Glintzer, p. 117)

I should explain this radical plan. The author is a Buddhist who believed, as did many at his time, that the Chinese philosopher Lao-tse went to the West and became the Buddha. Lao-tse taught "emptiness" and nonactivity. Buddha taught Nirvana and retreat from family and society. This text is one of not too many that would use religion as a way to "civilize," in this case to eliminate totally, another nation.

About the T'u-chüeh, a Turkish group that was powerful during the T'ang time, the official history says:

> The barbarians, though they have a human face, have an animal heart. Therefore, they are not as we are. When they are strong, they attack us and steal; when they are weak, they humbly submit themselves [to our rule]. They know neither gratitude nor [moral] duty: this is just their nature. (*Chiu T'ang-shu*, 194a)

An earlier, also official, text says about them:

> The T'u-chüeh prefer to destroy one another rather than to live together. The members of their hordes are not faithful people, as they come from a thousand, nay even ten thousand [different] tribes. They regard one another as enemies and kill one another, but then they mourn for them with great grief and swear to take revenge. (*Sui-shu*, 84)

Thus, these powerful neighbors of China are seen as immoral, like animals, and their behavior is irrational. One of the earliest such descriptions is from the first century B.C.:

> The Hsiung-nu, savage and wily, boldly push through the barriers and harass the Middle Kingdom, massacring the provincial population and killing the keepers of the

Northern Marches. They have long deserved punishment for their unruliness and lawlessness. (*YTL: Yen-t'ieh lun*, 1; trans. Gale, p. 5)

A text from the South says:

> The character of the Man and I is aggressive and they are quick-tempered. Their customs are uncivilized and strange. China for the time being treats them as a protectorate only. The people are often strong, quick and persevering. They use shoes made of leather and run up and down the mountains as if flying. (*Ling-wai tai-ta*, 10; trans. Netolitzki, p. 188)

The terms *Man* and *I* are general terms used for non-Chinese in the South; the text comes from the twelfth century, a time when the Chinese had instituted a kind of indirect rule among them. A sixteenth-century text recommends a different policy:

> The barbarians are like wild deer. To institute direct civil service administration by Chinese magistrates would be like herding deer into the main hall of a house and attempting to tame them. In the end, they merely bowl over our sacrificial altars, kick over our tables [with sacrificial gifts] and dash about in frantic flight. In a wilderness area, therefore, one should adjust one's methods to the character of the wilderness. . . . On the other hand, to leave these tribal chiefs to themselves to conduct their own alliances or to split up their domains is like releasing deer into the wilderness. . . . To fragment their domains under separate chiefs is to follow a policy of erecting restraining fences and is consonant with the policy of gelding a stallion and castrating a boar. (Wiens, *China's March*, p. 219, with some adjustments; from Wang Yang-ming)

To give some examples of how Chinese looked at some customs of Southern tribes, I quote from a twelfth-century text:

> After marriage, the son-in-law always goes around with a drawn sword [in his hands]. If the maid-servants of the wife were even slightly negligent, he would kill them. He is then praised as a courageous guy. Half a year after the wedding, the wife returns to the family of her husband. When the husband has killed several dozen maids since the wedding, he gains the respect of the family of his wife. If he should not do this, he would be regarded as a weakling. (*Ling-wai tai-ta*, 10; trans. Netolitzki, p. 191)

The same text describes the social system of a Chuang tribe in the hinterland of Canton, in which a man has several wives and lets them sell products to the Chinese at border markets; it does not indicate who produces these goods. The tone of this text indicates that the author finds such a society despicable.

> When I saw women in the hinterland of Canton, I was astonished that there are so many of them and that they were of excellent health, while the men were pitiful, their facial expressions were depressed. The married women have a dark skin, are well-fed, rarely sick, and very strong. In general, the women walk around with their merchandise on their backs in the markets inside and outside the cities, always trying to make a sale. But among the common people of Ch'ing province, every man has several wives and each of them walks around with merchandise on her back, following the markets, in order to provide for that husband. When they have only a pro forma husband, the reason is that people do not like to say they have no home. The men of these women only play and they carry their children around with them the whole day. When they have no children, they put their hands into their sleeves and do nothing. Each of the wives builds her own straw hut, separate from the others. The husband can come and leave, without arousing the jealousy of the other wives. Among the chieftains of the natives it is the rule to have a dozen wives. When a child is born, they make no difference whether it is a child of a main wife or of a concubine, otherwise quarrels and murder would "arise." (*Ling-wai tai-ta*, 10; trans. Netolitzki, p. 197)

There are innumerable texts of this kind, which indicate a biased, antiforeign view together with either an open or a veiled conviction that these people should accept Chinese customs. It is sad, though understandable under the conditions, that some Western missionaries accepted such judgments without criticism. For example, one well-known book about the tribes of the Southwest says about the freer premarital sexual relations of the Miao:

> Morally most of them are below, and some of them immeasurably below the Chinese. . . . There are no decent women among the Ta-hua Miao. . . . The Ta-hua Miao of Wei-ning district and around Chao-tung were, and in some cases still are, so bad that they could hardly be worse. This is describing their moral condition in very few words, but they are quite enough. (Clarke, p. 35)

Even in describing a group already under the political control of the Chinese government, the Chinese single out cultural elements they find queer or bad, and the authors cannot refrain from comparing them with animals. The acculturated Tanka of the Canton area in the twelfth century are described in this way:

> Those who live on boats and who regard the sea as solid land and those who live all the time on rivers or on the sea, are the Tan. Among the Tan are three groups: the first are the Fisher-Tan who are good at putting out nets and using fishing tackle. The second group are the Oyster-Tan who are good at diving in the sea and collecting oysters. The third group are the Lumber-Tan who cut wood in the mountains and produce good lumber.
> Usually the Tan are poor. Their dress consists of rags put together. When they once get a handful of rice, they divide it with their wives and children. Men and women live under a small mat shed. They produce numerous children, so that on one boat there are no less than a dozen children. As soon as the children can be carried around the mothers tie them with a soft cloth to their own backs and then handle the rudder as before. When the babies can crawl around, they tie long ropes around their hips. On the other end of the ropes are blocks of wood. Should the children suddenly fall into the water, they can be pulled out with the help of the rope. When the children can run, they run around under the matshed without any fear. When they can run, they also can swim and dive. When the boats of the Tan are moored, the children all play together on the sand. In summer and winter they wear no clothing. They are really like otters. Though the life of the Tan on the water may seem to be free and though it seems that their love for freedom cannot be limited, each one of them is tied to the administration, each has a special territory and each one pays taxes to the officials. Thus, we can see that nobody can hide, between heaven and earth. (Ling-wai tai-ta, 3; trans. Netolitzki, pp. 50–51)

Still another sign of the way Chinese looked at their minorities and tribes beyond their borders is the custom of writing the tribal names with the classifier *dog*, indicating that they were not real humans but related to dogs. Other names used for the tribes had a second derogatory element, as we saw with the tribal name Lolo, which has a meaning something like vagabond. The word can, however, be written with characters of the same sound but a nonderogatory meaning. Most of the people the Chinese called Lolo called themselves Nosu. There is, however, a significant difference between tribes in the North and West and tribes in the South of China proper. Those in the North and West who had social organizations that looked to the Chinese like a state and who were powerful were called by a term that attempted to transliterate their own names and which did not use the classifier *dog*. Today, derogatory names are replaced by other names.

The Chinese have always felt that the final stage for minorities should be total integration. This attitude is well expressed by the introduction to an album of pictures of tribes of Yünnan Province by an anonymous writer in 1788:

Under our dynasty the glory of culture spreads widely, and the barbarians who live intermixed with Chinese, accept most of Chinese culture. They learn to read and write; they understand the rituals [of good behavior]; not only do some of them go to schools, but a good number have even got an official rank. Their dress, marriage customs and mourning rituals have become totally Chinese; only their language still remains barbarian. Only in the frontier areas with their steep cliffs and dangerous valleys barbarian customs still are prevalent. (*Tien-sheng hsi-nan chu-I t'u shuo*)

It is interesting to note that this was written between the two periods of severe conflicts between Chinese and indigenous tribes, at a time when the tribes of Yünnan and Kueichou were vigorous. The author is a proud Chinese who wants to see that all minorities quickly become assimilated. Total assimilation is for him only a matter of time. Others had the same belief, but almost 200 years later Yünnan Province still has minorities.

In the following chapter we will see the different aspects of the problem of assimilation.

Diplomacy, Conquest, and Colonization

DIPLOMACY AND PERSUASION

In the following sections we will deal with the different Chinese methods and plans by which an independent neighboring society could become a Chinese colony (and its people ultimately a minority). Obviously, the most primitive method is an aggressive war. We must keep in mind that Chinese scholars never speak of an aggressive war, but always use such terms as *pacify*, or *an expedition to straighten them out*, as if they were forced by the enemy to establish order in the country or to correct their behavior. Such terms have as much value as the statements of Western nations that they were forced to defend themselves when they clearly started a war of aggression. Only in popular novels can we find passages clearly stating that the Chinese wanted to attack another country and provoked a war. However, in discussions between two parties about whether to start a war or not, we sometimes find the "peace party" making statements like the following:

> [The ruler and the feudal lords] should not talk about advantage and detriment, ministers about gain and loss, but they should cultivate benevolence and righteousness, set an example to the people, and widely extend their virtuous conduct to gain the people's confidence. Then will nearby folk lovingly flock to them and distant people joyfully submit to their authority. Therefore, the master conqueror does not fight; the expert warrior needs no soldiers. (*YTL: Yen-t'ieh lun*, 1; trans. Gale, p. 4)

Or, with direct reference to China's northern neighbors:

> Should your Majesty be unwilling to abandon them [i.e., our soldiers] to their fate, you have but to manifest your virtue towards them [the northern tribes] and the northern barbarians will undoubtedly come of their own accord to pay you tribute at the wall. (YTL; trans. Gale, p. 76)

It is hard to say whether such statements are just a way of stating that China is not in a position at the moment to make a war or whether the proposal truly expresses the belief that government in the neighboring societies is so bad, morality so low, and life so hard, that their people would voluntarily submit to a Chinese overlordship, expressed by the sending of tribute to China. Chinese scholars and officials certainly have always believed that life in China was much better than in any of the adjacent countries. There are some, but only a few, examples of educated Chinese who lived—voluntarily or otherwise—among the Hsiung-nu and other foreign states and served their rulers.

The fact that hardly any educated Chinese lived among non-Chinese, has been used to explain the supposed failure of Chinese scholars to develop original and alternative ideas about state and society. In Europe such an "expatriate" could always leave his country and go to another country, when he had to fear that he would be persecuted for his ideas in his own country. Life in the other country was similar to life in his own, except for the language, and the other country even might have been happy to accept such a man who could be useful. But in China emigration of a scholar to an "underdeveloped" country was not only technically difficult, but the man could not imagine that he could live there and that his qualifications and ideas could be used. Moreover, he had to fear that the government would retaliate and kill the remaining members of his family, who were considered as guilty as he was for his leaving China. Poems, stories, and plays describe in vivid words the sufferings of military leaders who were taken prisoner by the Hsiung-nu and had to gain their livelihood by herding sheep or other menial tasks. And, in addition, such a captive had to fear that the emperor would punish his family for his failure to gain a victory.

Marriage Ties

As in Europe before the nineteenth century, treaties between states were often accompanied by marriage ties between the rulers of both countries. Several motives were at work here: If one ruler married the daughter of the other ruler, he would not be likely to make a war against her father's country. Furthermore, if the other ruler had no son, his country might, after his death, fall to his daughter as inheritance. Since the early second century marriages were concluded between the Chinese emperor and the ruler of an adjacent country in the North or Northwest of China; and before that time marriages between feudal lords, the rulers of statelets inside China proper, had been common. In the T'ang period (618–906) twenty-one princesses were given to foreign rulers, often, but not always, in exchange for daughters of the foreign ruler. It is interesting that only three of the twenty-one women were true daughters of the emperor; they were given to the Uygurs in 785, 789, and 821, in times when China was relatively weak. The others were nieces or other relatives of the emperor. The foreigners had, of course, to give a "bridal dowry," in accordance with Chinese custom. As we saw earlier, the Tibetans in 641 paid 5,000 ounces of gold and other gifts for a "princess," but it seems this was regarded as worthwhile because of the gain in prestige of the Tibetan ruler. One consequence of such marriages was that the Chinese emperor was now the father-in-law of the foreign ruler, who called himself son-in-law of the Chinese emperor in his diplomatic correspondence.

Naturally, the princess did not go alone to the foreign country. She came not only with a whole staff of maids and maidservants but also with a large number of men who served in her office, prepared her correspondence, and kept her personal household stocked with the desired food and other objects a high-ranking Chinese was accustomed to. We must keep in mind that she was not usually the main wife of the foreign ruler; he, like the Chinese emperor, had a large harem, and each wife lived in her own quarters, either in a cluster of tents or in buildings in Chinese style, especially built for her comfort. When a princess was sent to the Uygurs in 821, she was accompanied on her trip by a Grand General of the Imperial Guard, a President of the Court of Imperial Banquets, a Commissioner for the Marriage Rites and President of the Court of Imperial Insignia, a Vice-President of the Court of the Imperial Clan, his assistant, who was a Secretary of the Ministry of Forestry, a man from the Court of Imperial Sacrifices, and a host of less important men. When they were back in China in 822, they reported:

> When the princess should still have had two nights to go before reaching the Uygur royal camp, the khaghan sent several hundred cavalry to come and beg that they could go ahead of the train with the princess by a different route. Hu Cheng said, "It cannot be done." The barbarian ambassadors said, "Formerly when the Princess of Hsien-an came, she went ahead when she was several hundred *li* from the Jua Gate. Why do you now resist us?" Cheng said, "Our Son of Heaven has proclaimed that we should escort the princess and hand her over to the khaghan. At present we have not yet seen the khaghan. How could it be fitting that we should let her go on ahead?" The barbarian ambassadors then desisted.
>
> When we got to the barbarian court, we selected an auspicious day to give the princess her appointment as the Uygur khatun. The khaghan first ascended his tower and sat facing the east. He had had a large felt tent set up below the tower to house the princess, and sent a group of barbarian princesses to teach her barbarian customs. Not until then did the princess remove her T'ang clothing and put on barbarian clothes, for which an old woman waited on her. She came out in front of the tower and made an obeisance towards the west. The khaghan was sitting looking at her. The princess bowed down a second time and, when she had finished, she re-entered her felt tent. She removed what she had previously been wearing and put on the clothes of a khatun, a single-colored robe and a large mantle, both crimson, and a golden decorated head-dress, pointed in front and straight behind. She came out to the tower and bowed down to the khaghan as in the first part of the ritual. The barbarians had set up a large sedan-chair with a curved screen in front of which they had arranged a small throne. Some ministers led the princess on to the sedan-chair. A minister of each of the nine clans of the Uygurs carried the sedan-chair and they followed the sun, turning to the right around the court nine times. Then the princess descended from the chair and went up the tower where she sat with the khaghan facing the east. From then on, whenever the ministers and the inferior courtiers made obeisance [to the khaghan], they bowed also to the khatun.
>
> The khatun had her own royal camp. (*Chiu T'ang-shu*, 195; trans. Mackerras, p. 120)

The fate of these princesses was not enviable. When in the eighth century the husband of one of these women died, the Uygurs wanted to bury her alive with her husband. She protested, saying she wanted to use the Chinese ritual, but she made a concession to the Uygur customs: She slashed her face and cried loudly. She was then allowed to return to China because she had no son. In China she asked the emperor to give to the successor of her husband a Chinese wife, and he was given the daughter of a high Chinese general of Uygur descent (*Chiu T'ang-shu*, 195).

Another custom, this time of the Hsiung-nu, embarrassed the Chinese; this played a role in the famous case of Miss Wang Chao-chün, a girl in the harem of the Chinese emperor. When the Hsiung-nu wanted a Chinese princess, this girl was sent, though she was not a princess at all. When her Hsiung-nu husband died, she had to marry his son (who, however, was not her own child) and later even her grandson, until finally she was allowed to return to China. Several operas describe her sad fate, and in T'ang times, according to a folk ballad, a temple in her honor was erected on the border. Today, her departure from China is depicted on the walls of at least two temples in Taiwan.

The Strategies of Chia I

One of the most interesting Chinese documents concerning policy in dealing with "barbarians" is an essay, supposedly written by Chia I, a scholar-politician in the beginning of the second century B.C., but more likely dating from the end of the second or the early first century B.C. This essay takes off from earlier essays about mass persuasion and books on strategy. To my knowledge it is the only document of its kind. We do not know whether what the author recommended was ever fully put into practice, but we can be sure that at least some of his recommendations were used. I will here give a simplified translation of its main ideas:

When in a country [the ruler] gives rewards, such rewards should never be distributed equally [to all who deserve them]. Because, when one distributes rewards equally, the country will be poor and yet, the [individual] reward is small and not large enough to stimulate people. Therefore, persons who are good in giving rewards provoke a competition [among possible recipients] and take them by surprise. Sometimes, they distribute much and see that [the reward] is tempting by merely looking at it, alluring when people speak of it. By such method one can gain the heart of a whole nation. If Your Majesty should give me the honor to listen to my plan, then I would use available funds, and if Hsiung-nu in positions higher than that of a chief of a family arrive [at court], I would dress them in embroidered clothes, and the members of their family would be dressed in ornamented brocade. We would make five chariots with rich carving and painting, we will equip them with four horses each, cover them with a green roof. Behind them, a couple of horsemen should follow, and then we would let them [at a parade] sit in the chariots which accompany the emperor. Even the parades of the shan-yü [the ruler of the Hsiung-nu] would hardly be comparable to this. If Hsiung-nu surrender to us, they should get something like this from time to time. Then, all people in their country who hear of this or see this, will eagerly tell one another, and each of them will hope: "If only I had such luck as to get something like this!" This [method] will spoil their eyes, and this is my first bait.

If ambassadors of the Hsiung-nu come [to our court] or if one of their important men surrenders to us, or if a great number of [Hsiung-nu] people be assembled, then Your Majesty should call them and given them a dinner. There should be prepared four or five dishes with lots of meat, cut in small pieces, broiled or fried meat, also pickled meat, each dish of the size of several feet. This should be put before them. Then that man should be asked to sit down [and eat]. I am sure that Hsiung-nu will stand by the hundreds around him to look. And this alone would make the rewarded one happy. He would smile and eat. All the dishes should be dishes he likes to eat but which he had never yet eaten. Hsiung-nu who come to us should from time to time receive such a dinner. Then all people who hear of this or see it, would find their mouth watering. They will tell it to one another, and they would hope, "If only we, too, could get this [treatment]." Thus, we shall spoil their mouths. This is my second bait.

If important men or ambassadors arrive [at our court], Your Majesty should send a person [to their lodging] and invite them. This invitation should be made public and any Hsiung-nu who wants to look at it should not be prevented from doing so. Then they should be served by twenty or thirty ladies, with faces powdered white and [around the eyes] painted black, dressed in embroidered dresses, sometimes openly, sometimes decently. During the dinner, these women should perform "Hunnic games" [acrobatic games]. Your Majesty should have the grace to ask [men from] the Department of Court Music to come and play music, blow the flute and beat the drums. Later, persons with masks should come forth, and still later dancers and jumpers. After a short intermission, the drums should be beaten and puppets should be made to dance. Finally, "barbarian" music [i.e., Hsiung-nu music] should be performed and they should be taken by hand and guided to the place of honor, with ten or more ladies serving them from front and behind. When persons who surrender get such a treatment from time to time, and when they like this, people in their whole country who hear of it or who have seen it will wide-eyed tell others. All their people will be excited and they will have only one fear, namely that they may be too late. This will spoil their ears. And this is another one of my baits.

People who surrender upon invitation of the emperor or persons who come upon an agreement, should also, sometimes, be made rich by the emperor. They should be [lodged] in a great hall and deep rooms, equipped with a fine kitchen and large, round storage units. In the stable there should stand rows of horses and in the sheds there should be chariots. In addition, there should be male and female servants, children and animals. Everything should be provided. Then, Hsiung-nu visitors should be invited and dinners given to Hsiung-nu ambassadors. Your majesty should ask [some of] his officials to equip them with all necessary implements and supply them with musicians, so that their lodgings are joyful and interesting. One should also take care that their property is larger than it was before [they came to China], so that the kings [of the Hsiung-nu] are afraid that such men may be richer than the shan-yü himself. When from time to time we make them such gifts and give them such lodgings, the whole country will long for [such a treatment] and will hope [to get it]. Everybody will be excited and will be afraid only of arriving too late. This is the way to spoil their stomachs, and this is still another bait.

Persons who surrender should from time to time be called by the emperor and he should console them. Then, he should invite them into the palace. It is difficult to come close to grandees of the Hsiung-nu. Your Majesty therefore should invite Hsiung-nu children and willing sons of grandees. Then Your Majesty should have the grace to invite not more than ten persons who should, dressed in embroidered dress and beautifully fitted out, accompany them [i.e., the children] when they go out and serve them when they are at home. When Your Majesty gives dinners to Hsiung-nu or arranges to have a big westling match for them or when Hsiung-nu ambassadors are [officially] received, high officials and military men should be there to serve them. Later the Hsiung-nu children will come to serve. Then the Hsiung-nu grandees will come closer and should be allowed to drink wine. Your Majesty would direct this and also distribute some money. Young maidens and puppets would provide entertainment. Later they [i.e., the guests] would be given embroidered garments, and sashes decorated with shells would be distributed to them when the reception comes to an end. Your Majesty would take interest in the Hsiung-nu children, you would encourage them, would play with them, would give them fried meat and would personally eat the same meat. He would give them heaps of beautiful dresses. And if Your Majesty would rise, the Hsiung-nu children would be sometimes in front of you, sometimes behind you, and the Hsiung-nu grandees would, after the wine and before leaving, dress in the garments and put on the sashes and stand there like high-ranking [Chinese] persons. If a few Hsiung-nu were treated this way, their whole country would get excited and people would have only one fear: of arriving too late. Thus, shall we spoil their hearts, and this is another bait.

Thus, one catches their eyes, catches their ears, catches their mouths, catches their stomach, and after one has caught these four, and then also catches their hearts: is there any doubt that they would come? Then we would control the Hsiung-nu. This I call my five baits.

The Hsiung-nu like the Chinese princesses and esteem the families of [the accompanying] ministers. They should in addition be given more [than the normal number] of officers, and all their house servants should be experienced politicians. They should be provided with sufficient money and implements of daily use. Then we will be able to exploit the esteem [the Hsiung-nu have for the princesses]. We can know their limits, can know their plans. Then our domestic and foreign policies will fit together and complement one another. Truly, how can their people withstand [such treatment] for a long time? Therefore, when my Three Plans [note: not translated here] are used and the Five Baits are carried out, there will be among the Hsiung-nu unrest and mutual mistrust. Then, their shan-yü will no longer be able to sleep restfully when he goes to bed; he will no longer enjoy the taste of the food when he eats. With his sword drawn and the bow ready, he will look to the right and to the left and regard everybody as his enemy. And his subjects—even when they do not run away from him—will be after him like tigers. His people will be afraid to come close to him because he may decapitate them. This I call politics.

But when the grandees [of his country] look at the shan-yü as if they had met a tiger or a wolf, then they will turn their faces toward the South [i.e., China] and return to China [as subjects] like the love of a weak child toward his loving mother. If the masses look at their officers and generals as if they had met a terrible enemy, then the turning of their faces toward the South and their wish to run over to the Chinese [side] can be compared to water which flows downward. But when the generals and the shan-yü have no more subjects whom they can employ and when they have no people who will protect them, what else could they do but come, their necks tied [like a criminal], beating the ground with their foreheads, and asking to be allowed to subject themselves to the justice of Your Majesty? This, we call "military virtue."

But even if the Hsiung-nu should understand our plan and move with all their folk far away, there is still a plan which concerns the frontier markets which they violate, but still covet. I would like that Your Majesty send ambassadors to them to concude a generous pact. They should not be allowed big markets, but rather the ambassadors should create spaces at strategical spots and conduct the masses [of Hsiung-nu] to them. There should be enough frontier officials and soldiers to be able to defend themselves. And at each such frontier pass there should be one or two hundred butchers, food-sellers and people who can make fine dishes. Then the Hsiung-nu would remain glued to the Great Wall. When their kings and generals are strong, they will go to the North and attack their rulers. When the Hsiung-nu are hungry, they would get soup and meat. When they are thirsty, they will get much wine. This will then go on without an end and we can wait. If we give them much, they would get even more hungry. If they had much wealth, they would get poorer and poorer. But that is what we Chinese wish to happen. When, then, one of the grandees of the Hsiung-nu comes [to surrender], we should give a reward to two or three men; when somebody surrenders with ten thousand men, we should reward ten or more men, because a reward is a way to entice the people [to surrender]. (Chia I, *Hsin-shu*)

This document contains every strategy that, over the course of history, has been used against the strong nomadic people of the North. It is a total plan of "fifth column" techniques: To create tensions in the leading stratum of the Hsiung-nu society and thus subvert their military strength; to subvert their economy by installing frontier markets (which we will discuss in detail later); to send great numbers of well-trained spies to the Hsiung-nu under the pretext that they will be service personnel for the princesses who are sent from China to the court of the shan-yü, the ruler of the Hsiung-nu. So-called princesses were sent from the early second century B.C. on, for more than a thousand years; frontier markets existed until recent time. The first Hsiung-nu who surrendered (though not because they loved China and hated their own government but because of dissension within the leadership of the Hsiung-nu) came at the end of the second century B.C. The main body of the Hsiung-nu indeed moved away from the Chinese borders to the far Northwest, and it is possible that units of these Hsiung-nu were integrated in the nomadic federation that terrorized Europe under the name of Huns. By the late second and early third century A.D. seventeen tribes of the Hsiung-nu surrendered to China and were resettled within China.

Ambassadorial Missions

Chia I speaks of Hsiung-nu who come to the Chinese court as ambassadors. There were always some foreigners in the Chinese capital on special missions, especially when a foreign princess was sent to China in exchange for a Chinese princess. We know that Hsiung-nu ambassadors and their corteges were indeed feasted and shown "Hsiung-nu games"—acrobatic performances, dances, music, and women. Some details of Chia I's plan were applied even as late as the eighth century:

An Uygur came to the court of China in 746. Honor guards stood at the Grand Audience Hall. The president of the Department of the Grand Imperial Secretariat summoned the man to his office and gave him the document of his appointment. The Ambassador left the Secretariat through the gate, mounted an imperial chariot and drove to the Imperial City's gate. There, he descended and walked. Preceding him were [men] carrying his pennants and emblems of office. (*Hsin T'ang shu*, 217a, according to Mackerras, p. 55)

There were other opportunities for spying on the foreigners as well. At the end of A.D. 756 the Chinese had sent the son of a Chinese prince to the Uygurs with a new title bestowed on him, accompanied by a "General for Friendship and Relations." The khan (ruler) of the Uygurs gave him one of his daughters, and together with some Uygur chiefs and some of the woman's relatives, she was brought to China. The emperor enfeoffed the woman and then received the Uygur khan, who came later (according to *Chiu T'ang-shu*, 195). When around 759 the khan of the Uygurs died, the Chinese sent an official for condolences. To express condolences by sending an ambassador to the foreign country was already a custom in the second century B.C. Each of these missions stayed for some time, probably several months, in the foreign country. Each mission had numerous members, down to servants and cooks, all of whom could collect information. Some of these personnel were given temporary high titles for the duration of the mission.

Some such missions, however, could be unpleasant for the Chinese ambassadors. In 762 a grandson of the emperor was sent to the Uygurs as ambassador. The Uygur ruler asked the Chinese prince to dance in front of the ruler's tent. This was regarded by the prince as very shameful and he excused himself, saying that he could not dance because China was in mourning for the death of two emperors. The Uygur ruler said that he and the Chinese emperor had concluded a pact of brotherhood and thus he, as an uncle of the ambassador, was above his "nephew," so that the ambassador should obey. The Uygur ruler then had all Chinese officials of the mission whipped with one hundred blows each, though he let the prince go free (according to *Chiu T'ang shu*, 195).

In 758 a daughter of the Chinese emperor was sent to the Uygurs as a bride. On her arrival the khan was sitting in a yellow robe and "barbarian" hat on a couch in his tent, surrounded by many bodyguards and insignia. But the Chinese chief of mission had to stand outside the tent. Then the khan blamed him for having a eunuch in his entourage (a eunuch was not a "real man" and should not be a member of a high mission). The eunuch quickly retreated. Then the mission head was asked to bow in front of the khan. All of the khan's behavior was a violation of the Chinese rule that a foreigner should be deferential when a Chinese ambassador arrived. When the woman was introduced as the true daughter of the emperor, not just a girl from the imperial clan, then the khan stood up, received the edict of the emperor and the diploma of appointment as imperial son-in-law. The next day, the woman became a khatun (wife of the khan). The emperor's gifts were now distributed to the officials of the khan, who gave the departing mission head five hundred horses and many furs (according to *Chiu T'ang shu*, 195).

In fairness, it should be said that foreign ambassadors coming to the Chinese court did not always behave correctly. They got relatively nice quarters to live in and had Chinese servants (who, of course, also served as spies), but with them came merchants who illegally sold products that had been declared parts of the gifts to the Chinese emperor. Other members of the staff went out and committed robberies, attacked harmless citizens, and stole openly (see Mackerras for the years 771–775 and later texts). We have a special memo to the emperor from the year 1490 about these conditions:

> Envoys from various regions are very cunning and often have intercourse with the personnel of the [Hui-t'ing]-kuan and [Chinese] merchants do not wait for the Ministry

of Rites to assign a period for trade, but ahead of time they bring in forbidden articles and sell them illegally [to the foreign envoys]. Recently, barbarians from Qamil and other countries have brought jade and other articles, which were bought on credit by treacherous people who for a long time did not pay, so that the barbarians stayed over one year. They also go outside [the Hui-t'ing-kuan] to drink and to commit evil. Interpreters repeatedly urge them to set out on the [home] journey, but they incite them to commit crimes: even though prohibitions are posted, they despise them and know no fear.

This led to edicts in the year 1500:

From now on, those who in violation of the regulations sell weapons to the barbarians shall upon investigation [and conviction] be punished by death. When the military or common people, whether in or outside of the capital, maintain illegal relations with the barbarians who come to court to present the tribute, or trade in their behalf, or incite [the barbarians] to harm the people, or leak information [to them], they shall be exiled to frontier guard duty, and their military functions shall be transferred to border garrisons. Interpreters and escorts who violate these regulations, if they are military, shall be dealt with according to military rules; if they have civilian positions, their names shall be stricken off the registers. . . .

Any official who should dare whether at the capital or along the road, to induce the barbarians to buy forbidden goods, or to frequent prostitutes, shall be punished on the spot with the cangue as a warning to the public. (Serruys, pp. 48–51)

TRIBUTE AND PRIVATE TRADE

Tribute Missions

Tribute is usually defined as a gift the ruler of a foreign country is obliged to present regularly to the ruler of a dominant country. In the case of China this definition is only partially accurate. It was, of course, prestigious for the Chinese court to receive "tribute missions," which brought valuable and often needed gifts. We can even use the reports on tribute missions to measure the international prestige of China; it was high when many missions came. President Nixon's 1972 trip to China was, at least in the eyes of the common Chinese, a tribute mission that brought gifts to Chairman Mao; this visit, indeed, raised the prestige of the chairman in China and the prestige of China in the world.

Tribute missions had two sides. The ambassadors and their staffs had to receive countergifts upon their departure, and the value of these Chinese gifts was usually equal to, if not higher than, the value of the tribute gifts.

The tribute gifts consisted usually of luxury items, as did the gifts President Nixon gave. If not, they were objects the court and the upper class could use, such as horses, camels, or falcons; or furs of ermine, sable, or squirrel. The emperor would later give some of these gifts to honored members of his government as rewards. The Chinese gifts in return usually consisted of silk, to be used for the official garments at the courts of the foreigners. In many periods of Chinese history, however, silk was paid as a tax to the government by the citizens and served as a kind of medium of exchange, so to give it away as a gift and to receive only luxury items was harmful for the Chinese economy. How much even the Mongols of the sixteenth century valued silk can be seen from the fact that Mongol women of high position presented tribute on their own to the Chinese court, most probably in order to get silk.

The tribute mission had to be lodged and provided for, and it usually included a great number of people. In the sixteenth century, for instance, the Jurchen embassies had between 800 and 1,800 men; a single horse that was part of the tribute might be cared for by ten men. And often they came months before the official reception, which could be at Chinese New Year or the emperor's birthday. As a result, in many periods of Chinese history not only was the number of embassies fixed, but the number of people within each mission was also limited in order to cut down the costs.

The moment an embassy crossed the Chinese border, it was provided with a military escort and interpreters and translators. The places close to the route the embassy had to take seem to have been especially prepared so that the foreigners would receive a good impression. Such places could even receive new names, such as "Calming down those from afar" or "Longing for those far away," whereas villages at a distance from these check-points had more aggressive names. Feeding the mission was an obligation of the local military outposts. The ambassadors even got special night-clothes when they were in China. Then the embassy had to be checked in order to find out whether or not some of the so-called ambassadors were pretenders.

Once in the capital the mission lived, as we mentioned, in a special quarter. When the capital was Peking, the quarter was the modern Legation Quarter (which now has a different name). In these quarters the foreigners had to be supervised constantly and often were not allowed to leave for fear they would engage in spying and illegal trade. Chinese in the service of the foreigners who came with the mission to China often were put under special supervision because they might be well-trained spies. Similarly, Chinese ambassadors to the Mongol court in the sixteenth century were frequently of Mongol descent and, because they could still speak Mongolian, were valuable spies. Though they were loyal to China, they were watched by the Chinese members of the mission.

Private Trade

Equal in importance to these official tribute missions were individual Chinese merchants who operated in the foreign country. A story from a twentieth-century Central Asian, though certainly not historically true, is a good indication of how the foreigners saw the situation:

> Once upon a time there came a merchant to China. That merchant had a beautiful female slave. Her name was Malika Dil Aram. That merchant fixed the price of 1000 gold coins on that female slave. The Khan of China thought much of paying 1000 gold coins and of buying the female slave. If he had bought the female slave and given the 1000 gold coins to the merchant, the tributes and contributions of China which were to be sent to him would have been finished. For this reason the Khan of China was not able to buy this girl.

However, when the Shah Bahram, a local ruler, saw the picture of this maiden, he was love sick and sent a minister with a letter to the Chinese emperor with the following message:

> "Give the tributes and contributions of one year to the merchant and buy the female slave and send her here. But don't take the tributes and contribution of China for three years from your subjects." They gave the letter to the Khan of China. When the Khan saw the letter he was very glad and went to the merchant. When the merchant heard

that the Khan had gone [to see him], he went to meet him and conducted the Khan to his inn. (Jarring, vol. 47, p. 78)

Reality was not always so romantic. A Russian report about a Chinese merchant who lived north of Vladivostok gives hard realities:

> The Chinaman Li Tan-juy was *tsaidun* or headman of the valley of the Imam. He exploited the natives mercilessly and punished them cruelly if they failed to deliver the fixed amount of furs by a given time. Many families he had ruined utterly, raping their women and selling their children for debt. At length two of the Udehé, Masenda and Somo by name, exasperated beyond endurance, had gone to Khabarovsk and lodged a complaint with the Governor-General. . . . Now Li Tan-juy heard of their visit to Khabarovsk. Then, as an example to the rest, he had Masenda and Somo flogged savagely. One of them died under the beating, the other survived but remained a cripple for life. (Arseneev, pp. 223–224)

Here, a Chinese merchant exploited non-Russian tribal people within the frontiers of Russia. In other cases merchants from one tribe, such as the Ko-lao in South China, lived in Chinese towns and conducted the trade between Chinese and Miao. At the same time, these acculturated Ko-lao were used to control the Miao. When the foreign country was powerful enough, it controlled the Chinese merchants:

> The whole of the Chinese employed in trade at *Urga* live a life of self-imposed banishment, being prevented by law from bringing their wives and families, and for the most part revisit their native land at intervals from five to ten years. (Gilmour, p. 134)

The typical consequence of this is prostitution: "Mongol women live off and with the Chinese" (Ma Ho-t'ien, p. 128).

The power of a private business establishment in what is now Outer Mongolia but was once territory attached to China can be seen in this report from a Chinese observer:

> The greatest Chinese merchant establishment in past days was the Shansi [province] house of Ta Sheng K'uei which has been doing business in Mongolia for more than three hundred years and was especially powerful during the Manchu period [to 1911]. (Ma Ho-t'ien, p. 71)

When independent Outer Mongolia canceled all debts, the house suffered a loss of one million Chinese dollars, but before the Communist revolution Ta Sheng K'uei had branches everywhere in Mongolia, and its capital was thirty million dollars. The Chinese businessmen lived separated from the Mongols. The city of Urga (now Ulan Batur) had four bath houses and one for Chinese only.

The same exploitation of minorities or weak neighbors is reported from the South. Chinese mining operations began in the present province of Kueichou in the eighteenth century, and, with government permission, the local Miao were exploited. They had to deliver fixed quotas of 10 percent of the tax in copper and 20 percent in lead. Usurers charged the Miao 5 percent interest per month, and after three months of nonpayment the interest was added to the capital. The payments could be made in the form of grain, and when there was not sufficient grain for payment, the land was taken away by the usurers.

Sources have noted the importance of markets in the Miao area. These markets were comparable to the Chinese intervillage markets; that is, they often were not in a village but between villages and thus visited by people from different regions and different tribes. I have seen a Shan village market directly on the Chinese border. It made a very impressive picture as all the tribal men and women arrived in their colorful dress. The individual traders had only minimal quantities of merchandise, such as a few pounds of vegetables or fruits, some knives, or some cloth. In addition to local folk, such a market is also visited by itinerant traders who migrate from market to market and replenish their wares by occasional visits to a town. Today, they often come by bicycle with their merchandise on the rack.

The so-called border markets, which Chia I recommended as a means to make non-Chinese turn toward Chinese luxury (see p. 110), were official state markets under the direct supervision of government officials and protected by Chinese soldiers. Although the strategist had recommended the establishment of such markets several centuries earlier, the first one mentioned in documents is in A.D. 594 (Serruys, p. 9). One of the main items of trade was Mongolian horses. (All through history China has imported good horses from its northern neighbors. In 1405 specific "horse fairs" were reported.) These controlled markets sometimes illegally sold embargoed items. For instance, the export of tea to peoples in the North who could not produce tea was often prohibited, for reasons that aren't clear. These border markets were also, as Chia I had recommended, places where buyers could find interesting restaurants, could see theatre or puppet play troupes, or could visit prostitutes.

Border markets were a specific institution of the northern border. In the South private markets, controlled at most by a local administrator, were common. A modern Chinese scholar studied the types of merchants who traded among the tribes of the south in areas administrated by t'u-szu (see p. 138) and described them thus:

> Before the borders [of China] were exactly established, the borderland was governed by some T'u-szu. The T'u-szu government only supplied tribute, paid taxes and asked the Chinese for hereditary recognition. When there were bandits, then they supplied services—that was all they had to do. Normally governing was done by the T'u-szu and there were only some scattered villages in which there was not even a T'u-szu. Therefore, when Chinese came into the area to make a living, they acted exactly like Chinese emigrants who went to Southeast Asia. Like them, each Chinese relied upon his own capabilities to work. Then, when later border districts were established, the local government behaved towards these Chinese as formerly our country's government did towards the Overseas Chinese [Hua-ch'iao]: they did not specifically protect them, did not help them.... The border district official's aim was to get rich.... Whether Chinese or natives, money was the only guideline. Whoever gave more money, received help. We can prove this, because border-area Chinese and natives curse the officials in the same way. Therefore we can say that the existence of Chinese was not based on the power of the government. As with the Hua-ch'iao, development did not rely upon government's help.
>
> Therefore, also, the border Chinese and Hua-ch'iao in their lifestyle have many similarities. One point here is that they made their living by trade. After some years of small business they had savings. The Hua-ch'iao invested that in large businesses or industries. In the border areas, because of traditional attitudes and environmental factors, most of them went from business to property-owning and became landlords. Chinese farming is highly developed; therefore, in suitable areas, they could expand greatly. And because of the traditional custom of hard working, they became more and more numerous, forming large families. And like Hua-ch'iao, they were quite conservative and had egocentric worldviews. Again like Hua-ch'iao, because of environment they acculturated in behavior to some degree to the natives; that is unavoidable. But in language, literacy, ancestor worship, morality and other important traits of Chinese civilization they remained conservative. (T'ao Yün in *Pien-Cheng Kung-lun*, 2, no. 1/2, pp. 28–29)

Itinerant traders bring objects of daily use to the natives on horseback to markets in rotation; they buy local products like medicine, furs and other things and bring them to the Chinese towns for sale. They, too, do not want to expand this trade, but with their savings mainly buy land, mostly in the Chinese areas. Most of them have special reasons for this: not all have luck, some get sick, are robbed, have enemies, meet wild animals and thus, their life comes to an end. . . . Other businessmen establish their shops in the native area. Some develop; others are branches of big shops in town.

The third type are Chinese who have contacts with the T'u-szu. They need the Chinese for their knowledge of the Chinese language, script, and customs in their contacts with Chinese. Usually these men are unsuccessful clerks, mostly over forty years old. More intelligent ones are rare: most of them are rascals. They get their income from the T'u-szu, often marry local women, have children. Because economically not independent and separated from other Chinese, they soon, in the second generation, become natives.

Group 1 often has several 1000 mou [Chinese land measure] land and cannot work it all, so they get tenants. Tenants usually are natives, from a large area around, because Chinese are rare. Thus former owners are now tenants. The natives are put down. (*Pien-Chiang lun-wen chi*, vol. 2, no. 9/10, pp. 28–30)

MILITARY CONQUEST

As we have said above, official Chinese historians do not speak of conquest but always seem to be on the defense. They pretend to have to "pacify" the tribes in the South whose unrest (when there was any "unrest") seems to have been occasionally robbing some Chinese merchants, even cutting off some heads for their sacrifices, or resisting when the Chinese took away their land. In the North the situation was different. The northern people were, in historical times, animal breeders (horses, cattle, sheep, and to some degree camels or mules) who did some simple farming, wherever this was possible, to supplement their diet. When and where contacts became closer, they traded animal products for cereals and slowly gave up their own marginally productive farming. Here, as we have seen, the Chinese had an advantage: Their grain could be stored and withheld, while the animal products were perishable. It seems that for such reasons of economic exploitation (withholding of grain or unfair pricing) the northerners began to attack Chinese settlements, and this led to wars. In later periods we see northern nomadic rulers who attacked China for the purpose of gaining better pasture land or simply for wealth or power. Because the nomads attacked mainly with cavalry, the wars between Chinese and Hsiung-nu in the second century B.C. often ended in defeat for the Chinese until they too had developed an effective cavalry. But for many centuries after the Han dynasty China lost control of the key productive area, the northeastern plain, and foreigners from the North ruled there. Only twice did foreigners rule all of China: during the periods of the Mongols (1279–1368) and the Manchus (1644–1911).

When the Chinese were victorious, they slaughtered many animals and captured many horses, thus weakening or even endangering the existence of nomads who were threatened with starvation. They also killed many foreigners. We hear of prisoners, but there is little information as to what happened to them. In only a few cases do we hear that they were settled in China. We mentioned earlier the Hsiung-nu tribes who were settled in parts of Shansi Province, near the border, and who about a century later were strong enough to attack China's capital and to create their own short-lived dynasties. In another case we hear that they were settled farther south, but we do not know what happened. Sources say that prisoners were generally enslaved. The women were given to high military and other officials, who used them in their houses as servants or concubines. The men were also enslaved, often castrated, and employed at the court or in powerful families. But we suspect that this was not the only way they were treated. In wars in the South captured men seem often to have been killed and not taken prisoner, while the women were of value as house slaves. In both cases the prisoners seem to have had only a minimal influence upon China. The gain of territory was, on the other hand, important.

Territorial gains in the North were mainly of strategic value because the land was basically unfit for Chinese agriculture. In medieval times China wanted to keep control over the trade routes to the west of Asia. In modern times the Chinese tried to prevent Russia from gaining control of Chinese Central Asia (Sinkiang). Thus, after a conquest military garrisons were established, in which the soldiers were farmers (in parts of Sinkiang this was possible) during peaceful times; in times of danger, being on the spot, they could hold the area until a larger army from China proper could arrive. Thus, from Han times on, we find Chinese military-agricultural settlements in Central Asia. These, naturally, attracted Chinese merchants, who supplied the soldiers with products from China, sold Chinese wares to the native population, and bought local products for sale in China. In many places in Sinkiang we find "double" cities: In one city lived the local population, while the Chinese lived in an adjacent one. This situation still exists in Sinkiang. Nowadays the settlers are not only soldiers but also people "sent to the land" because, it is said, they are not politically adjusted and should learn by living among the peasants. The Chinese aim here, as in the Soviet Union, is to fill up these colonies with their own people so that the native population will quickly become a minority. This policy is today close to achieving its desired end.

In the South the process was similar. There, too, the soldiers who had "pacified" the native population often remained in new settlements, very often small fortresses, dispersed all over the conquered area. They took over as much land as they needed and became successful farmers. The natives had several choices: Some retreated into the mountains, which the Chinese did not favor because farming was not good. Others became tenants of Chinese or simply servants. The Chinese government sometimes sent groups of prisoners from their prisons under military escort to the South, where they had to remain for life. In a few documented cases these men, with their wives, finally remained in the new place because they had land and could live better than they had been living at home. The last way of settling the new areas was through organized groups of farmers who had found for some reason that they could not make a living at home. With government permission and supplied with passports that allowed them to pass through several provinces, they came to the South, got some land from the government, and, cutting down the heavy forests and digging irrigation ditches, made new and fertile rice paddies.

Many of the Chinese families in the Southern provinces claim that their ancestors lived in Central or even Northeastern China and migrated southward. Some say that they had to leave their homes because the Liao, Chin, or Mongols (who all for a time had conquered North China) had taken away their land. With the exception of insignificant areas, today the whole of South China has a majority of Chinese in a country that some ten centuries ago was the homeland of various tribes. What happened to those tribes will be discussed in Chapter 10.

Before leaving the subject of colonization by conquest, we should note that military conquest in the South, and sometimes also in the North, was often the consequence of diplomacy and the actions of private or state merchants who had supplied information and who asked the government for protection when the native population turned against them.

RELIGIOUS POLICIES

In the European colonization of Africa and South America Christianity was an important element. Many missionaries certainly honestly wanted to save the souls of the heathens; but for others Christianity was a way to "civilize" the "primitives," to make them into real human beings who enjoyed the new rule that had displaced their own rulers. Chinese colonizers, too, from time to time used religion as an element of their policy, though in a way very different from the Europeans. Data on this topic are not numerous and are often so brief that we cannot assess the importance of what is reported.

Confucianism

In effect, Confucianism was the Chinese state religion until 1911; participating in Confucian rituals meant that one regarded oneself as a Chinese. The main teachings an individual had to learn and to apply, which could be acquired only by study of the classical books, were loyalty to the state (in other words, the emperor) and piety toward parents. Passing the civil service examinations was not only the symbol that indicated mastery of the texts, it also opened the door to state employment, even up to the highest offices. "Belief" was not required, as it was for a Christian; behavior and knowledge were sufficient. In Han times the sons of Hsiung-nu leaders often had to come as hostages to the Chinese court and to live there for a long time. These young men were educated like the sons of Chinese officials and learned the same Confucian rules and rites. In theory they, too, could compete for positions in the bureaucracy, though we know of no such actual case. The one Hsiung-nu who attained the highest possible position in the Han times, namely, a guardian of the young Chinese emperor, probably was not educated because he had surrendered to the Chinese as an adult. His descendants may well have been educated, but the sources do not tell us. It is extremely difficult to find out what became of such persons because, the moment they got some education and wanted to adjust to Chinese customs, they gave up their own, foreign, names and adopted typical Chinese names, and we cannot tell whether such people were foreigners or Chinese. The situation was different during the period between 220 and 558, when foreigners controlled North China. In this period some foreigners retained their native names, and official sources include the original foreign names of those who adopted Chinese names. During this time the foreign rulers usually accepted Confucianism, and many of their group studied the Confucian classics.

Buddhism

Between around A.D. 200 and A.D. 800. Buddhism spread all through Central Asia; it may have reached China even earlier, perhaps before 100 B.C. Buddhism was not originally tied to the state but rather ignored it; any person could become a Buddhist, even with no education. When Buddhism came to China, two difficulties arose. First, a true Buddhist was supposed to leave his family, not to marry and produce children. This violated the basic Chinese belief in filial piety. Of course, Buddhist lay people could marry, but the Chinese objected to the propaganda against the family that was taught by the monks. Furthermore, people who entered a Buddhist monastery or nunnery did not have to pay taxes to the government. A common complaint of Chinese scholars was that, for every person who did not work and did not pay taxes, another person would have to work and pay taxes. In medieval times, especially during the Sung dynasty, people who wanted to become monks or nuns had to buy a release form, the cost of which was, in effect a prepayment of taxes that the monk or nun would not pay from then on.

The second difficulty was more serious. The Chinese government had always controlled religion. In Confucianism the cult of Confucius is a part of the state cult; other religions were regarded as of little importance as long as they did not propagate doctrines or rituals that were regarded as dangerous to the state. But Buddhism rejected the state. What, then, would happen when a monk of high rank appeared in audience at court? Would he, like all Chinese officials, make the kowtow to the emperor? Or was the emperor of lower rank than the representative of Buddha? After long discussions a new formula was found: The emperor was not a normal human but a reincarnation of the Buddha of the Future, Maitreya. A monk had to make prostrations in front of the Buddha-emperor, and the emperor was thus acknowledged as superior.

In the first seven centuries A.D. Buddhism spread through most of the Central Asian states and China proper. Non-Chinese rulers of states neighboring China, or those ruling over parts of China, were particularly interested in Buddhism because no foreigner could acquire sufficient knowledge of Chinese classical books and of all the hundreds of rules of behavior a true Chinese scholar or ruler mastered. Thus, they were made to feel inferior to the Chinese. Everybody could accept Buddhism, however, and by the fourth century Buddhism was also a religion to which many Chinese adhered. Buddhist foreign rulers could feel equal to Chinese Buddhists and were friendly toward them.

On the other hand, Chinese from time to time sponsored Buddhism and Manicheism in the neighboring states because they believed that these two religions could weaken the military and political might of the unruly neighbors. In an interesting text a leader of the T'u-chüeh (Kök Türks) who planned to build fortresses, walls, and Buddhist as well as Taoist temples, was warned by one of his advisors:

> This should not be done. The number of us T'u-chüeh is very small, not even one hundredth of the population of the T'ang [Chinese]. That we again and again can resist them we owe to the fact that we migrate in order to find water and grass, that we do not have habitations and live off hunting. All our people are trained in the art of war. When we are strong, we let our soldiers go out on robbery and invasions; when we are weak, we flee into the mountains and forests and hide. Though the soldiers of the Chinese are numerically superior, this does not help them. But when we begin to build fortresses to live in; when we change, when we change our customs, then, one day we will be defeated and certainly be annexed by the Chinese. Also, the teachings in Buddhist and Taoist temples consist of doctrines of goodness and complaisance. This is not the way to war and power. Therefore, we should not build temples. (*Chiu T'ang shu*, 194a; trans. Liu Mao-tsai, p. 173)

Manicheism

Manicheism is an Iranian religion, founded by Mani (died A.D. 276), which contains elements of earlier Iranian Zoroastrism, Buddhism, and Christianity. It spread among the Uygurs and T'u-chüeh in the seventh century A.D. The most famous temple mentioned, the Ta-yün ssu (Temple of the Great Clouds), was built in the Talas River area around A.D. 748, according to the report of a Chinese who visited this temple in 750–751. At about the same time Manichean temples were erected in several districts of China.

Manicheans lived, like Buddhists, on a vegetarian diet and did not drink fermented milk (kumys) or other alcoholic drinks. Chinese anti-Manichean sources report that the believers assembled at night and that immoral behavior during these meetings was common—an accusation normally made by Chinese against religious communities that seemed potentially dangerous politically. At first, the Chinese were sympathetic to Manicheism because they thought this religion should weaken the nomadic societies whose main source of nourishment was meat and milk, and often fermented milk, making them less dangerous. (From time to time we also find Chinese advocating Buddhism among the Northern tribes for the same reason: Buddhist vegetarianism and antifamily attitudes would weaken the nomads.) However, in 843, in an action against Buddhism and other foreign religions, Manichean temples were secularized. From then on Manicheism seems to have gone underground, but its traces can still be seen several centuries later.

Interference in Religion as a Means of Control

The Manchu emperors (1644–1911) in general favored Lamaism, a special Tibetan-Mongol form of Buddhism, because in Mongolia and Tibet—both countries at that time under Chinese domination—Lamaism was widespread, and a fairly high percentage of young men were in monasteries and thus not subject to military service, as well as normally not producing descendants. The Mongols, in recognition of the favors done them, considered the Manchu emperor as an incarnation of the Buddha of Wisdom. When the Manchus strengthened their rule over Tibet, they directly interfered with the Tibetan Lamaism. Because, as we have seen (p. 71), it was possible to arrange that a desirable child became Dalai Lama, a child from a family of status and power was usually chosen. The Manchu emperors requested that the new Dalai Lama should be from a low-ranking family and that one of the Chinese officials in Tibet should "supervise" the selection. This was a way to tighten control over Tibet.

We hear of still other Chinese attempts to influence the religious attitudes of their neighbors. As early as the fifth century a translation of the Chinese classic book of filial piety (Hsiao-ching) was made for the Toba, a tribal federation that ruled over parts of China from the late fourth to the sixth century. The same book was sent to the Chin in the twelfth century and to the Mongols in 1307. In 1571 translations into the Mongol language of those Buddhist books that were most popular in China were sent to the Mongols. In the nineteenth century a Book of Rites (Li kitabi) was promulgated in Sinkiang. This book was not a translation of the Chinese Book of Rites (Li-chi) but an adaptation especially made for Sinkiang's predominantly Muslim and Uygur population.

In the late nineteenth and early twentieth centuries the Chinese government sponsored immigration into Mongolia and Manchuria. In fact, Manchuria soon had a majority of Chinese, and the Manchurian tribes there became a small minority. In 1909 a special school was created to train Chinese who were to become officials in Mongolia. In this school they learned more than just Confucian classics. A similar policy was instituted for the Miao in the South.

More direct policies were used in Sinkiang against the Muslim population. In 1731 the slaughter of cows was forbidden. This was for Chinese not an unusual law; already in the T'ang period slaughter of cows was forbidden from time to time (see p. 64). But the Chinese officials knew very well that Muslims ate only beef and lamb as their religion forbade them to eat pork. Preventing them from eating beef and thus robbing them of an essential part of their food supply was one of the causes for their rising against Chinese domination. Chinese opposition to the Muslims of Sinkiang and the Chinese provinces of Kansu and Shensi addressed itself also to their resistance to Chinese Confucianism and their rule against drinking any kind of alcohol or using opium, both of which were common among the Chinese administrators in the area. Chinese were also against Muslin endogamy—requiring any man or woman who marries a Muslim to become a Muslim before a wedding could be held. Furthermore, the Muslim religious custom of circumcision of boys violated a basic Chinese command of filial piety: No child has the right to mutilate the body his parents gave him. (At present, numerous Chinese, supposedly for medical reasons, practice circumcision of babies.)

In Central Asia the Chinese found not only Muslims as they knew them in China proper but also a new sect (Yasaviyya tariqat), which originated in the eighteenth century in Bukhara and quickly spread into Sinkiang and even into Kansu. The Chinese executed its leader, Ma Ming-hsin, in 1784. However, the sect was aggressive not only against the Chinese but also against the two traditional sects prevailing in Sinkiang (Afaqiyya and Ishaqiyya).

Thus, we cannot say that Chinese were tolerant of religions. As soon as a religion appeared to the government to be politically dangerous or influential, steps were taken toward its suppression. On the other hand, when the religion in a foreign country or a country under China's colonial rule seemed to contain elements that would weaken that society, they tried to sponsor this religion.

MARRIAGE POLICIES

We have mentioned mixed marriages between Chinese "princesses" and the leaders of strong federations of nomadic tribes in North and Northwest China. Such marriages had more than one reason: (1) Because the nomadic rulers also sent one of their daughters to the Chinese court to be the wife of a prince, we can regard these women as a kind of hostage and, therefore, to some degree a guarantee for peaceful relations between China and its northern neighbors. (2) On the occasion of such marriages the women were accompanied by large numbers of servants and other personnel who acted as spies. This was particularly the case of those Chinese who were sent to the court of the nomads. By contrast, the nomads who accompanied their princesses to China were, so far as we know, strictly controlled in their activities and movements.

For the process of ethnic assimilation marriages between ordinary Chinese men and minority women were much more important. Two factors were at work here. A Chinese man who wanted to marry a Chinese woman had to give a bridal gift with the value of at least one year's income. This was thought of as a repayment to the parents of the bride for the cost of raising their daughter from birth to the time of marriage. After all, as soon as she could be valuable to the family as helper in the house or as an income earner, she went to a stranger and worked for him. However, in the South a Chinese could get an indigenous woman for much less money because the standard of living of the minorities was much lower than that of the Chinese.

From the woman's point of view there also was an enticing factor. This could be clearly seen as late as 1974 in Taiwan, where a few (probably around 200,000) tribal people still live very much in their old way in the high mountains. There is hardly any level land, only mountain slopes all around. The slopes are sometimes so steep that the ploughing oxen have to pull the plough with their forelegs kneeling and their rear legs stretched. The work of cultivation cannot be done by a man alone; his wife has to assist him. Yet the wife still has to do all the traditional women's work: cooking, mending cloth, sewing, and raising the children. As the wife of a Chinese, she would not have to work in the fields. Moreover, she would have better clothing and would not have to sew them all by herself. So she is interested in marrying a Chinese when there is opportunity. Her father, too, is not unhappy because, even though the Chinese pays little for the bride according to Chinese prices, it is much more than an indigenous husband would pay.

On the mainland several tribal groups in the South had a relaxed attitude toward chastity. During the festivals the unmarried young people came together, danced together, and could disappear together in the forest. Young men could even visit their girlfriends regularly at night, supposedly in secret, without the knowledge of their parents (a custom which also existed in southern Germany under the name *bungling*). Even a pregnancy was no problem as long as the bride had not yet moved into the house of her husband. We know that Chinese men have taken advantage of such customs and that this has often led them to marry the woman. With modernization and industrialization, especially in Taiwan, almost all Chinese villages have lost most of their younger population to the factories in the cities. The old people often complain about this and state that they will not be able to keep their land much longer because they need the children as helpers, but the children very often do not come, even during harvest time. The same thing happens with the indigenous tribal people of Taiwan: Their sons and daughters, too, go into the cities and work in factories, earning much more than the income of the whole family in their native village. They seem to live together, usually in dormitories where missionaries and others try to protect them from the "evils of the city." But, in spite of this, the young have many possibilities to stroll around and to meet other young people, of their own tribe or Chinese. Women know that, when they marry a Chinese man, they can continue to live in the city, whereas if they married a man of their tribe, they would ultimately return to the mountains, at least for a time. All these factors contribute to the disintegration of the minority society.

We do not have detailed reports about this situation in South China, but we know that China's policy of family planning is applied in the whole country. Its main focus is to induce the population to postpone marriage and thus produce fewer children.

Reactions against Chinese Pressure

When the pressures toward colonization discussed in the last chapter reached a certain point, the thinkers among the minorities became conscious of the dangers threatening their society.

The situation in the North was and still is to some degree, easier than in the South: The northern non-Chinese were at times strong enough to defeat the Chinese and rule over them. When they were eventually defeated, they could retreat to the steppes and deserts of Central Asia, which were not inviting to Chinese settlers. At the worst, Chinese occupation armies would be stationed there, but these soldiers lived in solid houses by themselves, and the tribes did not have to have constant contact with them.

In the South there was much land fit for the Chinese type of agriculture; by force or by sale, therefore, the tribes quickly lost their land. They then had two choices: They could become tenants of new Chinese landlords. As such they had to work harder because of the intensity of Chinese agriculture and the high rent they had to deliver. On the other hand, they could retreat into the high mountains, as did the Taiwanese aborigines, who, we know, lived in the coastal plains down to the seventeenth century. But the mountains could not feed larger populations. In this situation there began a process that went on until the twentieth century and is perhaps still underway: In small groups, often consisting of only one family, the people moved from mountain to moutain, always southward. They crossed the borders of China and flooded into Vietnam and Laos, northern Thailand and Burma. These people, whom our newspapers call *montagnards*, are now outside Chinese jurisdiction, but they still have ties to their relatives within China, speak the same language, and continue their way of life as much as possible when they are not involved against their will in a war among the great powers.

Chinese have also moved south, but for different reasons: They have gone as merchants and have settled in towns and cities all over Southeast Asia, soon reaching higher standards of living than they had in China. The tribal people, meanwhile, continued to live much as they did before.

As we have seen, the tribal people who remained in their mountain retreats were forced into an economic crisis. This was often deepened by their greater and greater dependence on the alcoholic beverages Chinese merchants furnished them. Their own dances and festivals had always been a time of drinking, but their millet brews were not as strong as Chinese wine and especially Chinese brandy. Seeing many of their own men drunk and unable to work, they began to wonder about

Map 4   Chinese Central Asia and Tibet

themselves: Were we not once strong and warlike, and did we not resist the Chinese? Why are we now despised and oppressed by the Chinese?

One possible reaction against such self-doubts is the creation of a mythology that emphasizes the tribe's positive aspects. For example, we can see the version of the tribal myth of the Yao presented earlier (see p. 81) as the Yao's attempt to prove to themselves that they were better than the Chinese and, at the same time, relatives of the Chinese emperor. A similar story, from an area in which, at the time, Tibetan tribes lived, is reported in a source from about the fourth century A.D.: A man has to leave his family and go to war. When her husband does not return after a long time, the wife promises to give her daughter to the man who would bring back her husband. A horse runs away and finally brings the husband back. The horse wants to marry the daughter, according to the promise of the mother. Instead, they kill it and put its skin into the courtyard to dry. The daughter passes by the skin and curses it. Suddenly the skin rises up, envelops the girl, and flies with her onto a tree. This was the origin of the silkworm. This tale can possibly be explained along the following lines: The small-sized horses of China came, until late times, from Tibet to China. Furthermore, there is some indication that silk was invented in the Chinese-Tibetan borderland of present-day Szu-ch'uan Province. Though the mythology of this area is not yet well researched, we do know that the tribes of the area prided themselves that their horse was good and courageous, that the Chinese were treacherous, and that the Chinese owed the knowledge of silk to the tribes. This story can thus be interpreted as having the same theme as the dog story of the Yao: We, the tribal people, have as ancestors animals with special abilities who are better than the Chinese who benefited from the animal.

Among the Eastern Tibetan tribes for whom the horse and the monkey were holy animals, we find the following myth about the origin of the Lolo:

> On a Chinese river came drifting down an orchid-bamboo pipe. This pipe drifted to the shore and broke up. From it came a man. This man, A-tsa, could speak at birth. He lived in a hollow in the ground. He collected food and went hunting and saw, at the bottom of a pear tree, a female monkey which looked like a dog. At first, he was somewhat frightened and did not dare to pass by. Then, as the being did not move, his courage grew. He slowly came closer, picked up a pebble and let it fall. But the dog did not move. So, he came closer to her and touched her body. Soon after, both became enamored and their hearts came together and in the wilderness they became man and wife. Their children are the Lolo. (*Pien-cheng kung-lun*, 3, no. 9, p. 35)

A story told by a Miao, in that part of Szu-ch'uan south of the Yangtse River, contains an element which is already reported almost two thousand years earlier. I give here the modern version, according to Graham (p. 27):

An Ancestor of the Miao

> In ancient times a young unmarried woman was bathing in a pool. The pool was deep and of course she was naked. Suddenly she felt something hard enter her vagina. The water was not very clear, and she saw nothing and supposed that she had accidently run into a wooden snag in the water. She became pregnant and later gave birth to a son who, the son of the Dragon King, was an ancestor of the Miao.

In this and the earlier Lolo myth the tribes are descendants of a supernatural animal, identified with the Chinese dragon. Dragons play a role in Chinese belief as among other functions a symbol of the emperor. The mother of the first emperor of the Han dynasty was impregnated by a dragon; a dragon sat on the chest of the mother of the third emperor of the Han; and at least one of the mythical rulers of China before history also had a dragon as a father. Thus, again in this Miao story, the Miao are as good as the Chinese because their ancestor was an imperial animal.

Even more typical is the following story of the Miao:

The Ancient Miao and the Chinese Were Brothers, or In Ancient Times the Miao and the Chinese Were One Family

> In the earliest times the Chinese and the Miao were one family. The Miao was the older, the more powerful, and the more respected brother, and the Chinese was the younger.

The parents died and were buried. The brothers separated and lost all traces of each other. They both commemorated their ancestors at the same grave, but at different times so that they did not meet. The younger brother, the Chinese, worshipped later in the year, but finally the older brother noticed that somebody was worshipping at the grave of his parents. "Who is doing this, and for what reason?" he asked. Then he began to watch, and caught the younger brother. A quarrel ensued. They did not recognize each other, so each blamed the other for worshipping at his ancestral grave.

Instead of fighting they went to law about it. The official asked the Miao, "What evidence have you that this is your ancestral grave?" He replied, "I have buried a millstone, a certain distance to the right of the grave." He asked the younger brother the same question. He answered, "I have buried a brass gong a certain distance to the left of the grave."

The official sent men to dig and they found both the millstone and the gong. Then it became known that the two were brothers. But in the centuries that followed the descendants of the two brothers grew apart and forgot their common ancestry, and so the Chinese have forgotten it altogether. Moreover, the Chinese descendants have grown more and more powerful and numerous, so that the Miao are now the younger and weaker brothers, and the Chinese are the older and stronger brothers.[1]

This theme—that the tribal people and the Chinese are brothers—still plays a role in today's politics: The modern Chinese speak of the tribal people of the South as their "brothers." However, the Chinese language has no single word for *brother*, but only one for younger and one for older brother. Thus, for Chinese the tribes are the "younger brothers" of China, which means that they should obey their older brother and be guided by him. The story, however, maintains that the Miao were the "older brothers" and that the Chinese forgot this fact and now are stronger, so that they become the "older" brothers. In fact, a myth that seems to be only fragmentary even says that at one time "the Miao . . . gathered a million soldiers and took possession of China. This was a prosperous period for the Miao" (Graham, p. 28). There is no proof of such an event, and we should regard this tale as a part of the traditions discussed here, whose purpose is to show that the Miao tribes are equal to, or even better than, the Chinese.

The following story tells about a war between Chinese, the aggressors, and Miao, in which the Miao were victorious. Though not all details of the story are clear, the content is.

Raising a Big Elephant

When the mother elephant gave birth to the baby elephant, the father elephant loved the baby elephant as people love rice plants. The mother elephant pulled down three leaves and spread a bed for him. The elephant father also pulled some leaves and covered the baby elephant.

One day, when the baby elephant had grown up, they sold the baby elephant to some Chinese. Two Chinese named Wang Chin (King gold) took the elephant to battle and to attack a town and to attack strongholds.

One day the Chinese Wang Chin said something very clearly. He said, "My big elephant is like a general. My elephant is spotted. My big elephant can grab people with his trunk. My elephant's head and feet are spotted."

On another day the man who owned (fed) the big elephant said, "We will lead soldiers to the higher altitudes and go to the city of the emperor called Yin Hsiang City" (Silver flavor city). Then the two big elephants said, "We will lead soldiers and go up above. We will go to the Chinese new barracks. We will tie swords to our bodies" (we will go and fight the Chinese).

When the great elephants fought the Chinese, the Chinese died like clay. They

---

[1]A variation of this story states that when the two brothers first separated, they took a brass gong and broke it in two, each brother burying his piece near the grave. Later, at the official investigation, the two parts fitted together, proving their common ancestry. (Graham, pp. 27–28)

trampled Chinese to death like dust. The big elephants did not believe the words of the Chinese. They helped the Miao fight for land and cities. The big elephants were truly powerful. We want to raise other elephants. The song is ended. (Graham, p. 28)

Another story speaks of an emperor of the Miao who married the daughter of a Chinese emperor because he was so rich that he could make extravagant bridal gifts.

A Miao Prince Married a Chinese Woman

Roaming all over the world stirs my mind. I roam to the Chinese wife's home. The Chinese mother came at first because she wished to prepare silk clothing for her daughter Nts'ai Ngeo. The Chinese husband first came because he wished to prepare satin clothing for his daughter. The silk clothing was green. The satin clothing was a ware-red (pink) color.

That year was a fortunate year for the Miao emperor. He hired all the sedan chairs, coolies, and horses. He hired the players of the jointed bugles and horns to go. He really observed the same customs as the Chinese emperor in marrying a wife. He hired red-scissor people to blow (play) the jointed bugle.[2] He also secured a Lolo older brother to go and beat the great gong. The tunes the red-scissor people played were those of the hawk-cuckoo. They all went to the home of the Chinese woman.

At that time the Chinese girl Nts'ai Ngeo Fong also worked silk clothing and golden ornaments. She also wore silver ornaments and golden bracelets. At that time the Miao emperor brought 3,000 ingots of silver and placed them on the table. He used 300 carriers and carried them to a Chinese man's home.

When the Chinese man saw it he spoke a word about the Miao king having as much silver as there are stones. The Chinese emperor accepted the silver and put it away. His family went to prepare (for the wedding procession), because their daughter was about to start. The 3,000 soldiers of the Miao emperor went forward. Then the young daughter of the Chinese got into the sedan chair. The chair coolies walked very rapidly and in a short time arrived at the flat ground and also at a big field. They heard the iron cannon of the Miao emperor resound like the roar of thunder. The Miao emperor did not know whether the Chinese bride was old or young.

In a moment they arrived at the front door of the Miao emperor. She saw the emperor standing in the middle of the parlor. She also saw that many candles were lighted like bows and arrows.

At that moment the mother of the emperor came out to call into his home the soul of the bride, then, like the Chinese, led the bride out to pay respects in the hall. She first paid respects to the house gods, then to the stove door (this includes the whole stove), then to the Miao ancestors; then she paid respects to Nts'ai's highest heaven. Then she also paid respects to the level earth, then also to the groom's parents, and also to the distant guests of 300 fortified places. She also paid respects to the old people who lived nearby and to the hired help (brothers who helped them). After respects had been paid to all these, then the groom and the bride went into the bedroom. The groom said, "Now we have gotten a Chinese bride like a good official. This Chinese girl has come to make a good breed" (to help create a fine breed of people). (Graham, pp. 29–30)

All these stories tell about the better past in which the Miao were strong and equal to the Chinese. There are other stories in which it is acknowledged that the Miao lost their land and power to the Chinese, but owing to the trickery of the Chinese rather than an honest way.

Chinese Take Possession of the Land of the Miao

Na Bo Seo (great old woman with very long life) arose and opened up the universe. She planted some *mao bai*[3] and the five grains to eat. Her land was very broad. Ye Mang

---

[2]A reddish people, very clever like scissors, whose cleverness makes them excellent musicians when playing the jointed bugle, called in Chinese *sa la tzu.*
[3]*Mao bai* is a grain with fine seeds.

(an old Lolo) arose to turn the animals out to pasture. Ye Mang and a Chinese Yang Tsua arose to carry on mercantile business. Then all the people bartered foodstuffs with each other.

One day Na Bo Seo's many sons arose. The old Chinese man said, "We will all divide the land." The old Lolo men would not consent and arose and went to war. Then Chinese used a big bamboo tube and put in it sulphur and saltpeter and placed it on the road. The Miao used wood set on fire and torches to fight with. They fought several days. The Chinese could not defeat the Lolos and the Miao. The Chinese said, "We need not fight any longer. If we fight any longer more people will be killed. We had better determine the bounds of each other's land and each one himself mark his boundary." They all said, "Quite right." The Chinese went and used stones as boundary markers. The Lolos used wood to mark their boundaries. The Miao used grass and vines for boundary markers.

When they had all established their boundaries the Chinese said, "Such a forest is so big that we cannot see our boundaries. We should burn it with fire so we can see them clearly." Soon after he had said this the Chinese used a torch and burnt up the forest. Then all went to look at their boundaries, but only the Chinese then had boundaries, and the Miao had nothing dependable.

Then the Chinese brought their wives and children to live on the Miao's big plain and the large land by the streams. The Lolos were fierce and would not permit the Chinese to come and live there (on the Lolo lands), and afterward they fought several battles. The Miao could only be guests (renters) of the Chinese and must pay rent every year, and because of this the Chinese without farming are still able to get things to eat; hence they have been called Swa[4] because they are idle rich. The meaning of Mang is fierce, daring, brave, so the Lolos are called Mang. The Chinese saw that the hmong[5] did their farming well, so they called them Miao. This is the source of the three races. (Graham pp. 30–31)

The next story, from the Lolo and only recently collected, I would regard as symbolizing a later stage, the time when the Lolo were already under Chinese domination, had given up hope for a better future, and were trying to show that, morally at least, they were equal to the Chinese because they excelled in the virtue of filial piety and brotherly love.

Formerly there were two brothers, Chang Hsiao and Chang Li. Hsiao was son of the first wife and was very filial to his stepmother.

Once his stepmother got sick. He gave her medicine without any effect, so she awaited death. One day, suddenly, the stepmother said: "If you can get the heart of the phoenix in the emperor's palace, I could be cured." So, Hsiao secretly entered the palace, stole the phoenix, and mixed its flesh with other medicine, and gave it to his stepmother. It really helped her and in a few days she was totally healthy again. But the emperor found out that Hsiao had stolen the phoenix, so he had him apprehended and gave him the death sentence. When his stepmother heard this, she could not bear it, so she said to her own son: "Son, for my sake your brother got the death sentence. His filiality really touches me. You have to go and receive death in his place. Thus, you will do your duty toward him."

Chang Li really obeyed his mother's order, went to the execution place and wanted to be executed instead of his brother. Hsiao was a filial and dutiful son. How could he let his brother die for him? So the one brother would not let the other brother suffer. When the emperor saw that these two brothers were so filial and so dutiful, he was deeply touched. He could not bear to execute them. But as the law of the country was already fixed and punishment could not be stopped, he had the idea to make a straw figure of Chang Hsiao and had that figure executed. Thus, both were pardoned.

Others say that Chang Hsiao was a criminal of the T'ang who came back (to the

---

[4]Swa is the Ch'uan Miao word for Chinese. It means play or be idle and is applied to the Chinese because they are land owners and live on the income from rentals paid by the Miao people, who do the hard work on the soil.

[5]The Miao call themselves *hmong*, but have been named Miao by the Chinese. The word *Miao* means sons of the soil.

court) because of a vow: In a year of the T'ang dynasty there was a disorder in the plains. People suffered and were sick. The T'ang emperor vowed to sacrifice twenty-four heads to heaven. When the disaster was over, Huang Ch'ao and others were to be sacrificed in response to the vow. But Chang Hsiao was pardoned for the same reason as above, because the emperor was honoring his filiality and brotherly love, and sacrificed a straw figure instead. (*Pien-ch'iang lun-wen chi*), vol. 3, no. 9, pp. 27–28)

Here is another significant story, this time from the Mongols in the North. The great mythical hero of Mongol epics, Gesser Khan, upbraids the great emperor of China for his perverse love; instead of being grateful for Gesser Khan's morality, the emperor tries to kill him.

As soon as Gesser Chaghan, the ruler of the ten regions, had all his gifts together, he went to see the Küme Chaghan of China. When he had arrived there, he went straight to his house, his palace, and found Küme Chaghan sitting, holding his dead wife in his arms. Gesser Chaghan said to him: "Chaghan, aren't you acting completely wrong? It is not the custom that a dead and a living person remain united. If they remain united, this is a bad omen for the living. . . . Your reputation and your honor in the world require that you take a new wife and make the people happy and satisfied." Küme Chaghan said: "Who is this crazy man and where is he from? Not in a year, not even in ten years, I will let loose of this, my dead wife." "If this is so, the Chaghan cannot be helped," said Gesser Chagan and went out.

When Küme Chaghan was asleep, Gesser returned, took the dead wife from his lap and put a dead dog into the lap. When Küme Chaghan woke up, he jumped up and cried: "Oh, oh, this man of yesterday told the truth. While my dead wife was with me, she became a dog. Take it away and throw it out." When this was done, one of the doormen said: "Gesser Chaghan entered and took her, your wife away. I was too afraid to be able to cry out." The Chaghan said: "Oh, oh, this Gesser took my wife away. If he had taken what is sinful and pernicious for a living person, it would have been all right. But why did he place a dead dog in my lap? For this, he shall die." After he had said this, he had Gesser thrown into the snake pit.

Gesser, however, squirted some milk from the breasts of a female black eagle on the snakes. This poisoned and killed all the snakes. Then the ruler of the ten regions, Gesser Chaghan, used the big snakes as pillow and the small ones as mattress. After the night, he sang in the morning, when he woke up: "I thought that this Chaghan who had me thrown into the snake pit, was a Chaghan who thought he could kill me by the snakes, but it is just a Chaghan who can be happy that he had me kill his snakes for him. (And so on, with many other attempts to kill Gesser. In the end he forces the emperor of China to give him his daughter in marriage. He lives three years at the court.) (Schmidt, pp. 99–100)

The writer of this epic obviously had not the slightest knowledge of the Chinese court and conditions there, but that does not matter. The epic shows to its Mongol readers that Gesser, their man, is a hero greater than the emperor of China.

Another Mongol epic indicates that one of the most powerful emperors of the Ming dynasty actually was not a Chinese but a Mongol. The story, in brief, goes as follows:

Chu Hung-wu (Chu Yüan-chang, first emperor of the Ming dynasty, 1368–98), before his final victory, defeated the Mongol leader Toghun Temür and pursued him up to the capital city. There he caught a concubine of the emperor who was already two months pregnant. Twelve months later, she gave birth to a son. Two years later she got another son. The first one was Yüan T'ai-tse (First Crown Prince or Yüan Crown Prince), the second was Cheng (True Crown Prince).

After the death of the concubine, Chu Hung-wu had a dream, that a white snake embraced his right knee, a black one his left knee. Before this, they had a fight and the white had almost killed the black one. The next day, his sons had a fight and came to Chu and the older son embraced his right knee, the younger one his left. The emperor thinks now, that the older son is a Mongol. Dignitaries tell him to send him to the passes of Nan-k'ou and to remove all boats from the Yellow River which he has to cross. When he, therefore, cannot cross over and returns, you can kill him, because he has not obeyed your orders. Yüan T'ai-tse asks for the advisor Liu Po-en (1311–1375). He can cross over the river, though there was no ice visible, because under some water was solid ice. A miracle shows him that Peking should be his residence. He makes himself emperor. Chu makes himself emperor of Nanking. When Chu died, Yüan went to Nanking to see his brother. This man had made himself emperor, but he hanged himself, when Yüan arrived. He opened a posthumous letter of his mother which recommends to him to be good to the Mongols. Now, he wanted to abolish the custom of the Chinese who always on the fifteenth day of the eighth month stole Mongol men, killed them and sacrificed their head and their liver to the moon. He changed this to an offering of "moon cakes" made of dough, and from then on Chinese did not kidnap and kill Mongols. (Summarized from Mostaert, pp. 191 ff)

This epic contains a number of details of Chinese history but uses them for its own purposes. The "First Crown Prince" (Yüan T'ai-tse) is actually the greatest emperor of the Ming dynasty, Yung-lo. He is a Mongol, and his name Yüan in this story is at the same time the name of the Mongol dynasty that ruled China from 1277 to 1368 and was destroyed by Chu Hung-wu.

A similar development can be seen also among the tribes in the South of China in a famous Chinese novel, the *Story of the Three Kingdoms*. One of the main heroes in this novel is Chu-ko Liang (A.D. 181–234), the sage advisor of the weak ruler. Among the Nosu, an Eastern Tibetan tribe, Chu-ko Liang is the hero, wise and moral. His enemy Meng, the leader of a tribe from which centuries later came the ruling dynasty of the non-Chinese state of Nan-chao, is strong but mean. There are seven fights between Chu-ko Liang and Meng. Usually, Meng is victorious in the beginning because of his clever strategy and military power, but, finally, Chu-ko Liang always defeats him. In the end Meng surrenders to Chu-ko Liang's superior intelligence, wisdom, and leniency. As an illustration of this story I will give here the description of the fifth fight:

> A fifth time it happened. Mêng retired to a fastness in the mountains where there was a cave approached by only two paths, easily defended. In the valley below there were fevers in the air and four springs which would kill besieging troops. *At one spring dumbness and death came to the drinkers; Sores eating to the bone killed any who touched the second spring; The third turned any black who came near it, and they died; And those who drank of the fourth became cold in the throat, and died of spreading weakness.*
>
> When Chu-ko Liang's patrols returned afflicted with disease, the Marquis was dismayed, but Mêng Huo, rejoicing, complacently called dancers to amuse him in his cups and was betrayed by them and brought once more in bonds to his enemy's camp.
>
> Chu-ko Liang released him at once, for this was an unfair test, and Mêng returned to his mountains. He set guards at the rivers with cross-bows and poisoned arrows, and called in as an ally Prince Pa, who used tigers and leopards and wolves and naked men to fight for him. Chu-ko Liang's armies had never met such foes, and in the first encounter were defeated. But the Marquis quietly fanned himself. He had foreseen this danger, and in his equipment had imitation beasts of silk with clanging brass scales, and chemicals to make fire and smoke issue from their mouth. Ten soldiers manned each beast; a thousand waited for Mêng's host to charge. The living animals fled in terror and a slaughter followed.
>
> There was no need to arrest Mêng Huo and his court this time. They came humbly to the Marquis feigning submission, but the old man was too wise; he had them bound and searched. On every one were sharp knives to kill their arch-enemy. Mêng Huo's heart was not yet won.
>
> For the sixth time he has released. (Broomhall, pp. 140–145)

The process of adjustment to the Chinese is already so far advanced that the Nosu identify with the Chinese and oppose Meng, who after all was once one of their own men.

Still another Chinese hero, Chiang T'ai kung, glorified as the greatest hero in the Chinese novel *Feng-shen yen-i* (*Enfeoffment of the Deities*), became a hero of the Lolo. The Eastern Tibetan Nakhi people changed him into a shamaness, riding on a white horse and commanding the demons. A ballad about him exists among the Thai minority in Kuanghsi Province.

A simple form of reaction to Chinese oppression is to say that they are in reality Chinese. So the Chung-chia in Kueichou say that three tribes of their people left Hunan Province in the tenth century. The Sung-chia say they came from the old state of Sung, centuries before the common era. They claim they were defeated by the Kingdom of Ch'u (in Hunan), and resettled in Kueichou, so they slowly became "barbarians," but they now know Chinese and even Chinese script. Similarly, the Ts'ai tribe believes that their ancestors belonged to the state of Ts'ai in northern China and were resettled by Ch'u in Kueichou. We should perhaps not dismiss such legends as without basis. It is quite possible that individual groups of Chinese were forced or preferred to emigrate to the South in the last three centuries B.C. or in the tenth century A.D.

"REVERSE DISCRIMINATION"

Though the stories the Miao tell about their great victories over the Chinese in early history may be not true or not totally true, we can find numerous cases in which Chinese became slaves of minorities or were ill-treated by them. As we saw in earlier chapters, there were centuries during which the whole of China or larger parts of it were under the domination of foreigners. The most recent example of a minority group's gaining its freedom are the events that led to the creation of the People's Republic of Outer Mongolia. The Mongols there sing about the fights that ended with independence, expressing their hatred for their former masters:

> To take the fortress of Kiachta,
> one does not need a glass lantern.
> We will destroy with iron grenades
> destroy the Chinese invaders who came, decided (to destroy us).

> We set up, at the entrance of the square temple,
> four machine guns
> and defeated the illegal, evil Chinese invaders
> to a saving flight on the shortest road.

> The great People's general
> on the yellowish-red horse
> is a man of great mind
> who has clarified everything. . . .

> Thanks to the comrades who came to help us
> for the first time in the city of Bulak
> for the People's government was proclaimed.

> After they founded the People's Party
> and proclaimed the great aims,
> they brought peace to the masses
> after the destruction of different enemies.
> (Poppe, pp. 37–39)

And soon reverse discrimination is in effect, as we saw in the description on page 129. A Mongol proverb is a typical example of ethnic prejudices: "If a Mongol has nothing to do, he cleans his knife. If a Chinese has nothing to do, he kills his fleas"(Mostaert, p. 521).

Other cases in which Chinese came under the rule of a minority group are not so well documented because we have to rely mainly upon Chinese sources, and they, obviously, are not too interested in publicizing such events. It also seems difficult to establish the exact situation and conditions. I do not speak here of states led and populated by an ethnic group different from the Chinese whose people only later became a minority within China, such as the empire of the Hsiung-nu, which made masses of Chinese prisoners in a number of successful wars. We know of the fates of only a very few individuals. But through archeological discoveries we also know that many Chinese civilians went over to the Hsiung-nu as craftsmen and businessmen. Similarly, the state of Nao-chao, in the area of what is now Yünnan Province in Southwest China, attacked China and captured the provincial capital of Szu-ch'uan province in A.D. 892. Here, too, apparently many Chinese followed the conquerors of their own volition.

Perhaps all through the last centuries, though there are no records of exactly when, some Chinese became the slaves of Lolo tribes in Southwest China. These Lolo, who call themselves the Black Lolo, are the free men in their society; under them we find two other classes, the White Lolo and the Wa-tse. A recent report states that both are either caught or bought and are not Lolo but mainly Chinese. According to this 1943 report (*Pien-cheng kung-lun*, 1, no. 7/8, pp. 77–78, and no. 9, p. 22), they are customarily beaten severely, have to dress in Lolo costume, are not allowed to speak Chinese, have to work hard, are locked in at night, and are given poor food to eat. In addition, they are often tattooed in order to prevent their running away. They are hereditary slaves, and some of them belong to the Lolo "state." In time they are totally "Loloized" and are then allowed to do business for their master, at which point they have a considerable influence. Some are freed and may then own property and cannot be sold; they can even have their own slaves, who have to serve as soldiers as replacement for their White Lolo masters. Nevertheless, they still are lower class people. The reports are not fully clear, but it seems that it is not only Chinese who can become slaves of the Black Lolo, but also members of other tribes, who are then treated just like the Chinese.

So we see that the developments did not always follow only *one* line. Multiple factors decide what steps would occur. When Chinese power in the area in which minorities lived was weak—they had to try to stabilize their rule, and usually the minority-inhabited areas came last. On the side of the minorities, much depended upon their strengh and their morale. But the minorities, especially those in South and Southwest China, were divided into tribes, and resistance against Chinese armies required cooperation among as many tribes as possible, and old enmities between tribes, old jealousies between tribal leaders, were not easily set aside. Moreover, the Chinese did not fight by arms alone. They always tried to find a person, a group, or a tribe who was willing to cooperate with them against the tribes. Such people were won over by gifts or by being given a nominal title that elevated their prestige within their own and neighboring groups. So, overall, the final result of conflicts between Chinese and minorities (with the exception of Outer Mongolia) has always been a victory for the Chinese.

Assimilation and Breakdown (Becoming a "Minority")

THE WISH TO BECOME CHINESE AND THE WILL TO ABANDON ONE'S OWN CULTURE

The comparatively high level of Chinese culture and of the Chinese standard of living induced many of the surrounding people to admire China and made them willing to accept elements of Chinese refined culture. Two statements from Japan are typical of this attitude. The first is by Kumazawa Banzan (1619–1691):

> China is the Middle Country of Heaven and Earth. The heavenly-psycho-physical stuff is bright; the spirit of the land is extremely fine. That is why famous masters in every department of human activity are born there and teach the people in the north, south, east and west. This is as it should be. (quoted from Prasad, vol. 1, p. 19)

The second text is by Asami Keisai (1652–1711):

> The terms "Middle Country" and "barbarians" have long been customary in the Confucian books. In our country [i.e., Japan], Confucian books being flourishingly prevalent, all men literate enough to read them, think of China as the Middle Country, and of our country as barbarian. The more acute of these types sigh and whine—"Ah, that I should be born in this barbarian land!" (Ibid., p. 32)

Warnings against the Chinese

The leaders of neighboring countries as well as leaders of minorities inside China were conscious of the enticements China offered and warned against them. Thus, the Turk Tonyukuk, a man who knew Chinese civilization well because he was educated in China, in the years between 716 to 720 warned his lord, Bilge Khan, strongly against giving up the ancestral nomadic way of life, surrounding his domicile with a wall as the Chinese do, or building temples for Buddha or Lao-tse (see p. 119).

The epitaph for Kültegin, another ruler of the T'u-chüeh (Turks) says:

> In the Ötükän fastnesses there was no real leader, but the Ötükän fastness was just such a country in which it was possible to create a tribal alliance, and it was in this very country that, having settled down, I joined my life with the Chinese. The Chinese people, giving us limitless amounts of gold, silver, alcohol [grain], and silk always had

sweet speech and luxurious treasure, and seducing us with this sweet speech and luxurious treasures they so strongly attracted faraway peoples to themselves, who settled close by, and then absorbed their evil practices. . . . Having given yourselves over to seduction by their sweet words and precious gifts, you, O Turks, have perished in large numbers. . . . Evil people instructed a part of the Turks, saying, "To him who lives far away, the Chinese give poor gifts, but to him who lives close by, they give fine gifts." By these words they instructed you, and now you, people, not possessing true wisdom, have heeded their words, and having approached right up [to China] have perished there in great numbers. (Fairbanks, pp. 71–72)

How this leader (around A.D. 700) wanted to be seen by his people is seen in the following extract. It sounds quite different from the quotation above, as here Kültegin wants to make his men proud and, therefore, unwilling to establish friendly contacts with the Chinese.

Hear these words of mine well and listen hard! Eastwards to the sunrise, southwards to the midday, westwards as far as the sunset, and northwards to the midnight—all the people within these boundaries [are subject to me]. (Kültegin inscription; cited in Tekin, p. 261).

In spite of these words, his short-lived state soon came under Chinese domination.

About 1,200 years later the regent of the Torgut, a Mongol tribal federation, gave a similar warning:

We nomads have no need of the self-interested guardianship of alien powers. We have tolerated it for generations, and the consequence has been the decimation of our people and the corruption of our traditions and our way of life. . . . Our greatest danger lies in the transplantation of the ways of life of neighbouring nations, for these effeminize our people. A good horse and a free steppe under God's heaven is the Mongol's only need, and the nomadic life of his forefathers is his happiness. But so soon as we confine ourselves to the peaceful pastoral life, our restless neighbours seek to change our freedom to slavish subordination. . . . Now by cunning they have put our strength in chains, and our fierceness is powerless against their machines. We have been tossed to and fro between east and west, and we have sought help and sympathy from the one against the other. . . . China's overlordship does not threaten our traditions but brings with it the extermination of the nomads. (Gilmour, pp. 248–249)

And in the South, among the Yao, an *Investiture Book* supposedly dating from 1260–1261, gives their genealogy, the branch families, and the titles of these families, stating that their twelve lineages stem from the six sons and daughters of their first ancestor. The book states: "Daughters should not marry Chinese (*pai-hsing*), they should remain among the Yao, marry there, even marry within the same lineage" (*Pien-ch'iang lun-wen-chi* 1, p. 584).

Dangers from Tribal Leaders

As far as we can see, the danger for the minorities came not from the ordinary tribal men and women, but from their own leaders or leading class, who had to repay loans to the Chinese. So says an Ordos Mongol:

The Grandes who are above us have created a great number of districts. These strange taxes which you put upon us, the masses, cannot be sustained by us.

They are Grandes (venerable) like the sky, but the taxes which they have imposed are intolerable. After they have taxed (every district) by a number of camels and horses, they send (the taxes) to Hua-ma-ch'ih, Ting-pien and An-pien (places at the Chinese Great Wall).

What fine Grandes! What heavy taxes! How can we, who cannot survive any more, how can we pay? These are crazy and ferocious taxes. They tax us so that we give geldings and then the mean Chinese (to whom the Mongol banners owe money) set their value at the price of a donkey. (Our banner) is a flourishing banner. One taxes us to give fine horses and these Chinese beggars evaluate them at the value of a chicken, two years old. (Mostaert, pp. 394–395)

A Chinese text describes a minority leader in Southwest China in A.D. 794:

I-mou-hsün was always lamenting that his land was mean and barbarous, its culture and morality having no contact [with China], parted from and passed over by Chinese civilization, blocked and cut off from the fame and influence [of the emperor]. Thereupon he submitted a formal dispatch [to the court]. . . . He did not consult with his subordinates. He secretly decided on the great plan. Then he sent his envoys off [to the Chinese court] . . . around 794; later he rebelled again against China. (*Man-shu*, p. 28)

This leader must have received assistance from the Chinese in his war against the Tibetans because in the same year he attacked the Tibetans and resettled the prisoners in his own country. The Chinese at the time had attempted to resettle 200,000 free Ts'uan people from the area controlled by I-mou-hsün in districts they controlled, but they disappeared in the mountains. Here, the minorities are victims of an old principle of Chinese policy against neighbors and minorities. A Chinese minister says:

I have learned that for China the far-sighted plan is to fight barbarians with barbarians. . . . Therefore, I propose that intelligent and courageous officers and men . . . be appointed and that we everywhere make treaties with other barbarians in order to attack [the T'u-chüeh] together with them and to defeat them. This means "the tactic of war on two fronts." (*Chiu T'ang shu*, 194a; trans. Liu Mao-tsai, p. 166)

This maxim is repeated in almost the same words in numerous old and later Chinese texts.

As we have seen, the leaders of China's neighbors and minorities were particularly partial to marriage with a Chinese "princess." Here is a letter of the leader of the T'u-chüeh (Turks) to the Chinese emperor (who, however, was not yet officially the emperor):

On the tenth day of the ninth month in the year of the dragon [A.D. 584] the Khagan [name omitted] who is born by heaven, is wise and holy, the son of Heaven, addresses this letter to the emperor of the Great Sui dynasty: "The ambassador [name left out] came to me and transmitted your words to me. I took cognizance of them. Now the emperor [i.e., you] is the father of my wife [i.e., my father-in-law] and I am the husband of his daughter. Thus, I am like his son. Though we live in two different countries, our love for one another is the same. Now, our relationship is solid. May it be so with our children and grandchildren, nay, for ten thousand generations this way. I vow that I will never act against the will [of the emperor]. Heaven may be witness of this vow. All the sheep and horses in my country are also the emperor's and the silk in his country is also mine. Is there still 'mine' and 'yours' between us?" (*Sui-shu*, 84; trans. Liu Mao-tsai, p. 50)

The Turk seems to have hoped that he would be regarded at least as a son-in-law by the emperor. However, when the emperor sent a messenger with a letter to him and the khan did not rise because of his relationship, the ambassador nevertheless asked him to rise. So he had to stand up, kneel down, and put the letter on his head—but then he felt ashamed and he and his court cried (according to Liu Mao-tsai, p. 51). Still, the khans of the Turks did not learn the danger of affiliation with the Chinese.

> A leader of the T'u-chüeh, accompanied by his wife and advisors, received in his tent a Chinese ambassador. He said to him: "The T'u-fan [Tibetans] are descendants of a dog, but the Chinese made a marriage arrangement with them. The Hsi and Ch'i-tan [Mongolian tribes] were once our slaves, yet they, too, married princesses of the Chinese emperor. We, the T'u-chüeh, have several times asked for a marriage, but our request was the only one which was not accepted." The ambassador pointed out that the T'u-chüeh leader nominally is the son of the emperor, because he has received the right to carry the family name of the emperor's lineage, therefore, he could not marry a daughter of the emperor. The leader of the T'u-chüeh answered: "The two other barbarian tribes [Hsi and Ch'i-tan] also received the family name of the emperor, yet they were allowed to marry princesses. Why could one not follow that precedent? In addition, we have heard that none of the princesses which came to the barbarians [as wives] were real daughters of the emperor. When we now ask for a marriage, we do not care whether we get a real or a fake princess. We have often asked for a princess and never got one. We really feel shamed in the face of the other barbarians." (*Chiu T'ang shu*, 194a; trans. Liu Mao-tsai, p. 176)

The khan wants to have a Chinese wife purely as a matter of prestige; whether or not she is a real princess is unimportant.

Another ideal of the foreigners was to be allowed to live at the Chinese court and to participate in the glory of receptions. Here, a Chinese minister warns the emperor. He is against mixing foreigners and Chinese as this may only lead to espionage against China:

> I have heard that barbarians and Chinese were prevented from living together and the barbarians, already in earlier times, were caused to live far away, outside the borders. From time to time they came and had an audience and afterwards returned home when they had finished their business. . . . Since the Han and Wei times [A.D. 25–264] they have adopted Chinese dress and headgear and built houses in the capital. They were not permitted to go home. Comparing the advantages and disadvantages [of these two policies] . . . it is advantageous to protect the borders; but to keep the sons of barbarians as hostages is disadvantageous. . . . I have seen that the T'u-chüeh, T'u-fan and Ch'i-tan during their stay at court [as hostages] until now have all received preferential treatment. They have occupied military offices, entered the imperial school, changed their felt dresses and learned Chinese. They have studied the successes and failures in maps and history books and found out about the difficult as well as the easy passes in mountains and rivers. Our state has the glory to have civilized these barbarians, but the sons of wolves are ungrateful. They certainly will cause trouble later. (*T'ang-shu*, 112; trans. Liu Mao-tsai, p. 309)

Around A.D. 607 a ruler of the T'u-chüeh asked the Chinese emperor to be allowed to dress in the Chinese way as a symbol of his devotion to China. This was, of course, not really the reason he wanted a Chinese costume—he meant to get a court costume, which would give him status in the Chinese court ceremonial and would strengthen his prestige among his own people. The emperor of China, knowing this, rejected the request with the following words:

> Since the creation of the state by early rulers, the customs of barbarians and of Chinese are different; and in educating people, no sage would attempt to change the customs. . . . [To change] neither corresponds to the rule to adapt to [the conditions of] nature nor the sagacity of a ruler to accept everybody. The differences in dress are a [differentiating] symbol, differentiating between those who live far away and us. In general, the differences between people correspond to the will of heaven and earth. (*Sui-shu*, 84; trans. Liu Mao-tsai, p. 62)

FRONTIER FEUDALISM

The concept of a "frontier feudalism," suggested by Owen Lattimore, seems to be the best conceptualization of processes that went on along the borders between independent tribes and the Chinese Empire. We might even ask whether this theory would not explain the origins of feudalism in Europe better than the existing theories.

Steps in the Process

Let me outline the process in general. Once the Chinese state was created and began to expand, it came in contact with the surrounding non-Chinese. These were organized, with the exception of some very simple societies, in the form of tribes with a tribal leader, often supported by some assistants or councillors. As we have seen, the tribes that lived in the steppe and desert areas of the North created, from at least the third century B.C. on, tribal federations that were strong enough to resist China or, in some periods, even to conquer parts or all of China.

In the areas where groups lived either by a mixed economy (some animal keeping plus simple farming) or by simple farming (with digging stick or early forms of a plow), or even by collecting food and hunting, we also find tribes ruled by a tribal chief. Larger organizations were formed only in cases of military emergencies and lasted only a short time. The office of tribal chief seems to have been hereditary; a tribe may have had several clans, but only one clan supplied the leader.

The next step was an influx of Chinese merchants and probably also some settlers. When this situation created tensions or conflicts, the Chinese government stepped in and "pacified" the area; in other words, they created fortresses and walled towns for the protection of Chinese citizens. This was the time at which what we call frontier feudalism came into being. It was the time when Chinese were not yet interested in occupying and administering the areas in which the natives lived but were concerned only that the natives were quiet. Tribal chieftains were invited to visit the nearest Chinese administrator, the military governor or the civil magistrate. They brought gifts and received gifts in return, especially Chinese formal costumes. Some of them seem to have been allowed to go to the Chinese court and to appear at the official reception of the emperor. In this case they got official costumes and a title, as well as confirmation of their position. The title they received was not a rank within the Chinese bureaucracy but a special one, created for their position. For the Chinese all this meant only that the chieftain was pacified and would refrain from attacks against the Chinese in his area. For the chieftain it meant much more: He would now appear in the eyes of his tribe as a powerful man having close connections with the Chinese emperor or at least with the nearest Chinese military or civil administrator. Processes of this kind seem to have been common at least from the third century A.D. on. The fully developed form, known under the name *t'u-szu* (native administration system) began during the late fourteenth century and lasted almost to the present time.

Organization and Administration

The Chinese regarded the tribal chief not just as a head man (*t'ou-mu*) but as a special kind of official. Whereas all Chinese officials were constantly moved and could not stay in one place for more than three years (in most periods of history), this native administrator inherited his position. From the point of view of the natives, their former head man was now a glorified person of high status, and so he should have a staff as every high Chinese official had. His new dignity was visible in the way he dressed: in Chinese official costume and with the insignia of a Chinese official. Just as there were levels of provincial administration, there now appeared among the natives different levels of government. The highest one was equal to a Chinese prefecture (*fu*), the next to a Chinese larger district (*chou*), the lowest to a Chinese ordinary district (*hsien*).

The highest administrator set up a number of departments, such as Department of War, Department of Finance, and so on. The leaders of these departments were called "great chieftains" and were sons, brothers, or other relatives of the highest leader. Instead of salary, as in China, they each got a piece of land from which they would draw their income. One study, made in the province of Yünnan, states that, in all, the highest chief had 205 court officials. Apart from the great chieftains there were four lower grades, comprising the keepers of bows, the financial commissary, the generals, and the medical doctors. Next came the military advisors, chief of prisons, and hunting helpers; followed by the court historian, chief of the fish ponds, and controller of servants. Then came the master of ceremonies, the kitchen-chief, the controller of slaves, and 150 pages, that is, personal attendants of the chief. The administration's 205 court officials were all hereditary and all got their income from the rent of land. Ch'en Han-sheng reports that the income of the chief was 357,148 pounds of rice per year. Thus, we have here what we may call feudalism: an hereditary upper class that supplies the administrators. The latter are ranked in higher and lower classes and receive their income from land given to them by the leader as hereditary property.

The local units, that is villages or hamlets, were administered again by a hereditary native administrator (t'u-szu), formerly a tribal chief. To him belonged some pieces of land as personal property, just as the central administrator had such private property. This land was cultivated by the villagers collectively, and they had to give 30 percent of the harvest to their "lord," who paid his own servants from this income and whose total income was several hundred or thousand loads of rice. The rest of the land, mostly not rice fields, was "communal property." For example, in the case studied by Ch'en Han-sheng (*Frontier Land Systems in Southernmost China*), and confirmed by an earlier report (*Ti-li hsüeh pao*, 6, 1939, pp. 31ff), about three-quarters of the land was village land and paid no taxes. Each family had a lot, based on the household, not on the number of individuals, and every year the lots were redistributed. They usually cultivated only dry rice—that is, hill rice—whereas the administrators usually had irrigated fields that produced wet rice and gave a much higher yield. The unused forests and hills were also communal property. Whoever wanted to do so could cut down trees and create new fields; however, these fields still remained communal property. But nonrotating fields tend soon to become private property.

In China's Ming period (1368–1644), 359 t'u-szu existed in six provinces of Southwest and South China, the largest number being in the province of Kuanghsi (167), followed by Yünnan (151). Under the Manchu dynasty the number in Yünnan increased to 157. In 1935, 113 of these still existed (*Pien-ch'iang lun-wen chi*, vol. 1, no. 9/10, p. 12).

The Position of the Tribal People

In time, with the strengthening of the power of the Chinese government, one t'u-szu after another was replaced by a Chinese, until in the end the area came under regular Chinese administration. The natives thus became Chinese citizens, though they did not have all the rights of citizens. Their status down to the middle, or probably even the end, of the eighteenth century was the same as that of the castes discussed in Chapter 6. We also hear that there were occasionally expatriate Chinese who settled in such areas and got control over them, making themselves lords and governing independently of the Chinese government. Some are even said to have induced the basically peaceful Miao to join the Chinese.

For the Chinese the t'u-szu system had the advantage of keeping the native tribes relatively quiet, while their administration and control were not an expense. We do not know, because available reports are too incomplete, but we can imagine that the t'u-szu and the still higher great chiefs used their income to buy Chinese luxury articles and were more and more influenced by Chinese habits, while ordinary village people remained much as they had been.

An alternative development process is possible, at least in certain periods. We have several cases in which half-independent native societies developed into real states and gained their independence. This was possible when China was weak. The state of Nan-chao, which flourished in the modern province of Yünnan (629–937, followed by a state called Ta-li, which existed until about 1255) is the most important of such states. It came into existence when people of apparently Tibetan stock conquered a sedentary population of Thai. A class-structured society evolved, headed by the Tibetan Mêng family. One feudal state thus won total independence from China. China was for long periods forced to recognize Nan-chao. At first, there was a period of friendship because the Chinese wanted to use Nan-chao against the Tibetans, with whom they were at war. But the Chinese attempted to conquer Nan-chao in the eighth and early ninth centuries, resulting in large losses of Chinese lives. A political crisis in Nan-chao around 880 led to the end of the state, whose ruling family of some 800 persons was murdered. The successor state, Ta-li, was destroyed by the Mongol armies, and the Chinese Ming dynasty took the area over when they expelled the Mongols from China. Since then this area has been a Chinese province—one that has many minorities.

CULTURAL ASSIMILATION AND SOCIAL BREAKDOWN

Though Nan-chao's population was non-Chinese, they adopted Chinese culture fully. This can be seen in two areas. First of all, they learned the Chinese script and used it at home and in correspondence with China. Secondly, the rulers and their court adopted Chinese Confucianism. In both regards Nan-chao is an exception.

The Influence of Chinese Script

Other tribes along the borders of China or within China created their own scripts. The writing of the states of the Kitans (Liao) and Jurchens (Chin) was modeled upon the Chinese script; in other words, the symbols look almost like Chinese, but they have totally different meanings. The Lolo and other tribes, some of the Miao, for instance, seem to have started out with a pictorial script that does not attempt to express the sound of words, or even words, but only expresses concepts, which could, when necessary, be translated into sentences and words. Some of these scripts have been deciphered and experiments with them show clearly that a country without a writing system can easily create its own, unique system, once it has understood the basic principle involved. Therefore, the attempts of earlier sinologists to prove that the Chinese script is a loan from the Sumerians or Akkadians in the West are unconvincing. Even if the Chinese were in some sort of contact with western Asia around 2000 B.C. and created their own script later, the most they would have borrowed was the *idea* of writing.

Religion

Most neighbors of China understood that, even with a Confucian education, they would not be regarded as culturally or socially equal to the Chinese.

We mentioned above (p. 118) that rulers of China's neighbors or minorities in China had a tendency to embrace Buddhism, although their people seem to have retained their indigenous religions, which we often call shamanism.

There seems to have been an early connection between Chinese Taoism and shamanism. For instance, the "Step of Yü" (Yü-pu), an essential element in the Taoist ritual to the present time, is a form of shamanism (see Granet), and trance, a typical part of shamanism, is still today connected with folk Taoism. One of the centers of early religious Taoism was in the province of Szu-ch'uan, which at the time (in the second century A.D. and later) was still inhabited by many non-Chinese tribes, among whom shamanism flourished. Some highly interesting documents were discovered by Japanese scholars in northern Thailand among the Yao tribes; the documents, they say, came from China. Professor Y. Shiratori (pp. 334–335) says that "the language of the Yao in these documents is written in Chinese characters," but that they include so many modified Chinese characters and unique expressions peculiar to the Yao people that we cannot read them easily. The age of these texts is uncertain because, whenever the texts became "too tattered to read the titles or had many textual omissions on account of damage," they were recopied. Some texts are written in a good hand, most probably by a Chinese scribe, while others reveal the hand of a less educated man.

Some of the published texts contain prayers to be used in ceremonies by the shaman, such as ceremonials for the ancestral cult or prayers for the souls of persons whose corpses have not been found. There is a ritual that asks the spirit of the forest to move away so that good spirits can come and protect the new settlers, who want to build a house in the mountains. There are incantations used when children or domestic animals are sick; prayers to stars that influence the fate of individual persons; a prayer by women to the mythical ancestor of the Yao, P'an-ku; a booklet describing the hells and the judgment of good and evil there; and so on.

All these texts are quite similar to Taoist sacred texts; like them, they show some influence of Buddhism, but they are original creations to be used by the shaman-priests of the Yao. Are these texts a creation of the Yao influenced by Chinese Taoism? Or do they represent beliefs that were once dominant in Southwest China, whose early forms became the material on which Chinese Taoism grew? No sure answer is possible yet. On the basis of the fact that we have Taoist texts of similar character for more than 1,500 years, we can say that the Yao may have learned from Taoism. Furthermore, the Chinese script seems to be a late borrowing. Therefore, this religion may be an influence of China upon the original shamanistic religion of the Yao. We might add here that the use of Chinese script to express a non-Chinese language has its parallel in Chinese folk literature, which uses standard Chinese script to express a local Chinese dialect, making such texts almost unintelligible to educated Chinese who know only Mandarin.

Among the Lolo of Kuanghsi Province we also find holy texts. They are written not in Chinese but in Lolo script. Down to the present time the Lolo had two types of shamans. Those who use these texts are called *pei-mao*. Their profession is most often hereditary, but they undergo a training period of three to five years. The other type of shaman, called *tuan-kung*,[1] is illiterate and can use only incantations that are given by a deity. They often cure sick people, using a drum. When the drum is beaten for some time, they enter into trance and, in that state, are able to say which deity has possessed them. They continue to drum and dance and then begin to answer questions asked by the audience. The pei-mao venerate an ancestral master, and their performances are closely connected with their belief about the origin of the world and humanity, which has many parallels in other parts of Asia and the world. In addition, the pei-mao manipulate oracles of different kinds, one a type of oracle the Chinese also have.

Chinese officials have not recognized this cult of the pei-mao as a religion but have tried to restrict it, saying that such cults are "illicit"—a term used often even inside purely Chinese areas as a pretext to justify the destruction of temples. Chinese authorities declared that a temple should have an official permit to be allowed to exist. Moreover, they claimed that the local native cults wasted too much money, and their sacrifices of oxen were economically harmful. And they were opposed to the buffalo fights the Miao loved.

Law

As soon as they could, the Chinese also abolished the tribal system of justice. Most important in this practice was the custom of blood revenge, which formerly existed in China and still occasionally occurs among Chinese. Among the tribes it was abolished in 1666. This change of law had consequences similar to the introduction of British colonial law in India: The tribes became

> more litigious than the Chinese. . . . In many cases the affair is brought before the local headman, but on these occasions it is difficult to satisfy both parties, and the loser is almost certain to carry the case before the district magistrate. This love of litigation is encouraged by the secretaries and underlings in the various yamen, who depend for their living principally on the law cases, civil and criminal, brought before the magistrate. (Clarke, p. 27)

Next came the confiscation of the tribes' weapons and the prohibition against making weapons. Of course, ordinary Chinese citizens were not allowed to possess weapons either—only soldiers had them; but for the tribes this law meant that further resistance against Chinese became impossible unless they could acquire weapons by smuggling or bribery. As soon as possible, the tribes were required to remit taxes through their t'u-szu and to give military assistance when requested by Chinese authorities. In recent times they were not allowed to make political

[1] *Tuan-kung* is an antiquated folk designation for government officials used among Chinese.

agreements with foreign countries or with the Chinese central government; they were kept under the local, provincial administration.

Courtship and Marriage

The natives loved festivals and dances. Their "moon dances" took place in the open air under the light of the moon. The mouth organ was played, and much alcohol consumed. On this occasion young men and women met, and love affairs began, as we have seen (p. 82). Chinese officials tried to forbid these festivals and sponsored the Chinese form of marriage through a matchmaker who brought the parents of the young man and woman together. An early observer writes that

> many of their marriages are the result of mutual liking. Not infrequently, however, a girl is practically sold for money to a husband chosen by the parents, and in these cases the result is often disastrous. The young woman will probably run away from her husband's home and continue to meet her lover. (Clarke, p. 29)

According to Chinese morality, this was an impossible type of behavior. As in other parts of the world when marriage rules were changed, common reactions were an unusual number of suicides, mainly by young women, but double suicides are also reported. Such love suicides are not rare among the Taiwanese indigenous tribes when the parents object to love matches. After the Revolution the Chinese government began to introduce among the tribes the same system of partner selection sponsored in the whole country.

The theme of love and songs occurs in texts from the seventeenth century on in Kuangtung Province, in an area formerly inhabited by Chuang tribes. The heroine is Liu San-mei (the "third sister"). In a later version a *hsiu-ts'ai*, a young Chinese scholar, comes to her village with a boatload of lyrics because he wants to defeat Miss Liu in a song contest. In the first contest he cannot answer her poem with a counter poem, and when he rams the boat on a rock, the books are lost. He then has a second contest with her on a mountain. People admire the two, but the local Chinese gentry, thinking she is seducing the young Chinese, arrest her, and nobody knows what happens to her. A rock on which she had been sitting is venerated, and songs now come out of the rock. To stop this miracle, one of the gentry smears dog blood on the rock to silence it. In still another version, Miss Liu and the scholar sing for seven days, and in the end both change into rocks (Liang, pp. 156–158).

Chinese officials also disapproved of mixed marriages between a Chinese man and an aboriginal woman out of fear that such Chinese would turn into Miao (or any other non-Chinese ethnic group) and become anti-Chinese. Certain tribes had not only matrilocality (that is, the husband moves into the house of his in-laws) but also matrilinear inheritance rules (property and rank are inherited by the daughter), both customs disapproved by Chinese. When the t'u-szu system (and this was of course a Chinese-inspired system) was introduced, the t'u-szu practiced matrilinear inheritance but patrilocality, though people stuck to their customs until the Chinese could force them to change.

Chinese Influence on Other Customs

From the eighteenth century on the Chinese created schools in the minority areas for the t'u-szu's children. This was politically important because these children would later take over the jobs of their fathers. One of the most important texts they would study was the *Holy Edict* (*sheng-yü*), a moralistic document, from time to time revised and reissued, which the emperor issued as guidance for all Chinese. Here was one more way to make at least the rulers of the tribes good, reliable Chinese citizens.

Another, less important, change concerned burial customs. Some minorities practiced cremation of the dead. This may have been introduced among them by Buddhist missionaries; it also spread in Buddhist circles in medieval China. In later centuries Chinese officials forbade cremation among the tribes and forced them to adopt the costly Chinese way of burial. One reason may have been to help in introducing the ancestral cult for which it is essential that the dead person be buried, not cremated.

There is no doubt that the southern tribes always drank their own alcoholic beverages during their festivals. The same is true with the aborigines of Taiwan. Drinking is mentioned in early reports about them, and today alcoholism is a real danger in their society. They drink excessively during all festivals and believe that a man who does not drink, fight, or hunt is not a real man and will have difficulties in finding a wife. An early twentieth-century missionary says about the tribes in Kueichou:

> Drink is, we believe, in most cases the cause of their poverty and degradation. . . . We cannot remember that we ever saw an intoxicated Chinese woman. But Miao women glory in their shame and are not infrequently seen hilariously, helplessly drunk, parading or trying to parade, along the village street. (Clarke, p. 34)

And a Chinese visitor among the Mongols (Ma Ho-t'ien, p. 77) says that the Mongols drink more than either the Chinese, who are well known not to be great drinkers, or the Russians, who are, on the contrary, known as heavy drinkers. One can see Mongol men and women drunk on the streets. Chinese businessmen exploit this situation by making contracts with Mongols when the latter are drunk.

Drinking can be cause for impoverishment, which often forces women to become prostitutes. Ma says that Mongol girls live off and with Chinese. The same happened, and still happens, among the aborigines in the South. Another consequence of impoverishment is thievery. At the time when Clarke was a missionary in Kueichou (the mission there began in 1896), many local Chung-chia tribal people claimed to be Chinese. However, Clarke comments:

> We do not think the claim of the Chung-chia to be Chinese has done them any good. They appear to have all the defects of the Chinese and none of their better qualities. . . . The Chinese say that every Chung-chia is a thief, and from what we know of them, we should not feel justified in denying the charge. (p. 107)

Discrimination against Tribal Peoples

Chinese and tribal people lived together, as we have pointed out several times, often for centuries without changing their habits, language, or dress. Here, I give a report from Chou Ch'ü-fei who lived in Kuanghsi Province in 1172–1173 and writes about the Ch'in district:

> The population in the district consists of five groups. The first group are the natives, i.e., the old race of Lo-yüeh. They live in villages and look mean and coarse. They form with their lips and tongues the most diverse sounds which are impossible to understand and which are called the Lo language.

The second group is called the "North people." Their language is easy to understand, but mixed with southern elements. They are originally refugees from the Northwest who settled after the uprisings during the Five Dynasties period (907–960) in Ch'in and were entered into the population registers.

The third group are the Li people. This refers to those who in the history books are called "Li-yao." This group settled separately from the settlements of the other southern barbarians. They are superstitious and remind us of wild animals. Their language is totally unintelligible.

The fourth group are the so-called "Bow-plowers." They are really people from Fukien who perform police services and at the same time engage in farming. Their sons and grandsons speak only Fukienese.

The fifth group are the Tan who live in boats on the sea. Their language is similar to those spoken in the border area between Fukien and Kuangtung, but is also mixed with languages of Kuangtung and Kuanghsi. (*Ling wai tai-ta*, 3.24; trans. Netolitzki, p. 63)

Of these five ethnic groups the first and third are natives of the area. The second and fourth are Chinese, but immigrants from different parts of China, speaking different dialects of Chinese. The fifth group is also a minority (see p. 88) but one that immigrated along the rivers into Kuanghsi Province. What is of interest here is the way Chou Ch'ü-fei speaks of the indigenous people: "They look mean and coarse"; "they remind us of wild animals." Even in the twentieth century, when the Miao tribes of the borderland between the provinces of Hunan and Kueichou are integrated, serve (before the Revolution) in the armies of different warlords, and dress like Chinese, the discrimination remains:

At Chen-kan, within the circumference of the round city wall inlaid with stones, are Miao people comprising one out of every three persons, and Han people who have been transported here from elsewhere making up the other two-thirds, living together interspersed. Although the majority of the Miao still live outside the city, you can almost say that there has been a mutual assimilation in customs and ethnic characteristics, like the alloying of tin and lead in the making of a pot. This has been going on for more than a century. Therefore in recent times there has been a uniform type of person, which may be spoken of by the seemingly abusive term, "half-breed" (*tsa-chung*). They are very, very numerous. Those who have just come to the city from the area around Tsung-ping-ying ("Brigade General's Camp"), or the Miao districts near Kweichow, we can of course identify as "*lao-keng*" [Miao] just by looking at the way they walk, even though they may have changed [into Chinese] clothing. But if a person has to say on which side a particular Wu or Yang family ultimately belongs? This is not only difficult, it's impossible! If it can be agreed that "Miao women are particularly beautiful," then we can only say that all Wu and Yang families who have beautiful women must be Miao. But this, needless to say, is a joke. Perhaps the two families themselves have no way of knowing who are their ancestors. (Kinkley, p. 247)

The author, a very liberal man for his time, admits that racially there is no difference between Chinese and Miao, perhaps because of early intermarriages generations back. But those who want to discriminate still think they can detect ethnicity by observing such traits as manner of walking. The same is true for Taiwan: Many Chinese and, following them, foreigners, think that they can in every case say who is a "Chinese" and who a "montagnard" (*kao-shan hsiung-ti*). If one of the Taiwanese aborigine groups is physically different from local Chinese, it may be the A-mi,[2] who seem to have larger stature, a certain pink shade of skin, and larger, rounder eyes. Anthropologists believe that they may be related to aborigines of the Micronesian islands, such as Yap and Ponape, who came to Taiwan as result of

---

[2]Not to be confused with the Yami on Lan-tao Island (Orchid Island) at the south end of Taiwan.

shipwrecks. But all other tribes have the same height, eyes, and skin color as the Chinese. Their hair may have been a bit less straight than Chinese hair, but, with the spread of curling the hair by Chinese, even this trait cannot be relied upon for distinguishing them from Chinese.

Discrimination continues even when a minority lives where the military is supposed to protect them. Here is a report from Inner Mongolia from the early years of this century:

> Mongols under Chinese government seem to have no protection at all. A band of robbers has only to appear, and the country far and near is at their mercy. . . . The officers at the nearer military centers may bestir themselves as they like, the military organizations are such that no protective force can appear on the scene till long, perhaps months, after the country has been "eaten," and the inhabitants dispersed or slain. (Gilmour, pp. 366–367)

But even much worse things can happen. The following event, described by Shen Ts'ung-wen, one of the foremost writers of the twentieth century, happened in 1911 in his home town in western Hunan Province:

> A presage of change for the Feng-huang settlement and a reminder of the terrible racial conflict of the past came with a 1911 attempt at revolution. The uprising at Feng-huang, aimed at the circuit and *chen* yamens [administrative offices], was planned long in advance by the city gentry—including Shen's father and military uncles, as well as the Miao cousin—with the cooperation of merchants, who were mostly from outside provinces. Swords, spears, and home-made guns were the major weapons, although the Shens had some rifles. [Shen's] *Autobiography* intimates that Miao from the countryside served as much of the cannon fodder, but offers no hint as to whether they were under military or secret society organization. They were to scale the city wall late at night with freshly made bamboo ladders, but the garrison army could not be won over, and the revolt failed. Therefore when Ts'ung-wen awoke the next morning, his brothers and sisters were already hidden in Miao caves, but some of his uncles were among the several thousand revolutionaries killed. He gazed at a string of human ears, and searched for his Miao cousin's face among the 410 bloody heads dangling from slats of the captured scaling ladders displayed before the yamen. At this age, he could only understand "rebellion" through local operas and folk tales. Here was the concrete embodiment of "heads piled up in a mountain; blood, flowing to become a river."
>
> Yet the killing had just begun. Rather than acknowledge the presence of anti-dynastic conspiracy, local officials declared that there had been a Miao rebellion, and sent troops out to the Miao *chai* to arrest and summarily decapitate 100 "rebels" daily. In the confusion of mass executions, still accomplished by 20 swordsmen, the prisoners were not always stripped or bound. Prisoners who stood far away were mistaken for onlookers; a few gaping country people understood their plight only when made to kneel. Burial was neglected with the approach of cold weather; four to five hundred corpses were strewn along the river bank at any given time. After a month of this near genocide, several powerful gentry—themselves the undetected conspirators who had led the Miao into defeat—jointly petitioned the governor that further killing be limited and selective.
>
> The trial by ordeal then devised and the passive submission of innocent Miao peasants to their god's decision that they should die was an awesome demonstration of religious fatalism in the Miao country. The one or two hundred suspects arrested daily, nearly all innocent (as Shen no doubt learned from his father, a plotter), were made to throw bamboo divination rods before the Heavenly King (T'ien Wang, a Miao god) in his temple. The accused had only two chances in three of survival, but all accepted the heavenly verdict in silence. Shen Ts'ung-wen was allowed outside to watch these ceremonies and to test the keenness of his vision with little friends as they counted corpses across the river from atop the city wall. Shen reflected: "When I began to know 'human life,' what I knew was precisely this." (Kinkley, pp. 38–39)

Numerous similar examples of genocide can be found in Chinese history. Shen, who may have had Miao blood in his veins (his grandmother seems to have been a Miao), admired the Miao and expresses this many times in his diary. He accuses the Chinese officials not only of this bloodbath but for their policy in general and defends the Miao:

> Not allowing any of the Miao people an opportunity to learn, or to work, not permitting them to settle in the big cities, but only driving them up into the deep mountains to pass their lives in utmost simplicity, while still requiring them to pay grain and taxes, and to subscribe to unredeemable military bonds, let work obligations weigh down upon their bodies, and do drudgery into old age until they die—this is the kindness Han people show the Miao people. When taxes are too onerous and the harvest is meager, they sell their sons and daughters into lifelong bondage to the Han people at a very low price, hoping that this way they can save themselves and preserve their children—this, too, is the kindness the Han people show the Miao people. [The Miao] accept the fate decreed by the Han people and Heaven above, knowing neither ill will nor resentment, but living on, dispirited, because they are Miao-tzu, and not people. For the fact that they feel they are Miao-tzu and not people, we ought to thank the high level Chinese national officials of a past era. It was they who took these "things" to be a species apart and who wrote the laws with the blood of massacre, causing [the Miao] to be obedient ever after. (Kinkley, p. 278)

Especially in Ming times and in the eighteenth century there are reports of uprisings of the tribes in the southwestern provinces almost yearly. The most important ones in the province of Kueichou happened in 1734–1736 and 1795–1806. These uprisings are described in detail in special monographs edited by imperial order.

In this chapter we have discussed the problems that developed when Chinese settlers and, following them, Chinese administrators moved into areas originally inhabited by non Chinese only—whether land that had long been officially regarded by the Chinese government as "China" or whether it was integrated into China only after a more recent conquest. The idea that a minority should have a right to live according to its own customs and laws is really a very recent one, stimulated by President Wilson's statements at the end of World War I. Before this, Chinese, as well as people in other countries, were convinced that people living in what they regarded as *their* country should accept laws and customs of the country, be loyal to the government, and become "civilized." No doubt many administrators in China before the 1948 revolution acted in a humane spirit and tried to help the non-Chinese, to become "real," civilized Chinese. However soldiers, merchants, and often administrators too often behaved quite differently, exploiting the non-Chinese, taking their property and frequently their women by force.

The non-Chinese found themselves in a dilemma: Even if they had been of good will, they saw and felt that Chinese looked down upon them. So they created stories (fantasies, we may say) that they were better than the Chinese, or at least "brothers" of the Chinese with whom they once lived in harmony. At a later stage they fought the Chinese in wars that, as we have seen, sometimes lasted for centuries. At a still later stage they sank into despair, bought the alcohol the Chinese were only too willing to sell them in the hope that they might forget their misery and be happy for at least some hours. But the cost of the alcohol left them in debt, and so they lost their fields to Chinese settlers and—at best—become tenants of Chinese, if they did not have to move into cities as unskilled laborers. And they often lost their daughters to Chinese men as their wives or maid servants, so that their own young men had difficulties finding brides for themselves.

With the Communist Revolution, the situation has changed, as we will see in the next part.

The Minorities under Republican and Communist Regimes

Part Four

Changing Policies

11

THE EARLY REPUBLIC

In 1911, when the Manchu dynasty was forced to abdicate, more than 250 years of the rule of "foreigners" over China came to an end. The Manchu rulers and their officials from about 1700 on had tried as best as they could to become Chinese. They had lost their own language; their upper class had accepted Chinese culture and was as educated as any Chinese scholar. Their family names had early become the same as those of Chinese because they gave up their own names. Physically, they could not be distinguished from the Chinese of northern China; on the street only their different way of greeting another Manchu indicated that they were Manchu. Only in the government service were individuals of Manchu origin given preference, at least in the high offices at court.

Under the Manchu regime (1644–1911) China attained its greatest expansion and became the most powerful nation of the world. Before 1800 Europeans had admired China's culture and power, but subsequently, especially after 1841, they began to look down on China. The spread of the Industrial Revolution from its origin in England throughout Western Europe and the United States gave the Western countries vastly superior power. I am convinced that our descendants in the twenty-first century will recognize that this Western superiority was a short-lived, relatively unimportant event of history. By then most, if not all, countries will have industrialized, and some other society could be "superior." However, at the time intrusions of England, France, and other countries into China made it clear to the Chinese that, at least in military technology, they were now inferior to the West. Chinese intellectual leaders, formost among them Sun Yat-sen, began to hold the Manchus responsible. Because the imperial system under the Manchus was unable to modernize the country, the Manchus had to go. The Manchu government, including the young emperor, resigned, and, in 1912, China was declared a republic.

The first flag of the Republic had five colors, representing the five "races" of China: Han, Man (Manchu), Meng (Mongol), Hui (Sinkiang Muslims), and Tsang (Tibetans). Chang T'ing-hsiu writes:

> If we go into the border region of Southwest and Northwest China, we can meet people who differ in language, customs, or beliefs. They seem to be very different from those of China's interior. Customarily one gave them different names, probably because of their language or the area, like Miao, I, Ti, Mongols, Tibetans, etc. There are many such names and some people therefore thought that these are all different ethnic groups. (Quoted in *Pien-chiang lun-wen chi*, 2, pp. 1065–1066)

The point that Chang T'ing-hsiu wants to make is that there are no essential differences between these people. And, in fact, the five-colored flag was soon abolished

(1927) and replaced by the Republican flag, which symbolized the Nationalist Party (Kuomintang) not the ethnic groups.

NATIONALIST POLICY

Sun Yat-sen, the leader of the revolution of 1911 and for a short time president of China, was at first of the opinion that China's minorities should be quickly brought to a level similar to that of the Chinese, so that assimilation would be possible. Later he began to speak of the need to raise the cultural level of the minorities so that they themselves could decide whether they would like to be integrated or be allowed self-government. But he still admitted the existence of four minorities symbolized on the old republican flag.

What Is a Minority? A Contemporary View

The two best known cultural anthropologists of China (both foreign trained), Fei Hsiao-t'ung and Lin Yao-hua, published an article in the official newspaper of the People's Republic, the *Jen-min jih-pao* (August 10, 1958). They begin by attacking the minority policy of the Nationalist regime:

> Before the liberation, the Pan-Hanism of the Kuomintang led to its enforcement of a policy of oppression and discrimination in dealing with the various nationalities in the country. The existence of the minority nationalities was intentionally denied, and these peoples were considered merely as some "groups of people with different living habits." But such a subjective reactionary design could not change facts, and only served to aggravate hostility and misunderstanding among different nationalities.

Then they ask what an "ethnic group" really is:

> A self-reported name of a nationality cannot be used definitely for the establishment of the existence of such a nationality. For individuals may feel that they belong to a common community and this may not necessarily conform to facts. This situation still exists in modern nations. And since many of the minority nationalities in our country are still in the precapitalist stage of development, the possibility for the conclusion above mentioned is all the greater. Under certain historical conditions, some different tribes might develop into one single nation, and during a specific period of time, each constituent tribe might retain its original name. Under certain other historical conditions, a tribe might, in the course of its development, be split into several nations, but the original name of the tribe might remain unchanged in spite of the development. Moreover, during the precapitalist era, people still had regional concepts, concepts of native district affiliations, concepts of family connections, and these various concepts might overshadow their consciousness for the communal entity which they had jointly formed. Thus we cannot simply use the names of nationalities as the basis for the establishment of actually "different" nationalities.

The authors enumerate nine different situations that can occur and which, in their opinion, make it difficult to decide whether a group is a "nationality" or not. One of the situations is:

> A minority nationality might at one time ascend to the status of the ruling group in history, and its people became scattered over different parts of China. Later they lost their ruling status and became discriminated against. They changed their language

and other national characteristics in the attempt to conceal their true nationality, but they still retain their national consciousness.

And another one:

Some Han people who had resettled in minority areas have retained the characteristics of the Han nationality, but they are not definitely sure whether they are actually Han people. They have become known under the names given them by the minorities in the neighborhood and have been looked upon as minority nationalities.

The first situation seems to refer to the Manchus, rulers over China between 1644 and 1911. But as early as the eighteenth century, most Manchus had given up their language and had accepted Chinese customs. True, like many immigrants in the United States, they knew that they had originally been Manchus, but in the twentieth century only a very few of them, still living in Manchuria, could speak the Manchu language, and even they could not write the Manchu script. The second case seems to refer to people said to have been captured by tribes in Southwest China and to have become slaves of those societies. Nobody knows much about their history and origins. To enumerate such cases as serious problems for the establishment of "national minorities" seem to indicate an attempt to make the question unsolvable.

Most remarkable is the eighth case:

Han Chinese who moved to different minority areas had gone in different groups and at different dates. Those who had moved earlier had been separated from the Han people in the interior for a longer period of time, and some had come under the influence of the minority nationalities, so that there arose definite differences of language and customs and living habits between the early groups and those who have moved to the same areas at a later date. Such early resettlers admit differences from the Han Chinese, and after liberation demand to be treated as minority nationalities.

Here, the implication is that some groups that seem not to be "Han" Chinese actually are "Han." In fact, there are some tribes claiming to be Chinese who immigrated to South China very long ago and, over time, became so similar to the surrounding tribes that they were counted as non-Chinese (see p. 82).

By enumerating all these possible situations, the authors reject attempts to define a minority by its special customs or living habits, by language, or by tracing of racial origins. After referring to Stalin's *The National Question and Leninism*, they state that "the special characteristics of tribes and clans are the special characteristics of nations in their rudimentary stage, that is to say, the common nature, to a certain extent, of their language, territory, economic ties and psychological factors." In other words, when these underdeveloped tribes develop and become socialistic, they will be like the majority, that is, Chinese.

The Pre-Communist Period

From 1914 to 1927 the Chinese government maintained a special ministry for Tibetans and Mongols, which later became only a "commission." During the last years of his life Sun Yat-sen became more and more impressed by the Russian Revolution, and his policy of 1924 spoke of *self-determination* and *autonomy*, the same terminology that Lenin had used. The government should help and guide small, weak racial groups toward ultimate self-determination and self-government—this was Lenin's important change of the original Marx-Engels theory that each society would have to develop stage by stage from a primitive society to a socialist society. Lenin proclaimed that this long process could be shortened by the guidance of a "developed" country.

The actual developments in China were different, as they were in the Soviet Union. In the 1920s the Nationalist regime had some influence upon only one minority area, the so-called Inner Mongolia, that is, the part of Mongol-inhabited land closest to China, in which there already was a very considerable Chinese minority. In 1928, instead of gaining the right to self-government, Inner Mongolia was divided into four provinces—Jehol, Chahar, Sui-yüan, and Ning-hsia. As provinces, they were on the same level as the older eighteen provinces of China and under the control of the central government, at least in theory. The Mongols in these provinces had no special rights.

Similarly, Manchuria, the country of origin of the Manchus and, since the beginning of this century, so heavily settled by Chinese farmers that the Manchus had become a tiny minority, was divided into three Chinese provinces. Here, as we have seen, during the Japanese occupation of 1931–1945 a new state was proclaimed, called Manchukuo, "the State of the Manchus." This puppet state even created a special region, Hsing-an, for the minority of Mongols living in that part of the country. The so-called state of Manchukuo and its autonomous region disappeared with the defeat of Japan in 1945. Since then the area has been an integral part of China and was divided into three provinces.

As we have seen (p. 43), Outer Mongolia achieved its full independence early, but Republican as well as Communist governments continued to claim it as a part of China. Sinkiang, whose population was only about one-quarter Chinese, was from 1911 on practically independent; the Republican regime was unable to consolidate its control over the area.

The Years of Revolution

During the years of revolution, from 1920 on, Soviet influence in the Far East became stronger and stronger, the more Soviet armies pushed toward the Pacific coast of Siberia. There were also a considerable number of "White Russians" who had fled from the Communists to Sinkiang. When Soviet Russia was still weak (1919–1928), the Chinese rulers sponsored the immigration of Chinese into Sinkiang. In 1944 there was a revolt in the Ili area, the part of Sinkiang closest to the Soviet Union, and an East Turkestan Republic was proclaimed. In 1946 Chiang Kai-shek entered into talks with the local Chinese rulers of Sinkiang in the hope of establishing closer contacts with his Republican regime in Nanking. Though the local rulers would have liked to get assistance in their resistance to Soviet influence, they knew that the Chinese did not have the power to help because the whole area between Sinkiang and China proper—provinces of Kansu, Ch'ing-hai and Ning-hsia—was ruled by leaders of the Muslim Ma family.

They were nominally under the control of the Chinese government, but in fact they did what they wanted—carve out a Chinese Muslim state. This was prevented from actually happening by competition among the different generals and, perhaps more important, by the defeat of Japan, which had tried to help the Ma generals, in World War II.

The situation in the province of Yünnan, in the Southwest corner of China, was quite similar: The government of China was too weak to appoint loyal governors, so after the 1911 revolution the province was factually independent. Until 1928 the "governor" T'ang Chi-yao ruled there. Some of the indigenous people collaborated with him, even to the point that his successor, Lung Yun, was a member of the Yi, a new name for Lolo. Lung Yun's half-brother, who was more sympathetic to the Republican government, succeeded him after the end of World War II.

The fate of Tibet was discussed in Chapter 5. It remained practically independent until the Communist conquest (1950). However, under the Republican regime Chinese influence, at least over Eastern Tibet, was strong, so that it was given the name of Hsi-k'ang (Tibetan, Kham) and made a Chinese province in 1939.

Thus, until the end of its regime on the mainland of China (1949), the Nationalist government exercised little or no control over most of the areas inhabited by minorities. When evaluating this, we must keep in mind that, since its beginning, Chiang Kai-shek's regime had no single year of peace. First, from 1927 on, he attempted to gain control over the "warlords" who had created their own centers of power. Then came, one after another, various Japanese attempts to gain control first over Manchuria, then over all of China (1930–1934). At the same time, the Nationalist regime tried to eliminate the small Communist nucleus in Kiangsi Province (1933–1935). They were successful in so far as the Communists had to leave Kiangsi and begin their "Long March" (1935), during which they evaded Nationalist armies, mainly by passing through provinces not under Nationalist control, often through minority areas. The Long March cost many lives, through not only battles with Nationalist Chinese forces but also fights with minorities. Finally, the Communists settled in Yen-an in Shensi, which the Nationalists did not control. Then the Sino-Japanese war began in full scale (1937–1945), the Soviet Union occupied Manchuria, and the Nationalist regime broke down (1948).

COMMUNIST POLICY

Development of a Position

During the years before the Chinese Communist Party came to power, it gave consideration at various times to the problem of minorities. After the foundation of the Party in 1922 the idea was that Mongolia, Tibet, and Turkestan (Sinkiang) should be "autonomous states," which would be voluntarily united with China as a federated republic. In a decision of 1930 it was decided that these regions should have the right either to federate or to secede. Discussion on these matters had their parallels with discussions in the Soviet Union around 1921–1922, when some leaders of minorities demanded the right to secede, which, of course, was denied.

During the confrontations with the minorities in Southwest China at the time of the Long March the Communists became aware of the problem of minorities. They often needed help from the minorities through whose areas they marched, or at least their permission to pass through. When they settled in Yen-an, they were again in an area in which ethnic problems existed: tensions between Chinese and Muslims of non-Chinese ethnicity. Mao Tse-tung now reformulated the Party's position: All minorities should be given equal rights with the Chinese. They should not be forced to learn Chinese but rather be encouraged to develop their own cultures. They also should control their own affairs—but they must live in a unified state together with the Han Chinese. Mao's statement of November 6, 1938 led to the adoption of the concept of "autonomous areas," which Lenin had developed. Combined with this was a tactic used in Europe by Communist parties before they had gained full control of a country, the so-called united front: All groups should work together against the common enemy, under the leadership of the Communist Party. Consequently, the Yen-an regime was friendly toward the local minorities. They opened a special Nationalities Institute destroyed during an attack; from 1945 on this was not a research institute but a cadres' training school in which the selected future minority leaders were also taught Chinese.

Even before their victory, the Communists had been joined by a few individuals of minority origin, such as Ma Chün, a Muslim who lived in Manchuria and had established early contacts with Chou En-lai. Most important for a long time into the period of the People's Republic was Prince Yün Tse of the Tümet federation of the Mongols. Although he had forgotten how to speak the Mongol language, under the Mongol name Ulanfu he became the only minority member in the Central Committee of the Communist Party. He had been trained as early as 1923. Sinified, alienated, and dissatisfied members of minorities were important in the early endeavors to bring the minorities under Communist control. During the war against Japan, which, in the main, took place in those parts of China proper in which there were only few minorities, the only event of significance involving minorities was an uprising of Li tribes on the island of Hainan in the South, who joined with local Communists against the Nationalists (1943).

When the Nationalist regime was overthrown, the Communists had to decide what attitude they would take in the minority question. They applied in general the same tactics the Soviets had used in the conquest of Russian Central Asia. Perhaps the first action characteristic of the new age was a criticism of the situation of Tibet in 1949: The Party attacked the "independence" of Tibet but also promised Tibet help in case of an attack by England—an easy promise to make because England at this time was hardly in a position to conquer Tibet. The second step was a Chinese attack on Tibet (October 1950), which ended in a compromise: The People's Republic promised autonomy for Tibet (May 1951). In 1952 the Tibetan army was included in the People's Liberation Army, and cadre schools for the training of future leaders were created in Lhasa. The Party made use of tensions between the Tibetan nobility and the Lamaist church, between the Dalai Lama in Lhasa and the Panchen Lama in Shigatse, and between provinces and the central government of Tibet. The traitor who in 1955 helped in upsetting the Lamaist regime in Lhasa became the first general secretary, while the Dalai Lama became chairman, but without any actual power. The wife of a traitor was made the head of Lhasa's women's organization.

Social Mobilization

Such movements were a part of the social mobilization that began in 1950 and 1951. At this time the Party sent activists into the minority areas to start mass meetings similar to meetings held in China proper. At these meetings discussions were conducted in order to find out whether there were tensions within the minority, and who were the "conservative" (in other words, anti-Communist) leaders or leading groups. The meetings were combined with theatre performances or film shows, which naturally attracted and enthused the people, the content of which was to show the oppression that supposedly existed and how to get rid of it. Such troupes toured in 1952 through all parts of China and later also visited foreign countries. I saw them in 1957 in Pakistan, performing as "Chinese folk dances" the dances of Sinkiang people and of Yao and Miao tribes, and "Chinese" ballets in Russian style.

At first, the Chinese activists who were sent to the tribes to win them over to the new policies had to contact the traditional tribal leaders, because these men could speak or understand Chinese, whereas the activists could not speak the native languages or dialects. The second step was then to mobilize the youth against their elders by promising them a role in the new society. In addition, certain able persons of low social position were elevated for various reasons and used against the old elites; slaves were encouraged to run away, and, if they were recaptured, the capturers got into trouble.

The theory behind all these activities was Lenin's phrase: "national in form, social in content." So, beginning in October 1951, the idea of the independence of specific ethnic groups was given up and branded as reactionary and dangerous because it would necessarily lead to imperialism. Instead, the Party tried to inculcate the spirit of patriotism and to project the image of the "older brother" who helps his "younger brothers" to develop their own languages, literatures, and folk arts. From this period, in which we hear that large collections of folk tales and folk plays were made and stored, we have a number of Chinese-language texts. In some cases the Chinese editor admits to having adapted the tales or made certain "corrections," which we can discover when we compare a tale collected before 1951 with the new one. Unfortunately, before the Revolution few Chinese collected folklore materials from minorities, and the missionaries were only slightly interested and then only in tales they regarded as beautiful or significant in some way. We guess, for instance, that before the Revolution there existed among Chinese as well as among the minorities stories, songs, and proverbs about bad landowners and bad government officials; they could not be published at that time. The Communist cadres have collected such material, but we do not know whether what they collected is real folklore that existed before the collectors came or material that was composed specifically for purposes of propaganda against the Nationalist regime.

Classification and Organization of Minorities

These missions and meetings also aimed at finding out more about the size and character of individual tribes or groups; the anthropologist Fei Hsiao-tung mentioned above was a member of one such mission. He found more than 100 minorities. As such diversity was politically not admissible, he attempted to work out a classification that would reduce the total number. In August 1952 the concept of autonomous area was therefore refined. Areas inhabited by only one minority were accorded the rank of chou (prefecture), but when in such an area there was a second minority, this area could become an autonomous hsien (district, comparable to an American county). An area in which two or more relatively strong minorities lived could become a "multinational area," but when one of these minorities lived in a compact, cohesive unit, it could establish its own hsien.

By 1952 there existed 130 autonomous areas and over 200 coalition autonomous governments. In that year the land reform in China proper (which cost the lives of millions) was completed, but minority areas were advised to conduct their own land reform only when the majority of the masses demanded it. What such "will of the masses" means is hard to say, except that it excluded the former leadership of the minorities and others, such as priests. But we also should keep in mind that voting was for the minorities a totally unheard-of process. Thus, in 1954, in a further attempt to define autonomous areas, the voters were asked to say to which nationality they belonged. The report states that they "did not know what their nationality was." Some of them may have known but were uncertain as to what answer their new leaders wanted to hear. In 1955–1956 land reform and collectivization was carried out in the minority areas; in Tibet it was done as late as 1958. After the end of the so-called period of the Hundred Flowers (a short period during which dissenters were invited to express their ideas, for which they later were punished) minority areas that tried to avoid collectivization of their land, which some people had just received through Communist expropriation from the landlords, were branded as antisocialist.

From 1956 on the minority areas went through several organizational changes. There were forty-six such groups in 1957, and we hear of autonomous regions, prefectures, counties, and even villages. Later, some new autonomous regions were created, while other areas came under regular Chinese administration. There was an important rule that the language of the minority was not the only language spoken in a minority area and that the leaders in such an area did not have to be members of the minority; in other words, they could also be regular Chinese. Also important is that areas of China proper with unique dialects or customs, such as Fukien Province, Canton Province, or Taiwan, could not be counted as autonomous areas.

Within the minority areas minority languages were studied and dictionaries were prepared for the cadres; their old script was modernized, and Latin alphabets were developed. The term *pu-lo* (tribe) was abolished, and derogatory place names (and, as we have seen, there have been quite a number of them) were changed. Formerly, the Chinese symbols for tribal names had been written with the character for *dog*, indicating the nonhuman nature of the tribes; now they had to be written with the character for *man*, an innovation already introduced by the Nationalists.

We have pointed out several times that the minority policy of the People's Republic took the policy of the Soviet Union as a model, even after the friendly relations between the two countries came to an end. There are, however, some differences, which Professor Dreyer (pp. 263ff) points out: The minorities in the Soviet Union are republics and, in theory, can secede from the Union; this is not true of the autonomous areas in China. In the Soviet Union there is more freedom in the development of national languages and cultural forms. The country is pluralist in culture, but the Russian language is the common language and the socialist economy covers the whole federation. Individuals of minority origin can and do reach key positions in the government; Stalin, for instance, was a Georgian, not a Russian. To my knowledge in China thus far no Party leader of minority origin has been assigned work in Chinese areas or areas of other minorities, which means that their advancement is limited. China has a much more assimilative policy than the Soviet Union and one that is closer to the policy of the Nationalist regime before 1948. The overall stress is on the superiority of Chinese culture.

Current Problems and Policies

Both the Soviet Union and China have tried to reduce the percentage of minority populations within the minority areas by stimulating or even forcing migration of members of the dominant ethnic group into those minority areas. The so-called *hsia-fang* tactic, which sent millions of young men and women to distant places, especially to Sinkiang, had three aspects: (1) to make potentially or actually disenchanted young persons politically harmless; (2) to populate minority areas and change the ethnic balance; (3) to use these exiled persons to control minority areas; the exiles would tend to look down on the underdeveloped minority and represent China, rather than cooperate with the minority.

The influx of Chinese into Sinkiang is the most important of these movements and presents special problems. It is assumed that up to 1911 the population of Sinkiang and its agricultural development did not change much; it is even possible that agricultural production decreased during the eighteenth century. In 1911 the amount of cultivated land was estimated as 1,600,000 acres. In 1943 this had grown to 3,606,400 acres; and in 1961 to 7,900,000 acres. All these data are unreliable, because there is no exact census available, but it is known that some of the rivers in Sinkiang have been used for irrigation of desert land. However, the rapid expansion of irrigation and the consequent overuse of land have already begun to show the usual consequences, which plague even the United States: salinization of the soil. At the present time the new acreage serves mainly for the supply of the Chinese armies and settlers in Sinkiang, and further expansion seems unlikely. On the other hand, Sinkiang is becoming more and more important as a source of oil and minerals.

In 1959 the above-mentioned Ulanfu proposed an expansion of the livestock industry for Mongols inside China, similar to that already carried out by the government of the Outer Mongolian People's Republic, a country that, like Sinkiang, suffers from lack of water. The livestock industry could also be expanded in Sinkiang; perhaps this would stop the flight of Sinkiang people into the Soviet Union (in 1963 an estimated 70,000, according to Dreyer, p. 170). Animal husbandry also could be a means of livelihood in Tibet, where farming is marginal. But such a policy seems to be blocked by an old Chinese prejudice against nomadism and cattle breeding.

There are still other problems, which, though minor at present, may someday become more important. Anthropologist Fei Hsiao-t'ung has already pointed out that there are tribes in Yünnan Province that are also represented in Burma. Others live partly in China and partly in Laos, both in areas where the international borders are not perfectly clear and where the Chinese government was never fully in control. Thus, even in 1976, the People's Republic admitted that there were some ethnic groups on the borders continuing their old style of life, without communes, language reforms, or application of the new marriage laws. Moreover, there are larger groups of Miao and Yao living in the mountains of Vietnam, Laos, and Thailand. According to their own traditions, their ancestors migrated not long ago from China, always following the mountain ranges and not causing trouble to the governments in these countries. They still know their relatives in China. After the Revolution remnants of Nationalist armies lived on the borders between China and Burma, out of reach of the People's Republic but, at least in name, subjects of that country. (They have earned some international notoriety because they seem to have gained their living by cultivating and selling opium. As far as we know, many of the cultivators were not Chinese but minorities.) I have seen a number of families resettled in Taiwan, as well as Chinese refugees settled in the Shan states of Burma. These settlements indicate that Chinese overflowed the borders of China and settled in neighboring countries, usually as successful businessmen or traders in the plains. But in addition, minorities from China have also resettled outside China, usually as poor farmers living in the mountains. What will their future be? Will they simply be forgotten?

The Dilemma: What Is the "Right" Policy?

12

Readers may feel that this book has been partial—partial in favor of the minorities in China. This is true to a certain degree; I have tried to show the situation of minorities rather than to show the rationale behind the attitudes of the majority, the Chinese. Although I have referred to some Chinese attitudes toward minorities, these references have not been comprehensive. The real question is: Should the Chinese have behaved differently toward the minorities? There is no sense in blaming any society for what its ancestors have done; whatever has been done cannot be undone. American society is perhaps an exception in that we feel obliged to pay for what our ancestors of a hundred and more years ago have done. Though this is a highly altruistic attitude, it may have consequences we have not foreseen and which will perhaps make life even more complicated in a later generation. Let us here speak only of China, though the same may be valid for other societies.

For our purpose it seems useful to divide the minorities into two large groups: One consists of numerous, often very small, tribal groups in Southwest China, remnants of populations that once inhabited all of South China and parts of today's Central China. The other comprises large, compact groups that once had political identity as states and until very recently maintained diplomatic and other contacts with China's neighbors.

THE SITUATION IN THE SOUTHWEST

We mentioned that the groups in the Southwest were not "barbarians"; they were tribal and only occasionally in their history developed into states. In other periods they were characterized by what I have called frontier feudalism. Many of them had developed a script, though it was not a means of general communication, but rather limited to use in religion. In the last 150 years they were split into many small tribes, living more and more isolated in the mountains on a low level of subsistence. The present regime has put together groups of such tribes, sometimes giving them a new general name, such as Yi for tribes that mostly seem to belong to what were formerly called Lolo, and these groups live in their autonomous districts or even autonomous villages. Their old leadership is replaced by cadres now being trained in Peking, who try to change the economy and attitudes of their areas so that they become similar to or even identical with the economy and attitudes of the nation.

Schools exist in which the students are taught Chinese, though their own language seems also to be taught in the early years of schooling. This is similar to what has been done in the Soviet Union. Putting together tribes whose languages, though related, are not the same naturally creates tensions among them, decreasing the possibility that a trend toward nationalism could grow in these new units. The tribes may resent this, but what else could be done when the aim is to integrate them into the Chinese economy? Only by these means can their standard of living be raised; only by these means can they receive an education that allows them to compete with Chinese. It is probably impossible to develop their languages to a level on which modern technological and scientific knowledge could be transmitted to them; and even if this were possible, it would be unfeasible to translate all the new knowledge into their languages and make it widely available. The tribes will have to learn standard Chinese if they want to reach equality. But hundreds of millions of Chinese have to do the same: They have to learn standard Chinese, the so-called Mandarin (Chinese: *Kuo-yü*, national language), while among themselves they continue to speak their dialects. This was already a policy of the Nationalists. When I traveled in Kuanghsi Province in 1937, I could easily communicate with educated officials and with school children but not with small businessmen or the ordinary people.

It is possible that intermarriages of Chinese men with women of the minorities will continue, but no longer for the reason that minority brides require a lower bridal price. With the new Chinese marriage law the formerly obligatory bridal price is abolished. Thus, if present policies continue, it is quite possible that these minorities will slowly be absorbed and become "Chinese," even though some foreigners have a kind of nostalgic love for these "freedom-loving" people and regret what is going on. Such a romanticism may even be present among the tribes themselves. But I see no other way if they are not to become a living museum, the object of tourists who look at them as if they were exhibition pieces in a museum—quaint, but not fully human.

THE SITUATION IN THE NORTH AND THE NORTHWEST

The other group—the people in the Northwest and the North—presents a totally different problem. This population was formerly to a large extent nomadic and cattle breeding. Therefore, the only sedentary population is in the cities, which were centers of intercontinental caravan trade in the old times and are now centers of local commerce and trade with China proper. Even with modern technology it seems impossible, or at least economically unfeasible to attempt to change the area of Sinkiang and Tibet into farmland. As we saw in the last chapter, the expansion of farmland in Sinkiang may already have reached its limit. However, development of extractive industries (oil and minerals) seems to be promising, and I imagine that at least some of the steppes could be upgraded by development of new varieties of grasses, so that modern cattle breeding and meat production could become feasible.

The social aspects are, however, more difficult. Both countries are border areas. Sinkiang has a very long border with the Soviet Union. Tibet has a border with India or countries under Indian protection, such as Nepal, Sikkim, and Bhutan; it even has contact with Afghanistan and Pakistan, two countries whose future is questionable. We could add here the northern provinces of China that formerly constituted Inner Mongolia and which are adjacent to independent (but Soviet-linked) Outer Mongolia. In all these areas the minorities inside the borders of China have close relatives beyond the border. Thus, there always exists the possibility that a strong power on the other side of the border will spread propaganda among the minority peoples, and the consequences of such penetration could someday become serious. We mentioned that thousands of inhabitants of Sinkiang fled to the Soviet side of the border. At least some of them later returned after having been indoctrinated and having seen the higher standard of living in the Soviet Union. This condition is not new: In the nineteenth century Imperial Russia tried to cut off as much as it could from Sinkiang; Tibetans have lived for centuries inside Nepal; Mongol tribes were separated from their brothers only by the Russian Revolution and the political disorders in China after the end of the Manchu dynasty. Since the nineteenth century the political leaders of China have recognized the danger of the situation and have kept Chinese soldiers in Sinkiang. Now masses of settlers are coming into Sinkiang, while there are only some parts of Tibet, especially the northern parts, being settled by soldiers and immigrants from the mainland of China.

As far as we can see, the long-range policy of the People's Republic seems to be the same as in the Soviet Union: To give the areas a degree of autonomy that allows them to continue for the time being to practice their own customs, including their religion, their language, their own script (or a newly developed script based on a Western alphabet), and limited self-government, until the immigration of Chinese slowly changes the character of the population, making the original inhabitants a minority. The fight against organized religion and the economic power of religion seems to have been easily won in Inner Mongolia and Tibet; but the mainly Islamic people of Sinkiang—like their brothers on the other side—offer more resistance. Their religion ties them not only to their brothers but also to the numerous and newly influential Islamic countries such as Pakistan, Iran, and the Arab states. Experiences in the Soviet Union and Turkey have shown that expropriation of land held by the Islamic communities does not weaken their religiosity because, in theory, the properties in the name of Islam belonged not to any church or person but to Allah.

To conclude: When we put ourselves in the position of the Chinese government—and it does not really matter what the character of that government is—it is hard to think of any other feasible policy toward these compact, large minorities in the West and Northwest or even, to some degree, in the North of China. If China should allow them to develop totally on their own and become independent states, it is more than likely that they would ally themselves with the neighbor on the other side and become a serious danger for China. By saying this I am in a way expressing what Chinese emperors of Han and T'ang times, as well as the Manchu emperors in the eighteenth century, felt and tried to achieve—control over Central Asia, the Mongolian steppes, and Tibet. China wants to create a situation in which the danger of aggression across her border will be minimized. The question as to whether the people living there like it or not is of secondary importance. One can call this imperialism or colonialism, but after the experience China has had in the last 150 years, and with the situation of the world today, its policy is understandable.

Bibliographical Notes

RECOMMENDED ADDITIONAL READING

Introduction and Part One:

For the archeology and the earliest periods of China's history the work by Kuang-chih Chang, *The Archeology of Ancient China* (New Haven: Yale University Press, 1968), is by far the best. Use the most recent edition! Usable also is Ping-to, *The Cradle of the East* (Chicago: University of Chicago Press, 1975). For questions of ecology Kuang-chih Chang (ed.), *Food in Chinese Culture* (New Haven: Yale University Press, 1977) is very highly recommended.

Parts Two to Four:

The data for these parts come mostly from original Chinese sources. Some analysis of these data was made by the author in *Kultur und Siedlung der Randvölker Chinas*, 2nd ed. (Leiden: E.J. Brill, 1979); *Lokalkulturen im alten China: Erster Teil: Die Lokalkulturen des Nordens und Westerns* (Leiden: E.J. Brill, 1942); and *Lokalkulturen des Südens und Ostens* Monumenta Serica Monograph 3 (Peking: The Catholic University, 1942). Only the second volume has been revised and translated into English, under the title *The Local Cultures of South and West China* (Leiden: E.J. Brill, 1968). This volume discusses, on pages 1–31, the general theory of the author's book *China und seine westlichen Nachbarn* (Darmstadt: Wissenschaftliche Buchgesellschaft, 1978). Numerous articles in American and European journals are relevant to the Republican and Communist periods. *Pictoral China* (Peking) contains pictures and short essays about China's minorities, as does *Beautiful China* (Taipei). Both are propagandistic journals that represent the viewpoint of their governments. The booklet by Henry G. Schwarz, *Chinese Policies towards Minorities*, Occasional Paper No. 2 (Bellingham: Western Washington State College, Program in East Asian Studies, 1971) provides translations and analysis of numerous documents.

Bibliography

Adam, Thomas R. *Modern Colonialism: Institutions and Policies.* Garden City, N.Y.: Doubleday, 1955.

Arseneev, Vladimir K. *Dersu, the Trapper.* New York: E.P. Dutton, 1941.

Aziz, Barbara N. *Tibetan Frontier Families: Reflections of Three Generations from D'ing-ri.* Chinese Materials Center, Taipei, 1978.

Bacon, Elizabeth E. *Central Asians under Russian Rule. A Study in Cultural Change.* Ithaca: Cornell University Press, 1966.

Bretschneider, E. *Medieval Researches from Eastern Asiatic Sources.* 2 vols. London: Kegan Paul, Trench, Trubner, 1910.

Broomhall, A.J. *Strong Tower. The Nosu, Kweichow.* London: China Island Mission and Morgan & Scott, 1947.

Burman, B.R. *Religion and Politics in Tibet.* New Delhi: Vikas, 1979.

Chang, Kwang-chih. *Shang Civilization.* New Haven: Yale University Press, 1980.

Chavannes, Edouard. *Documents sur les Tou-kiue (Turcs) Occidentaux.* St. Petersburg: Académie des Sciences, 1903.

Ch'en Han-sheng. *Frontier Land Systems in Southernmost China.* New York: Institute of Pacific Relations, 1949.

Chia I. *Hsin-shu (The New Book).* Written probably second century B.C.

Chiu T'ang-shu (Old History of the T'ang Dynasty). K'ai-ming ed. Shanghai, 1934. Covers period between A.D. 618–960.

Chu Wen-djiang. *The Muslim Rebellion in North China 1862–1878. A Study of Government Minority Policy.* The Hague: Mouton, 1966.

Clarke, Samuel R. *Among the Tribes in South-West China.* London and Philadelphia: China Island Mission, 1911.

Dardess, John W. *Conquerors and Confucians. Aspects of Political Change in Late Yüan China.* New York: Columbia University Press, 1973.

de Beauclair, Inez. *Tribal Cultures of South-West China.* Asian Folklore and Social Life Monographs, vol. 2. Taipei, 1970.

Demiéville, Paul. *Le Concile de Lhasa.* Bibliothèque de l'Institut des Hautes Études Chinoises. Vol. 7. Paris, 1952.

Dreyer, June T. *China's 40 Millions.* East Asian Series, vol. 87. Cambridge: Harvard University Press, 1976.

Eberhard, Wolfram. *China und seine westlichen Nachbarn.* Darmstadt: Wissenschaftliche Buchgesellschaft, 1978.

Eberhard, Wolfram. *Kultur und Siedlung der Randvölker Chinas.* 2nd ed. Leiden: E.J. Brill, 1979.

Ekvall, Robert B. *Cultural Relations on the Kansu-Tibetan Border.* Chicago: University of Chicago Press, 1939.

Fairbank, John K., ed. *The Chinese World Order. Traditional China's Foreign Rela-*

tions. Cambridge: Harvard University Press, 1968.

Fei Hsiao-t'ung and Lin Yao-hua. *A Study of the Question of "Different Nationalities" among the Minority Nationalities in China. Jen Min jih Pao* (Peking), August 10, 1958.

Feng Han-yi and J.K. Shryock. "The Historical Origin of the Lolo." *Harvard Journal of Asiatic Studies*, vol. 3, 1938, pp. 103–127.

Fields, Lanny B. *Tso Tsung-t'ang and the Muslims, Statecraft in Northwest China 1868–1890.* Kingston, Ontario: The Limestone Press, 1978.

Fitzgerald, Charles P. *The Southern Expansion of the Chinese People.* London: Barrie and Jenkins, 1972.

Franke, Otto. *Beiträge aus chinesischen Quellen zur Kenntnis der Türkvölker und Skythen Zentralasiens.* Berlin: Preussische Akademie der Wissenschaften, 1904.

Frontier Affairs. See *Pien-cheng kung-lun.*

Frontier Studies. See *Pien ch'iang lun wen chi.*

Fujisawa, Yoshimi. *The Historical Studies of the Tribes in South-west China: Historical Studies of the Nan-chao Kingdom.* Tokyo: Daian, 1969.

Gabein, A. von. *Das Leben im uigurischen Königreich von Qoĉo (850–1250).* Veröffentlichungen der Societas Uralo-Altaica, vol. 6. Wiesbaden: Steiner Verlag, 1973.

Gilmour, James. *Among the Mongols.* London: Religious Tract Society, 1883.

Golomb, Ludwig. *Die Bodenkultur in Ost-Turkestan.* Studies Instituti Anthropos, vol. 14. Fribourg, 1959.

Graham, David C. *Songs and Stories of the Ch'uan Miao.* Smithsonian Miscellaneous Collections, vol. 123, no. 1. Washington, D.C.: Smithsonian Institution, 1954.

Grousset, René. *L'empire des steppes.* Paris: Payot, 1939.

Herzog, Rolf. *Sesshaftwerden von Nomaden. Geschichte, gegenwärtiger Stand eines wirtschaftlichen wie sozialen Prozesses.* Forschungs-Institut für internationale technische Zusammenarbeit an der Rheinisch-Westfälischen Technischen Hochschule, Aachen, no. 1238. Köln, 1963.

Hoffmann, H. "Tibets Eintritt in die Universalgeschichte." *Saeculum*, vol. 1, 1950, pp. 258–279.

Hou Han shu (History of the Later Han Dynasty). K'ai-ming ed. Shanghai, 1934. Covers period between A.D. 25 and A.D. 220.

Hsiao-ching (Book of Filial Piety).

Hsin T'ang shu (New History of the T'ang Dynasty). K'ai-ming ed. Shanghai, 1934. Covers period between A.D. 618 and A.D. 960.

Hsü Wen-ch'ang chi (Collected Works of Hsü Wei). 1521–1593.

Huan K'uan (see *YTL*).

Irons, William and N. Dyson-Hudson, eds. *Perspectives on Nomadism.* Leiden: International Studies in Society and Social Anthropology, 1972.

Israeli, Raphael. *Muslims in China.* Scandinavian Institute of Asian Studies, Monograph Series, no. 29. London: Curzon Press, 1980.

Israeli, Raphael. "The Muslim Minority in Traditional China." *Asian and African Studies*, vol. 10, no. 2, 1975, pp. 101–126.

Jack, Robert L. *The Back Blocks of China: A Narrative of Experiences among the Chinese, Sifans, Lolos, Tibetans, Shans, and Kachins, between Shanghai and the Irrawadi.* London: E. Arnold, 1904.

Jagchid, S., and P. Hyer. *Mongolia's Culture and Society.* Boulder, Colorado: Westview Press, 1979.

Jarring, Gunnar. "Materials to the Knowledge of Eastern Turki," Part 3 and Part 4.

Lunds Universitets Arsskrift, N.F., essay 1, vol. 47, 1951.

Jen-ming jih-pao (People's Daily). Peking.

Kani, Hiroaki. *A General Survey of the Boat People in Hong Kong.* New Asia Research Institute, Chinese University of Hong Kong, Monograph Series 5, 1967.

Katanov, N.T. *Volkskundliche Texte aus Ost-Turkistan, II.* Aus dem Nachlass herausgegeben von Karl Menges. Berlin: Als Manuskript gedruckt, 1943.

Kinkley, Jeffrey C. *Shen Ts'ung-wen's Vision of Republican China.* Ann Arbor: University Microfilms, 1978.

Kui-chou t'ung-chih (Gazetteer of the Province of Kui-chou). 1692.

Kunstadter, P. *South East Asian Tribes, Minorities, and Nations.* Princeton: Princeton University Press, 1967.

Krader, Lawrence. *Peoples of Central Asia.* Bloomington: Indiana University Press, 1963.

Kwanten, L. *Imperial Nomads. A History of Central Asia 600–1500 A.D.* Philadelphia: University of Pennsylvania Press, 1979.

Lantzeff, George V., and R.A. Pierce. *Eastward to Empire. Explorations and Conquest on the Russian Frontier to 1750.* Montreal: McGill-Queens University Press, 1973.

Lattimore, Owen. *The Mongols of Manchuria.* New York: John Day, 1934.

Lattimore, Owen. *Nomads and Commissars. Mongolia Revisited.* New York: Oxford University Press, 1962.

Lattimore, Owen. *Studies in Chinese Frontier History.* London and New York: Oxford University Press, 1962.

Lee, Robert H.G. *The Manchurian Frontier in Ch'ing History.* Cambridge: Harvard University Press, 1970.

Leslie, Donald D. *The Survival of the Chinese Jews.* T'oung Pao Monographs, vol. 10. Leiden: E.J. Brill, 1972.

Li Chi. *The Beginnings of Chinese Civilization.* Seattle: University of Washington Press, 1957.

Li Kitabi (The Book of Rites, in Uygur language).

Lin Yao-hua. *The Lolo of Liang Shan.* New Haven: Human Relations Area Files Press, 1961.

Lin Yao-hua and N.N. Čeboksarov. "Die wirtschaftlich-kulturellen Typen Chinas." *Jahrbuch des Museums für Völkerkunde zu Leipzig*, vol. 22, 1966, pp. 189–240.

Linck-Kesting, Gudula. *Ein Kapitel chinesischer Grenzgeschichte. Han und Nicht-Han im Taiwan der Qingzeit (1683–1895).* Münchener Ostasiatische Studien, vol. 22. Wiesbaden: Steiner Verlag, 1979.

Ling-wai tai-ta. = Almut Netolitzki. *Das Ling-wai tai-ta von Chou Ch'ü-fei.* Münchener Ostasiastische Studien, vol. 21. Wiesbaden: Steiner Verlag, 1977.

Liu Mao-tsai. *Die chinesischen Nachrichten zur Geschichte der Ost-Türken (T'u-küeh).* Göttinger Asiatische Forschungen, vol. 10. Wiesbaden: Steiner Verlag, 1957.

Lombard-Salmon, C. *Un example d'acculturation Chinoise: La Province du Gui-Zhou au xviiie siècle.* Publications de l'École Francaise de 'Extrême-Orient, vol. 84. Paris, 1972.

Ma Ho-t'ien. *Chinese Agent in Mongolia.* Translated by John DeFrancis. Baltimore: Johns Hopkins University Press, 1949.

Mackerras, Colin. *The Uigur Empire. According to the T'ang Dynastic Histories.* Columbia: University of South Carolina Press, 1972.

Man shu (The Book about the Southern Barbarians). Translated by G.H. Luce. Data Paper No. 44, Southeast Asia Program. Department of Far Eastern Studies, Ithaca: Cornell University, 1961.

Maunier, René. *The Sociology of Colonies, and Introduction to the Study of Race Contact.* 2 vols. London: Rutledge and Kegan Paul, 1949.

McMillen, Donald H. *Chinese Communist Power and Policy in Xinjiang 1949–1977.* Boulder, Colorado: Westview/Dawson, 1979.

Medlin, W.K.; W.M. Cave; and F. Carpenter. *Education and Development in Central Asia.* A case study on social change in Uzbekistan. Leiden: E.J. Brill, 1971.

Meskill, Johanna M. *A Chinese Pioneer Family. The Lin of Wu-feng, Taiwan, 1729–1895.* Princeton: Princeton University Press, 1979.

Michels, Robert. "Die Theorien des Kolonialismus." *Archiv für Sozialwissenschaft,* Frankfurt, vol. 67, 1932, pp. 693–710.

Moseley, George V.H. *The Consolidation of the South China Frontier.* Berkeley: University of California Press, 1973.

Moseley, George V.H. *The Party and the National Question.* Cambridge: M.I.T. Press, 1966.

Moses, Larry W. "T'ang Tribute Relations with Inner Asian Barbarians." In J.C. Perry and B.L. Smith (eds.), *Essays on T'ang Society.* Leiden: E.J. Brill, 1976.

Mostaert, Antoine. *Folklore Ordos.* Monumenta Serica Monographs, no. 11. Peking: The Catholic University, 1947.

Pa Shin, ed. *Essays Offered to Gordon H. Luce by His Friends.* Ascona: Artibus Asiae, 1966.

Petech, L. *China and Tibet in the Early 18th Century. History of the Establishment of Chinese Protectorate in Tibet.* 2nd ed. Leiden: E.J. Brill, 1972.

Philipps, Eustache D. *The Royal Hordes. Nomad Peoples of the Steppes.* New York: McGraw Hill, 1965.

Pien-cheng kung-lun (Frontier Affairs). Chungking, 1945.

Pien-ch'iang lun wen chi (Frontier Studies). Chungking, 1943–1945.

P'ing-ting Miao-fei fang-lüeh (Plans Concerning the Pacification of the Miao Bandits). Reprint, Taipei, 1968.

Poppe, N. *Mongolische Volksdichtung.* Wiesbaden: Steiner Verlag, 1955.

Prasad, S.A. *Studies in Sinological Sex, Religion, Racism, and Nationalism.* Northern Ridge, Australia 1979.

Rock, Joseph Fr. Ch. *The Na-khi Nâga Cult and Related Ceremonies.* Serie Orientale Roma, vol. 4. Rome, 1952.

Rubel, Paula G. *The Kalmyk Mongols: A Study in Continuity and Change.* Uralic and Altaic Series, vol. 64. Bloomington: Indiana University Press, 1967.

Ruey, Yih-fu. *(1)83 Aboriginal Peoples of Kweichow Province in Pictures.* Academia Sinica, Institute of History, The Aboriginal Peoples of South China in Pictures Series, no. 1. Taipei, 1973. *(2)16 Aboriginal Peoples of Kweichou Province in Pictures.* As above, no. 2, Taipei, 1973.

Schmidt, Isaak J. *Die Taten des Bogda Gesser Chans.* St. Petersburg: W. Gräff, 1839.

Schmidt-Glintzer, Helwig. *Das Hung-ming-chi und die Aufnahme das Buddhismus in China.* Münchener Ostasiastische Studien, vol. 12. Wiesbaden: Steiner Verlag, 1976.

Schran, Peter. *Guerilla Economy. The Development of the Shensi-Kansu-Ninghsia Border Region, 1937–1976.* Albany, New York: State University of New York Press, 1976.

Schwarz, Henry G. *Chinese Policies towards Minorities.* Occasional papers, vol. 2. Bellingham: Western Washington State College, Program in East Asian Studies, 1971.

Schwarz, Henry G. "Ethnic Minorities and Ethnic Policies in China." In William Petersen (ed.), *The Background to Ethnic Conflict*. Leiden: E.J. Brill, 1979.

Secret History of the Mongols (Yüan-ch'ao pi-shih). See Erich Haenisch, *Die geheime Geshichte der Mongolen*. Leipzig: O. Harrassowitz, 1941.

Serruys, Henry. *The Mongols in China during the Hung-wu Period (1368–1398)*. Mélanges chinois et bouddhiques, vol. 11. Brussels, 1959.

Serruys, Henry. *Sino-Mongol Relations during the Ming, II: The Tribute System and Diplomatic Missions (1400–1600)*. Mélanges chinois et bouddhiques, vol. 14. Brussels, 1967.

Shen Ts'ung-wen. See Kinkley.

Shiratori, Yoshiro. *Yao documents*. Tokyo, 1975. (Japanese and Chinese)

Stalin, Joseph. *The National Question and Leninism*. Moscow: Foreign Language Publishing House, 1950.

Stein, Sir Mark Aurel. *Innermost Asia*. 4 vols. London: Oxford-Clarendon Press, 1922–1928.

Sui-shu (History of the Sui Dynasty). K'ai-ming ed. Shanghai, 1934. Covers period between A.D. 589 and A.D. 617.

Tekin, Talat. *A Grammar of Orkhon Turcic*. Bloomington: Indiana University Press, 1968.

Tien-sheng hsi-nan chu-I t'u-shuo (Illustrated Description of the Barbarians of the Province of Yünnan). Peking, 1788.

Ti-li hsüeh pao (Journal of Geography). Peking: K'o-hsüeh ch'u pan shê, 1953ff.

Tjioe, Long E. *Asiaten über Deutsche. Kulturkonflikte Ostasiatischer Studentinnen in der Bundesrepublik*. Frankfurt: Thesen Verlag, 1971.

Tung-fang tsa-chih (Far Eastern Miscellany). Shanghai, 1904–1945, and Taipei, 1967–present.

Vernadsky, G. "The Eurasian Nomads in Their Art, in the History of Civilization." *Saeculum*, vol. 1, 1950, pp. 74–86.

Wiens, Harold J. *China's March into the Tropics*. Hamden, Conn.: Shoe String Press, 1954.

Wiens, Harold J. "Cultivation, Development, and Expansion in China's Colonial Realm in Central Asia." *Journal of Asian Studies*, vol. 26, 1966, pp. 67–68.

Wittfogel, Karl A., and Feng Chia-sheng. *History of Chinese Society: Liao*. Philadelphia, 1949.

YTL: Yen-t'ieh lun, by Huan K'uan. See E.M. Gale. *The Discourses on Salt and Iron*. Leiden: E.J. Brill, 1931. Reprint, Taipei, 1967.

Index

Toba (T'o-pa), tribal federation and dynasty
    of, 36, 37, 53, 54, 67, 120
Tocharians, ethnic group of, 12, 22, 56
Tongking (Vietnam), 88
Tonyukuk, 133
Torgut (Turgut), Mongol federation of, 134
Trade relations, 43
    with foreigners, 112; with minorities,
        113, 114; role of, 115; routes and, 117;
        with West Asia, 56
Tribal councils, 39, 65
    federations of, 5, 29, 37, 46, 137; organi-
        zation of, 35, 36; Tibetan organization
        of, 66
Tribes
    formation of, 36; names of, 22
Tribute, 37, 40, 52
    missions of, 112, 113; payments of, 38;
        relations, 10
Ts'ai, 82
Ts'ai tribe, 131
Tsang (Tibetans), 151
Tsang-ko, 77
Tso Tsung-t'ang, 61
Tsong-kha-pa, 71
Tsou Yen, 99
Ts'uan, tribal group of, 135
T'u-chüeh (Köktürks), tribal group and
        state of, 54, 101, 119, 120, 135, 136
Tu-chün, district of, 84
T'u-fan, city of, 70
T'u-fan, tribal federation of, 67, 136
Tu-ku tribe, 53, 54
T'u-szu type of administration, 115, 116,
        138, 139, 141, 142
Tu Wen-hsiu, 58
T'u-yü-hun, tribal federation of, 67
Tuan-kung, 141
Tümet, Mongol tribal federation of, 156
T'un-t'o caste, 93
Tung-hu, tribal group of, 34
Tung-ming, 29
Tungus
    language of, 14, 28, 35, 98; tribes, 28, 29,
        33, 34
Turfan, city of, 59. *See also* T'u-fan
Turgut tribe, 60, 62
Turkestan (Sinkiang), 155
    importance of for China, 51; East
        (Chinese) and West (Russian), 55, 56;
        West (Soviet Central Asia), 38
Turkey, 39, 162
Turkic
    languages, 54, 64, 98; tribes, 40, 46, 54,
        55, 63, 67
Turks, 59, 67

Udehé tribe, 114
Ulan Batur (formerly Urga), city of, 42

Ulanfu, 156, 159
Umma, 64
Ungern-Sternberg, 43
United States, 97, 151, 153
Uralo-Altaian language group, 14
Urga (Ulan Batur), city of, 114
Urumchi (Ti-hua), city of, 61, 62
Usury, 114
Uygur, tribal federation of, 30, 41, 55, 58,
        64, 98, 106, 107, 110, 111, 120
Uzbek, tribal group of, 98

Vegetarianism, 120
Vietnam, 40, 57, 88, 90, 97, 99, 123, 159
Volga river, 60

Wa-tse tribe, 132
Wang Chao-chün, 107
War, 105
Warlords, 155
Wedding, 84, 89
Wei, 52, 53
Wei dynasty, 66
Wei-ning, district of, 103
Wen-ti, 51
West Asia, cultural influence of, 56
Wheat, 16, 25
White Lotos sect, 60
Wiens, H., 90
Wilson, W., 146
Wittfogel, K., 15
Women
    organization of, 156; power of, 69; rights
        of, 35
World concepts of Chinese, 9
Wu
    ancient state of, 88; partial state of, 52
Wu-huan, tribal group of, 34, 35, 36
Wu-man tribes, 76, 77, 78, 79, 80, 90
Wu San-kui, 30, 31
Wu-ti, 51, 56, 57

Yak, 69, 70
Yami tribe (Taiwan), 144
Yao, mythical emperor, 82
Yao
    language of, 98; tribal group of, 80, 81,
        82, 83, 86, 90, 124, 134, 159
Yaqub Beg, 61
Yellow Church (Lamaism), 71
Yellow River (Huang-ho), 129
Yen-an, city of, 45, 73, 155, 156
Yen-lang, 77
Yi
    language of, 98; tribes, 76, 155, 160
Yin and Yang, 6
Yü, 140